36 Stratagems Plus:

Illustrated by
international cases

T0381518

36 Stratagems Plus:

Illustrated by international cases

Douglas S. Tung
and
Teresa K. Tung

TRAFFORD

Order this book online at www.trafford.com
or email orders@trafford.com

Most Trafford titles are also available at major online book retailers.

Printed in Victoria, BC, Canada.

ISBN: 978-1-4269-2806-2

*Our mission is to efficiently provide the world's finest, most comprehensive book publishing
service, enabling every author to experience success. To find out how to publish your book, your
way, and have it available worldwide, visit us online at www.trafford.com*

Trafford rev. 3/1/2010

 www.trafford.com

North America & international
toll-free: 1 888 232 4444 (USA & Canada)
phone: 250 383 6864 ♦ fax: 812 355 4082

Table of Contents

List of illustrations for the stratagems.   ix

Preface.   xv

Chapter:

1.   Introduction to Chinese war strategy books and stratagems.   1

2.   A systematic approach to the stratagems based on basic behaviors.   13

3.   To watch, to find out, to plan, to await and to take advantage of.   29

Stratagems:
Watch the fire across the river.
A straw will show which way the wind blows.
Find the way in the dark by throwing a stone.
Take counsel in one's temple.
To win hands down.
Wait at one's ease for an exhausted enemy.
Loot a burning house.
Take away a goat in passing.

4.   To pretend to be ignorant, to feint and to deceive.   69

Stratagems:
Play dumb.
Hide one's light under a bushel.
Make a feint to the east and attack the west.
Pretend to advance along one path while secretly going along another.

Point at the mulberry only to curse the locust.
Cross the sea by deceiving the heaven.
Retreat in order to go forward.

5.   To bluff, to substitute and to conceal.   99

Stratagems:
Empty castle ploy.
Raise a corpse from the dead.
Steal the beams and pillars and replace them with
    rotten timber.
Hide a dagger in a smile.

6.   To be circuitous, to make use of, to borrow and
        to shift off.   117

Stratagems:
Besiege Wei to rescue Zhao.
Beat somebody at his own game.
Push the boat along with the current.
Kill with a borrowed knife.
Turn around one thousand catties with the strength
    of four liangs.
Make a cat's paw of someone.
Shift the misfortune to somebody else by moving the
    corpse to his place.

7.   To procreate.   149

Stratagems:
Create something out from nothing.
Fish in murky waters.
Decorate the tree with bogus blossoms.

8.   To transfer and to take away.   165

Stratagems:
Lure the tiger out of the mountain.
Remove the firewood under the cooking pot.

9.   To attract, to warn, to prod and to chart the
        best course for action.   179

        Stratagems:
        Cast a brick to attract a piece of jade.
        Entice snakes out of their lairs.
        Beat the grass to startle the snake.
        Prod somebody into action.
        Befriend a distant state while attacking a
            neighbour.
        Lengthwise and breadthwise, opening and
            closing.
        Play double-faced and attack somebody from
            behind.

10.   To strike, to monitor and to block the
        opponent's retreat path.   213

        Stratagems:
        Their name is Legion.
        Offend in order to defend.
        Gain the initiative by striking first.
        Work on the hearts and minds of others.
        Outwit by novelty.
        Break the cauldrons and sink the boats.
        Defeat the enemy by capturing their chief.
        Remove the ladder after the accent.
        Borrow a safe passage to conquer Guo.
        Shut the door to catch the thief.
        Not to be bound by fixed rules, but vary the plan
            according to the situation of the enemy.

11.   To avoid and to reverse.   259

        Stratagems:
        Avoid the important and dwell on the trivial.
        Aim at swift victory and avoid prolonged campaign.
        Turn the guest into the host.

12.   To use some special stratagems.   277

        Stratagems:
        The beauty trap.
        Let the enemy's own spy sow discord in the
            enemy's camp.
        Inflict injury on one's self to win the enemy's trust.
        The Stratagem with a set of interlocking
            stratagems.

13.   To abandon and to run away.   303

        Stratagems:
        The plum tree dies fro the peach tree.
        In order to capture, one must let loose.
        The cicada sheds its shells.
        Retreat is the best option.

14. Sun Tze's teachings and the stratagems.   325

Appendices.

A   A Chronology of Chinese Dynasties.   339
B   Map of China, Warring States Period   341
            (475-221 BC).
C   Stratagems: A Synopsis.   342
D   Answers to odd-numbered exercises.   349

Bibliography.   353

Indexes.

A   Stratagems and basic behaviors.   355
B   Names of people.   358

List of illustrations for the stratagems

	Section number
Winston Churchill would like to watch Adolf Hitler and Josef Stalin exhaust each other.	3.1.1.3
2006 Lebanon War (July 12 – August 14, 2006).	3.1.1.3
A Persian cat revealed a military secret.	3.1.2.3
Mud and snow could also be tell-tale signs.	3.1.2.3
Adolf Hitler tested the British and the French respones by breaking the Versailles Treaty.	3.2.1.3
The Bush administration lobbied for support to U.S. attack on Iraq, 2002.	3.2.1.3
Japan plotted to fight Imperial Russia on Another occasion.	3.3.1.3
The Gulf War (August 2, 1990-February 28, 1991).	3.3.1.3
Napoleon Bonaparte's confrontation with Michel Ney at Laffrey.	3.3.2.3
The Cuban Missile Crisis (October 16 –28, 1962).	3.3.2.3
Maximus Fabius wanted to exhaust Barca Hannibal in a long war of attrition.	3.4.1.3
Napoleon Bonaparte's invasion of Russia.	3.4.1.3
Japan got its opportunity to seize Chinese territories when China was in chaos.	3.5.1.3
The adventure at Vigo Bay, 1702.	3.5.2.3
The Soviets annexed the Baltic States in 1940.	3.5.2.3
Josef Stalin played cool to take Harry Truman's message.	4.1.1.3
Feigned deafness could be used as a sale promotional tactic.	4.1.1.3

Anwar El Sadat ascended to the presidency of Egypt in 1970.	4.1.2.3
Taking a low profile could help to win a business deal.	4.1.2.3
Napoleon Bonaparte's invasion of Egypt.	4.2.1.3
Deceptive tactics in the North African Campaign, 1942.	4.2.1.3
The Trojan Horse.	4.2.2.3
Dwight D. Eisenhower feigned to invade Calais.	4.2.2.3
Franklin D. Roosevelt changed his attitude on the research of atomic bomb.	4.2.3.3
A satirical comment deserved another satirical remark.	4.2.3.3
A Japanese samurai story.	4.3.1.3
Henry Kissinger's secret trip to China.	4.3.1.3
How the Russian delegation got its diplomatic status.	4.3.2.3
Harold Wilson's ploy on the Soviets did not work.	4.3.2.3
The adventures of Ian Robert Maxwell.	5.1.1.3
Matsushita Konosuke was "the god of management".	5.1.1.3
A mysterious Anti-Nazi resistance leader in the Netherlands during WWII.	5.2.1.3
Coazon Aquino carried on her husband's mission.	5.2.1.3
Marshal Tukhachevsky was set up by the Germans.	5.2.2.3
Adolf Hitler, Josef Stalin and Saddam Hussein all had their doubles.	5.2.2.3
"Speak softly and carry a big stick".	5.3.1.3
Japanese diplomatic talks before Pearl Harbor attack.	5.3.1.3
The tales of one thousand and one nights.	6.1.1.3
The Battle of Tsushima (May 27-28, 1905).	6.1.1.3
Franklin D. Roosevelt beat his enemy in the enemy's own game.	6.2.1.3
A make up artist tricked the fugitive.	6.2.1.3
The Suez War of 1956.	6.2.2.3

Johann Strauss II and his orchestra avoided prolonged performance.	6.2.2.3
Religious doctrines could be used as knives.	6.3.1.3
Let the Germans clear the way for the communist rule in Poland.	6.3.1.3
Leonardo da Vinci scared away the prior who hounded him.	6.3.2.3
A strong feudal lord (daimyo) was scared Away by small tricks.	6.3.2.3
The British agents made use of a U.S. senator to prompt Nazi Germany declaring war on U.S.	6.3.3.3
Most favoured stratagem used by the Japanese militarists.	6.4.1.3
Operation Himmler gave the excuse for attacking Poland in 1939.	6.4.1.3
Tsar Peter the Great tricked his enemy with his "concealed armies".	7.1.1.3
A native of Formosa taught in Oxford College during 1704-06.	7.1.1.3
Otto Skorzeny was labelled "the most dangerous man of Europe."	7.1.2.3
Kambe made the water murky to have his way.	7.1.2.3
Search lights could enhance the dispositon of an army.	7.1.3.3
The U.S. President's comments and no comments.	7.1.3.3
The founding of the German Labor Front in 1933.	8.1.1.3
Conspirators plotted to oust Premier Nikita Khrushchev during his vacation in the Black Sea.	8.1.1.3
Attempts to break the Mitsubishi shipping monopoly in 1880.	8.2.1.3
The Norwegian heavy water sabotage.	8.2.1.3
Josef Stalin made use of his agreement to fight Japan as a brick to get pieces of jade.	9.1.1.3
Small gift tokens promoted sales.	9.1.1.3
A sheriff cracked a case of theft.	9.1.2.3

A ploy that helped to solve a case of burglary.	9.1.2.3
The aftermath of the Battle of Sante Cruz, 1942.	9.2.1.3
Chrysler's CEO beat the grass by showing his convertible to capture the attention.	9.2.1.3
A map to prod the U.S. public.	9.3.1.3
A German U-Boat officer was prodded to give information about German acoustic torpedoes.	9.3.1.3
Imperial Japan attacked China but strived to befriend with the U.S. in the 1920 s -1930s.	9.4.1.3
The Molotov-Ribbentrop Pact signed on August 23, 1939.	9.4.1.3
European powers pulled together to contend Napoleon Bonaparte, 1805.	9.4.2.3
Otto von Bismarck had a master plan to build up a military strong Germany.	9.4.2.3
The manipulations of King Frederick II of Prussia.	9.4.3.3
Otto von Bismarck was a power manipulator.	9.4.3.3
The appeasement policy.	10.1.1.3
The Heroes in the North African Campaign 1942.	10.1.1.3
The wisdom of an ice cream and lollipops merchant.	10.1.2.3
Surviving the consumer electronic retail competitions.	10.1.2.3
The Munich Beer Hall Putsch, 1923.	10.1.3.3
Israeli pre-emptive attack in the Six-Day War 1967.	10.1.3.3
Psychological warfare used in the Falklands War, 1982.	10.1.4.3
US$10 million as the training expenses.	10.1.4.3
Ingrid Berman's choice of an aria for her audtion.	10.1.5.3
The fall of the Empire of mechanical watch-makers.	10.1.5.3

Peter Rumantsiev knew "When death is certain, the soldiers will live."	10.1.6.3
Hitachi Comp[any instilled high employee morale during the recession 1974-75.	10.1.6.3
Nazi Germans rescued Benito Mussolini for setting up a new Italian Socialist Republic.	10.1.7.3
The "Shock and Awe" air campaign in the War in Iraq, 2003.	10.1.7.3
The Battle of Salamis, September 480 BC.	10.1.8.3
Hermann Goering plotted to remove Werner Von Blomberg.	10.1.8.3
The Prague Spring, 1968.	10.1.9.3
The North Atkabtuc Treaty Organization (NATO) agreements.	10.1.9.3
Henry Ford II recruited a skilled technician By buying a company.	10.2.1.3
Higuchi Drug Store strategically located its shops to bring in more customers.	10.2.1.3
The Second Battle of El Alamein marked a turning point in WWII.	10.3.1.3
Tommy Franks maintained that war should be fought based on adaptability and flexibility.	10.3.1.3
Edward Kennedy's accident at Chappaquiddick in 1969.	11.1.1.3
The Iran-Contra Affair in 1985.	11.1.1.3
Nazi Germany's Blitzkrieg (Lightning War).	11.1.2.3
The Vietnam War 1969-1975.	11.1.2.3
Toyota surpassed General Motors in global auto sales in April 2007.	11.2.1.3
Mark Twain: The magician muttered, and knew not what he muttered.	11.2.1.3
Mordechai Vanunu fell into the beauty trap.	12.1.1.3
The KGB's ploy on Christina Onassis.	12.1.1.3
Tricked the enemies using thier own agents.	12.1.2.3
A deadly hoax committed by the British Intelligence.	12.1.2.3
Rudolph Hess, number 3 man in Hitler's Germany, flied to Scotland, 1941.	12.1.3.3
Double agents misled Nazis.	12.1.3.3

The Battle of Khalkhin Gol, 1939.	12.1.4.3
"Hold to the last man" to keep control of the	13.1.1.3
bridgehead.	
Sidney Carton died for Charles Darnay due	13.1.1.3
to his love for Lucie Manette.	
Vernon Kell cracked the German spy ring in	13.1.2.3
1914.	
The Hitachi conspiracy, 1980.	13.1.2.3
Nikolai Vatutin moved his 3ʳᵈ Guards Tank	13.2.1.3
army north without being noticed.	
How Amadeo Pietro Giannini got around	13.2.1.3
the Federal Reserve Board's order.	
Evacuation at Dunkirk.	13.2.2.3
Charles de Gaulle carried with him "the	13.2.2.3
honour of France" in his escape to	
London.	

Preface

Our theses.

The Thirty-six Stratagems is a unique collection of ancient Chinese tactics that describe some of the most cunning and subtle stratagems. A stratagem is a strategic plan that contains a trap or a ruse for the enemy. Many of these stratagems had their origins in events that occurred during the Warring States Period (475-221 BC) and the Three Kingdoms Periods (220-280) in China.

Ever since our book *More than 36 Stratagems: A systematic classification based on basic behaviors* (coauthored with Kenneth Tung, and published by Trafford, 2003) was published in April 2003, there has been a tremendous response from readers throughout the world on this "concise and thought-provoking look at the replaying of ancient Chinese stratagems in recent military and political occurrences and anecdotes."

In 2008, another book *Sun Tze's stratagems: A systematic approach based on basic behaviors* (coauthored with Joseph K. Tung) was published by Trafford. It was another exercise to establish our theses:

(1) Since there are hundreds of philosophical aphorisms and heroic exploits in the Chinese history, and

many of them have heavy content of strategic measures, obviously the number of stratagems is more than thirty-six.

(2) The number "36" used to denote numerous was a practice in the Chinese olden time. Each stratagem is related to an outcome of the arrangement of the hexagram of the *I-Ching*. A hexagram is a grouping of six unbroken and broken lines. Mathematically there should be 64 (or 2^6) outcomes from these six lines, each of which has two states (unbroken and broken). Subsequently, there should be 64 stratagems for the perfect match when the hexagram concept is used. Apparently the elements of *I-Ching* numerology were added merely to create an aura of mystery and antiquity.

(3) The original text of *The Thirty-six Stratagems* is divided into six categories of six stratagems each. The six categories are said to correspond to six situations. They are stratagems to use:

(a) when one is on the favored side of the combat with regard to the strength, resources available and the prevailing condition.
(b) when one has to defend himself against the opponents.
(c) when one is well prepared to launch the attack on his opponents.
(d) when the outcome is unpredictable.
(e) when one plots for gaining ground.
(f) when one is on the unflavored side of the combat.

We think that the classification does not provide a guide to the reader when a stratagem is most appropriate, especially when a sequence of schemes has to be formulated as the scenario develops. A systematic approach to classify these stratagems according to the basic behaviors of each stratagem can enable the reader to acquire a better perspective, especially in determining the right time to do the right things. This is the rationale for us to call the stratagems presented in this book "36 Stratagems Plus".

Current research.

At this point, we would like to differentiate strategy from stratagem. A strategy is a detailed plan for achieving success in situations such as war, politics, business, industry or sport; or the skill planning of such situations. A stratagem is a carefully planned way of achieving or dealing with something often involving a ruse. (*Cambridge Advanced Learner's Dictionary*). Thus, a strategy is a careful plan which may or may not incur a ruse while a stratagem must contain deceit and deception.

In this book, we are neither concerned with the military theories nor its technicalities. We cover sixty stratagems to illustrate the enlightened exploitation of strategic power. For each stratagem, we present an eclectic discussion of its theme and tactical aspects. Then, we trace its source that is usually the exploit of some of the Chinese generals, statesmen and ordinary people. The source may also be folklore, myth or story. For illustrations, the exploits and anecdotes of generals, kings, emperors, and people in the West and the East (Japan and the Philippines) are used. For the readers who are interested in the exploits and anecdotes of Chinese sources, they should refer to our two published books mentioned above.

Exercises are provided to enhance the conceptual understanding the materials presented. Answers to odd-numbered exercises are included.

This work is partly fiction and partly based on recordings in other media. Any resemblance to existing people, corporations and organizations are purely coincidental.

Moral support from a friend.

One of Douglas' college friends happened to read *More than 36 Stratagems: A systematic classification based on basic behaviors.* We have lost contact for forty years. He spent some time tracing Douglas' existence and where about; and he was able to locate me by going through other people.

We were able to communicate through the phone and then through the internet. He believed that our research efforts to broaden the scope and the dimensions of the thirty-six stratagems are challenging, and he would like us to read the story of Liu Xin. According to *History of the Han Dynasty* by Ban Gu (32-92), Liu Xin (??-23) was interested in mathematics, astronomy, poetry, and learning. He designed a cylindrical standard measure to unify national measurements. He calculated the pi value that is the ratio of the circumference of a circle to its diameter, as 3.1547. Once, when he found out *Zuo Qiuming's Chronicles* among some ancient books, he advocated that the imperial court should establish a study of ancient literature. However, some powerful officials rejected his proposal. Liu said, "These people cling only to the outdated matters, reluctant to accept new ideas."

We are more fortunate than Liu Xin, because we live in an Age of Innovations which can tolerate new ideas and alternate ways of thinking. We believe that pragmatism is the key to our case. On November 4, 2008, the Americans elected Barack Obama as thier first black president. It came half a century after the civil rights movement led by Martin Luther King. Mang middle-aged people confessed that they never expected they lived long enough to see something like this. Likewise, it is time to look at stratagems with a fresh perspective.

Acknowledgments.

We would like to acknowledge the following people for inspiring and encouraging us in the creation of this book. My son's in-laws, Mr. and Mrs. Kenneth Leung brought us a souvenir on their trip to China in 2004. It was an excerpt from Chapter VIII of Sun Tze's book, with words engraved and brush written with paint on bamboo strips, bound together by ropes.

We wish to express our sincere gratitude to many people for help with the preparation of this book: particularly to Mr. L. Kong and Mr. Joseph Tu, ex-member of the

Department of Computer Science, The Chinese University of Hong Kong. Our thanks go also to Kenneth Tung's colleagues at the Primerica Financial Service, Toronto for their helpful comments and suggestions on the manuscript. We also want to thank Walter Lee, Fiona Tung, Eddie Lai, Renee Lai, Nicole Phung, Tony Phung, Ma Yeung Ling, Kenneth Tung and Joseph Tung for their enthusiasm and editorial assistance. And finally to Douglas' wife or Teresa's mother, Beverly a thousand loving thanks, and to Douglas' grandson Brandon our best wishes.

We must emphasize we are entirely responsible for any error of commission and omission that may still exist in the book. Corrections, comments, and suggestions from readers are appreciated.

March, 2010, Toronto,
Douglas S. Tung and Teresa K. Tung.

Chapter 1.

Introduction to Chinese war strategy books and stratagems.

1.0 The Spring and Autumn Period and the Warring States Period.

In China, the half-millennium precedent the downfall of the Zhou Dynasty (c. Eleventh Century BC to 221 BC) was marked by frequent and intensive warfare. For instance, during the Spring and Autumn Period (770-476 BC), there were over 150 kingdoms coexisting with the Zhou Dynasty, among them Qi, Lu, Jin, Yan, Qin, Chu, Wu, and Yue were the stronger. These powerful states with their military and economic advantages waged wars to expand their territories, exerting their dominance as overlords to the smaller states. According to historical records, during this period, a total of thirty-six kings were killed and fifty-two vassal states were destroyed.

The Warring States Period (475-221 BC) was a time of endless brutal wars that were fought among the seven overlords, Qi, Chu, Yan, Han, Zhao, Wei, and Qin. Unlike the wars of the Spring and Autumn Period when the armies were small and battles lasted only a day, much like the pre-Napoleonic wars, this period featured massive armies (half a million per army was not an uncommon figure), long battles and sieges. This unfortunate situation could end only with one state unifying all others into one Empire.

During these periods, Chinese learning flourished at a level unsurpassed in all times. The atmosphere of reform and new ideas was attributed to the struggle for survival among warlords who competed in building strong and loyal armies and in increasing economic production to finance warfare as a means to survive and to prosper. To effect these economic, military, and cultural developments, the warlords needed ever-increasing numbers of skilled, literate officials and teachers, the recruitment of who was based on merits.

Another factor conducive to the learning prosperity was the end of the monopoly on learning by government coupled with the flow of scholars to the courts of the warlords to offer their services in military science, diplomacy and public administration. For instance, Confucius, the famous philosopher (551-479 BC), and his contemporary Sun Tze (540-485 BC), author of the famous *The Art of War* lived in the Spring and Autumn Period.

Then comes the era known as that of the Hundred Schools of Thought (late Spring and Autumn Period and early Warring States Period). During this era, Mencius (372-289 BC) and Xunzi who belonged to the Confucius school compiled their theses. There were other philosophers such as the Legalists (e.g. Han Fetze, Li Si), the Taoists, the Mohists, the Astrologists, the Logicists, the Diplomatists, the Eclecticists, and the Agriculturalists etc. "Tze", "ze" or "zi" were honorific titles, meaning "Master".

1.1 Chinese military writings.

Since warfare was a matter of vital importance to the state, some military people spent much time to study the art of war. Unfortunately many of the literature were lost. Another reason could be due to books on military matter were not favorably regarded in China after the spread of Confucianism as the national orthodoxy. Some of the

Chinese military classics, not necessarily in chronological order, and despite of the uncertainty regarding the authorship, dates and extent to which these works are composites drawing upon common ground and lost writings, include the followings:

(a) *Liutao*, or *Six Secret Teachings* by Tai Kung (also known as Lu Shang or Jiang Ziya) recorded his political advices and tactical instructions to King Wenwang (c. 1100 BC) and King Wuwang (c. 1050 BC) of the Zhou dynasty. Tai Kung has commonly been honored in China as the first famous general and the progenitor of military studies.

(b) *The Art of War* by Sun Tze (540-485 BC) has been considered the greatest extant Chinese military classic. Sun wrote this in the years 515-512 BC,

(c) *Sima Fa* (or the *Methods of the Minister of War*) by Tien Jangchu in the Fifth Century BC. Tien was instrumental in the great victories achieved by Duke Jinggong (547-490 BC) of the Qi State. The book was subsequently compiled during the reign of King Weiwang (378-343 BC) of Qi to record Tien's strategic concepts.

(d) *Wu Tze* by Wu Ch'i (c. 435-381 BC) and his disciples. Wu has been widely regarded as China's first great general, never been defeated, and credited for administrative reforms and impressive innovations. The book considers all aspects of war and battle preparation, and suggests applicable techniques for resolving tactical situations.

(e) *Military Methods* by Sun Bin (c. 378-320 BC). This book was considered to be lost in the Han Dynasty period. In 1972, the archaeological findings in Shandong Province of a Han Dynasty military official's tomb recovered Sun Bin's book. Bundles of damaged bamboo strips that preserved numerous ancient writings on military, legal and other subjects were found. This book gave an account of Sun Bin's thoughts and teachings, and apparently, it was compiled and edited by his disciples.

(f)   The *Wei Liaotze* by Wei Liao who lived in the last half of the Fourth Century BC. The book was based on Wei Liao's court conversations with Huiwang (Liang) of the State of Wei (reigned 379-335 BC), citing passages from numerous military writings. Someone from Wei Liao's family or school after Wei's death enhanced it with materials about Qin's military organization. Wei Liao was strictly a theoretician, because he had not been historically noted as a commander. A short historical note in the *Records of the Historian* by Sima Qian suggests that a descendant of Wei Liao offered advice to the youthful king of Qin, who eventually unified China in 221 BC and became known as Emperor Qin Shihuangdi (reigned 246-210 BC).

(g)   *Three Strategies of Huang Shihkung* was written at the end of the First Century BC. A reclusive adherent of the Taoist school who had profound knowledge of military matters enhanced it. The book incorporated materials attributed to Tai Kung (also known as Lu Shang or Jiang Ziya). These materials were secretly preserved by successive generations of the court officials of the Qi State.

(h) *Questions and Replies between Tang Taizong and Li Weikung.* Tang Taizong (reigned 627-649), was commonly known as Li Shimin. He reportedly commanded troops by the age of fifteen. He was instrumental in assisting his father, Li Yuan, to subdue numerous challenges to found the Tang Dynasty. Li Ching (571-649) with the honorific title Li Weikung, was one of Taizong's earliest associates and supporters. He commanded troops to suppress both internal and external uprisings.

1.2 Sun Wu (Sun Tze) and *The Art of War.*

According to the historian Sima Qian (145-86 BC), Sun Wu (also known as Sun Tze, 540-485 BC) was given an audience in the State of Wu. Having read the thirteen chapters of Sun's *The Art of War*, King Helu of Wu (reigned 514-496 BC) invited Sun to demonstrate the drilling of troops with the King's concubines. Impressed with Sun's military ways, King Helu appointed him Grand General of his army. In 511 BC, Sun led an army of 30,000 men to defeat the State of Chu who had 200,000 men. Sun made the Wu State the mightiest State during his lifetime by conquering the States of Yue and Chu.

Sun Tze's book on military strategies dictates an absolutely pragmatic approach. He declared that all warfare was based on deception. He was extremely clever and observant of ways to take advantage of the enemy's situation. Nonetheless his goal was not to kill the enemy but to break the enemy's resistance without fighting if possible. Taking over the opponent's territory was preferable to destroying him. His first aim is to conquer the enemy by strategy, second to prevent the joining of his forces (with his allies), third to attack him in the battlefield, and the worst policy is to besiege a walled city. For Sun, knowledge of oneself and the enemy is what leads to victory. Thus, Sun offered intelligent advice for military commanders, but he never questioned the ethics of a system that uses violence and deceit to take advantage of other people's weaknesses.

The Art of War has been exercising tremendous influence on Chinese military thoughts. From the emperors, the generals to the common people, it has been the most widely read book for the conduct of warfare. It has been influential throughout the Chinese history, and is still respected by military minds today. The Chinese Communists studied it for tactics and manoeuvres against the Japanese and the Chinese Guomindang (the Nationalists).

A Jesuit missionary J. J. M. Amiot first translated *The Art of War* into French in 1772. In 1910, Lionel Giles translated it into English and the Luzac Company of London published it. Today, this book is being used in military academies not only in China and Japan, but also in the U.S. In the Gulf War of 1991, General Norman Schwarzkopf, the Allied Commander, openly admitted in order to win the war, he had made a lot of references to this book. In the Operation Iraqi Freedom of 2003, General Tommy Franks, the U.S. Commander of the coalition forces, acknowledged the well-known principles of adaptability and flexibility were from Sun Tze.

1.3 Chengyu.

In China, throughout these years, literary gems, historical deeds, philosophical aphorisms and heroic exploits have been summarized into phrases, often in four Chinese words, called chengyu. Both educated class and the ordinary people have been familiar with them. In English, there are idioms, proverbs and sayings that serve similar functions. Of these synonyms, perhaps the closest equivalent to chengyu is saying.

Most of these sayings made their first appearances in the Spring and Autumn Period (770-476 BC) and the Warring States Period (475-221 BC). Some of their sayings have heavy content of strategically measures. They embody much tactical content to remind people the ways of dealing a situation, whether they are on the favored side or on the unflavored side. These sayings became the heuristics or ad hoc rules of thumb for the strategists and for those who wanted to win most or to lose the least in situations. For example, if there are dark clouds in the sky, so we think it is likely to rain, then we carry umbrellas when we go out. The dark clouds are the cause, and the heuristic of carrying umbrellas helps us to keep as dry as possible when we are out. But, sometimes it may not rain despite of the forecast.

Therefore, heuristics cannot guarantee absolute success; likewise the strategies may not achieve its full purposes due to various random factors. Though these sayings have been evolved with much Chinese culture, thought and customs, yet they are valid in other cultures, because they are primarily concerned with winning and losing.

1.4 Strategies and stratagems.

A strategy is a detailed plan for achieving success in situations such as war, politics, business, industry or sport;

or the skill planning of such situation. A stratagem is a carefully planned way of achieving or dealing with something often involving a ruse. (*Cambridge Advanced Learner's Dictionary*). Thus, a strategy is a careful plan that may or may not incur a ruse while a stratagem must contain deceit and deception.

Basil Henry Liddell Hart (1895-1970), the British military strategist viewed strategy as a way to minimize the need for armed conflict through moral and physical dislocation of one's opponents. He believed that direct attacks against an enemy firmly in position almost never worked. Therefore, to defeat the enemy, one must first upset his equilibrium before the main attack can succeed. He called this the "indirect approach", with a theme similar to one of Sun Tze's teachings.

The Thirty-six Stratagems is a unique collection of ancient Chinese sayings that describe some of the most cunning and subtle stratagems. Whereas the Chinese military texts such as Sun Tze's *The Art of War* emphasizes on military organization, leadership, and warfare strategies, the stratagems are more suitably applied in the fields of politics, diplomacy and espionage. These stratagems are especially useful in tactical maneuvers to undermine both the enemy's will to fight and his sanity. Many of these stratagems had their origins in events that occurred during the Warring States Period (475-221 BC) and the Three Kingdoms Period (220-280).

1.4.1 *The Thirty-six Stratagems.*

The origins of *The Thirty-six Stratagems* are unknown. The first historical mention of the thirty-six stratagems dates back to the Southern Qi Dynasty (479-502) where it was mentioned in the *Nan Qi Shi* (History of the Southern Qi Dynasty). The story begins with the ascent to the throne of King Mingdi (reigned 494-499) of Southern Qi Dynasty. He was suspicious of the loyalty of the courtiers appointed by his predecessor, and he purged them one by one.

General Wang Jingze (435-498) was the Commander-in-Chief. He watched the matter closely; and he thought instead of waiting for the disaster to come upon him, it would be better to lead the rebel against Mingdi first. Mingdi was ill at that moment. When his son, Xiao Baojuan, Marquis of Southern Qi, knew that General Wang led the rebel, he fled away from the capital. Wang said, "Of the thirty-six stratagems of Master Tan, running away is the best" to laugh at Xiao.

Master Tan was the famous General Tan Daoji (d. 436). But there is no evidence to either prove or disprove his authorship of *The Thirty-six Stratagems*. Tan assisted Liu Yu to found the Liu-Song Dynasty (420-479). After Liu had passed away, King Wendi (reigned 424-454) succeeded him. In 431, Wendi gave order to Tan to recover the Province of Honan from the State of Wei. Tan won thirty engagements within a short period of time, and penetrated his army deep into the territory of the Wei State. However, Tan had the problem of stretching his supply lines, and he was running short of food and provisions. This secret was revealed to the enemy by the soldiers defected to the Wei camp.

Tan planned to retreat but this would leave his army extremely vulnerable to rout and slaughter. He thought of a ploy. At night, he ordered his soldiers to carry baskets of sand, pile them up and pretend to weigh them as if it was grain, shouting "One *stone*, two *stones*..." ("*stone*" was a unit of weight). On top of the baskets, they sprinkled a layer of grain.

In the morning, these heaps of sand baskets looked like grain at a distance. The Wei scouts were surprised to see this, and they reported what they saw. The Wei generals deferred to attack Tan's troops. They suspected that the deserters' report was a ruse to lure them into a trap, and had all of them executed. Meanwhile, Tan led his troops in a leisure way out of the area dominated by the Wei Army. The Wei generals thought there must be troops hidden to guard the supplies in Tan's camps, and they dared not attack the camps either. Tan was successful to bring his army safely back home.

What Tan did was to evade from being attacked in his retreat. General Wang only focused on the retreat action in the case of Xiao, the Marquis of Southern Qi, and made sarcasm of it, as "running away is the best". While this is the first recorded mention of the "Thirty-Six Stratagems", some of the stratagems are based on events that occurred up to a few centuries earlier.

For example, the stratagem "The beauty trap" was based on the beauty trap classic - story of Xishi - that happened around 500 BC. The stratagem "Besiege Wei to rescue Zhao" was named after the ploy devised by the military strategist Sun Bin (descendant of Sun Tze) in 353 BC to relieve the siege of Handan, the Capital of the State of Zhao by sending troops to besiege Da Liang, the Capital of the State of Wei instead. (Refer to 6.1.1.2).

1.4.2 Modern versions of *The Thirty-six Stratagems*.

All modern versions of *The Thirty-six Stratagems* are derived from a tattered book found at a roadside vendor's stall in Szechwan in 1941. It turned out to be a reprint of an earlier book dating back to the late Ming or early Qing Dynasties in the Fifteenth Century entitled, *The Secret Art of War: The Thirty-six Stratagems.* There was no mention of who were the authors or compilers or when it was originally published. A reprint was first published for the general public in Beijing in 1979.

Without any other information, current speculations about the origins of the *Thirty-six Stratagems* suggest that there was no single author. More likely they were simply a collection of sayings taken from popular Chinese folklore, myths and stories. General Tan Daoji might have done some compilation, and passed the materials verbally or in manuscripts for centuries. It is believed that sometime in the Fifteenth Century an unknown scholar published them in the form that comes down to us today.

The original text of *The Secret Art of War: The Thirty-six Stratagems* is rather short, consisting of 138 Chinese words. It merely gives the name for each stratagem followed by a brief explanation. The author himself did not pay much respect to it. It is because the stratagems are taken as traps, ruses, and schemes. A book on these tricks cannot attain the status equal to that of the military work of strategies or history of wars, not to mention other Chinese literary work. In addition, the military strategies books have at least paid lip service to the Confucian notion of honour, but the stratagems make no pretence of being anything but ruthless. The stratagems focus on the use of deception, subterfuge or hidden tactics to achieve the objectives.

Today, *The Thirty-six Stratagems* is classified into six categories of six stratagems each. The six categories are said to correspond to six situations. (Detailed in 2.0) This division is based on the hexagrams of the *I-Ching*. A hexagram is a grouping of six broken or unbroken lines. In addition, the explanation of each stratagem is likewise said to be based on the interpretation of each hexagram as found in the *I-Ching*. The number "36" denotes numerous as a practice in the Chinese olden time.

Throughout the Chinese history, there are hundreds of philosophical aphorisms and heroic exploits; and many of them have heavy content of strategic measures, thus the number of stratagems is not limited to the conventional figure of 36. Further, the association of the stratagems with the hexagrams of the *I-Ching* has been ascribed to garnishing with an aura of mystique and antiquity. In fact, the population of outcomes of a grouping of six broken or unbroken lines should be 2^6 or 64. The number 36 falls short of the total outcome.

1.5   A systematic approach to the stratagems.

In this book, we are neither concerned with the military theories nor their technicalities. We think that a systematic study of the stratagems is more important.

For each stratagem, we present an eclectic discussion of its theme and tactical aspects. We present the classic case of the stratagem supplemented by two international cases to illustrate the use of the stratagem. For these international cases, the exploits or anecdotes of famous generals, kings, emperors, merchants, and ordinary people in the East and the West are used. As these stratagems offer insights into the workings of human nature to maximize gain and to minimize loss, they should encompass not only the epoch-making battles but also the successful negotiation of a much better business contracts, and the problem solving by ingenious minds.

Chapter 2.

A systematic approach to the stratagems based on basic behaviors.

2.0   Classical classification of the Chinese stratagems.

Around three hundred years ago, during the end of the Ming Dynasty and the beginning of the Qing Dynasty in the Fifteenth Century, there was an unknown scholar who compiled the Thirty-six Stratagems. He named the book as *The Secret Art of War: The Thirty-six Stratagems.* The stratagems were grouped into six sets with six stratagems in each set. Each set corresponded to a scenario that could take place in combat.

(I)   When one is on the favored side of the combat with regard to the strength, resources available and the prevailing condition.

1. Cross the sea by deceiving the heaven.
2. Besiege Wei to rescue Zhao.
3. Kill with a borrowed knife.
4. Wait at one's ease for an exhausted enemy.
5. Loot a burning house.
6. Make a feint to the east and attack the west.

(II)   When one has to defend himself against the opponents.

7. Create something out from nothing.
8. Pretend to advance along one path while secretly going along another.
9. Watch the fire across the river.
10. Hide a dagger in a smile.
11. The plum tree dies for the peach tree.
12. Take away a goat in passing.

(III)   When one is well prepared to launch the attack on his opponents.

13. Beat the grass to startle the snake.
14. Raise a corpse from the dead.
15. Lure the tiger out of the mountain.
16. In order to capture, one must let loose.
17. Cast a brick to attract a piece of jade.
18. Defeat the enemy by capturing their chief.

(IV) When the outcome is unpredictable.

19. Remove the firewood under the cooking pot.
20. Fish in murky waters.
21. The cicada sheds its shells.
22. Shut the door to catch the thief.
23. Befriend a distant state while attacking a neighbour.
24. Borrow a safe passage to conquer Guo.

(V)   When one plots for gaining ground.

25. Steal the beams and pillars and replace them with rotten timber.
26. Point at the mulberry only to curse the locust.
27. Play dumb.
28. Remove the ladder after the ascent.
29. Decorate the tree with bogus blossoms.
30. Turn the guest into the host.

(VI)   When one is on the unflavored side of the combat.

31. The beauty trap.
32. Empty castle ploy.
33. Let the enemy's own spy sow discord in the enemy's camp.
34. Inflict injury on one's self to win the enemy's trust.
35. The Stratagem with a set of interlocking stratagems.
36. Retreat is the best option.

So far many books, (except *More than 36 Stratagems: A systematic classification based on basic behaviors*, Trafford Canada, 2003, and *Sun Tze's Stratagems: A systematic approach based on basic behaviors*, Trafford Canada, 2008) whether written in Chinese or in translated versions of other languages follow this format. However, this classification does not provide a guide to the user when a stratagem is most appropriate, especially when a sequence of ploys has to be formulated as the scenario develops. In fact, a systematic approach to classify these stratagems enables the readers to acquire a better perspective of the stratagems, especially in determining the right time to do the right things.

2.1 Systematic Classification of the Stratagems based on basic behaviors.

Prof. Chien Chiao advocated to examine the basic behaviors in each stratagem, and to classify the stratagems accordingly. The theme of this classification is to focus on the basic actions or behaviors of each stratagem in simple terms, and to avoid the duplications found in the classical classification. The sequence of actions in a ploy can also be designed.

The following is an enhanced and modified revision of Prof. Chien's classification, making it more systematic and meaningful.

2.1.1 Actions 1-5 stress on patient but alert waiting, careful observation and investigation of the scenario, formulating a plan and quick grasp of the opportunity when it is available.

Action 1: **To watch.**

In view of a possible confrontation, it is always safer to watch, preferably from a distance, before getting involved in the matter. One should be observant and avoid any involvement if the scenario is not clear, or it does absolutely no good to be involved.

The stratagems are:

(I) **Watch the fire across the river.** (One of the classical 36 Stratagems).
(II) **A straw will show which way the wind blows.**

Action 2: **To find out.**

This is a fact finding technique in which inquiry or investigation of the scenario is conducted on the opponent's situation and intention.

The stratagem is: **Find the way in the dark by throwing a stone.**

Action 3: **To plan.**

Sun Tze emphasized the need of careful planning because "The general who is able to make careful deliberations beforehand can win." (Chapter I).

The stratagems are:
(I) **Take councsel in one's temple.**
(II) **To win hands down.**

Action 4: **To await.**

One has to keep track of the changing internal and external conditions of a scenario. He has to take action when the right moment comes. Premature or delayed action can ruin the chance.

The stratagem is: **Wait at one's ease for an exhausted enemy.** (One of the classical 36 Stratagems).

Action 5: **To take advantage of.**

As a result of Action 4, when the right moment comes, one has to take action without hesitation.

The stratagems are:
(I) **Loot a burning house.** (One of the classical 36 Stratagems).
(II) **Take away a goat in passing.** (One of the classical 36 Stratagems),

2.1.2 Actions 6-11 have feint as their theme, because "war is primarily a game of deception" (*The Art of War*, Chapter I).

Action 6: **To pretend to be ignorant.**

When the right moment has not come, one has to keep a stolid look so as not to arouse the opponent.

The stratagems are:
(I) **Play dumb.** (One of the classical 36 Stratagems).
(II) **Hide one's light under a bushel.**

Action 7: **To feint by misleading.**

The action is a deliberate feint which serves as a cover for other actions to follow.

The stratagems are:

(I) **Make a feint to the east and attack the west.** (One of the classical 36 Stratagems).

(II) **Pretend to advance along one path while secretly going along another.** (One of the classical 36 Stratagems).

(III) **Point at the mulberry only to curse the locust.** (One of the classical 36 Stratagems).

Action 8: **To deceive.**

This action is to deceive the opponent by passing off something as something else.

The stratagems are:

(I) **Cross the sea by deceiving the heaven**. (One of the tradtional 36 Stratagems).

(II) **Retreat in order to go forward.**

Action 9: **To bluff.**

If the opponent is on the favoured side, but he does not have much information on our side, we can bluff him away.

The stratagem is: **Empty castle ploy** (One of the classical 36 Stratagems).

Action 10: **To substitute.**

When it is impossible to remove something undesirable, or to prevent something undesirable happening, one may try to substitute the target with another substance so that less harm is done or the outcome of the happening becomes more acceptable to him.

The stratagems are:

(I) **Raise a corpse from the dead.** (One of the classical 36 Stratagems.)

(II) **Steal the beams and pillars and replace them with rotten timber.** (One of the classical 36 Stratagems).

Action 11: **To conceal.**

One may conceal a hostile scheme or aggressive intention with a smile.

The stratagem is: **Hide a dagger in a smile.** (One of the classical 36 Stratagems).

2.1.3 In Actions 12-15, a third party or object is involved in all actions.

Action12: **To be circuitous.**

This action does not aim at the primary target due to the presence of many difficulties. Instead it is carried out on a secondary target first. After achieving success, it will help to attain the original objective.

The stratagem is: **Besiege Wei to rescue Zhao.** (One of the classical 36 Stratagems).

Action 13: **To make use of.**

This action refers to the way with which one can win by making use of the thrust from his opponent. It is derived from the Chinese martial arts in which one can knock down his opponent by making use of the force put forward by the opponent. One can also win by exploiting the momentum of the battle situations and conditions.

The stratagems are:
(I) **Beat somebody at his own game.**
(II) **Push the boat along with the current.**

Action 14: **To borrow.**

One has to borrow the name, its authority and the influence of a notable third party (or object) so as to impress or to gain a favour from his opponent. He can also make the third party an instrument.

The stratagems are:
(I)   **Kill with a borrowed knife.** (One of the tradtional 36 Stratagems).
(II) **Turn around one thousand catties with the strength of four liangs.**
(III) **Make a cat's paw of someone.**

Action 15: **To shift off.**

The aim is to find a scapegoat, and to shift something undesirable such as blame or disaster on to the scapegoat.

The stratagem is: **Shift the misfortune to somebody else by moving the corpse to his place.**

2.1.4 Action 16 is to fabricate some pre-conditions favourable to the strategists before any action is taken.

Action 16: **To procreate.**

This is to fabricate or to make up when there is no such thing, to stir up the matter, and to elaborate or exaggerate things even it is a very minor issue.

The stratagems are:
(I) **Create something out from nothing.** (One of the classical 36 Stratagems).
(II) **Fish in murky waters.**   (One of the classical 36 Stratagems).
(III) **Decorate the tree with bogus blossoms**. (One of the classical 36 Stratagems).

2.1.5 Actions 17-18 aim at the removal of the condition that favours the opponents.

Action 17: **To transfer.**

In actual operations, the environmental conditions are most important in affecting the outcome. It is one measure to create a more favourable scenario to the strategist.

The stratagem is: **Lure the tiger out of the mountain.** (One of the classical 36 Stratagems).

Action 18: **To take away.**

This action is to remove the means which support the opponent, and to do this thoroughly.

The stratagem is: **Remove the firewood under the cooking pot.** (One of the classical 36 Stratagems).

2.1.6 Actions 19-24 deal with the opponents faced directly and openly, but only actions 22-23 are real confrontations with the opponents.

Action 19: **To attract.**

To give an allurement for the sake of gaining benefits is a delicate matter. Unless the strategist has good judgement as to what and how much should be given, and when and how frequently the allurement should be made, this action may work the other way to hurt the financial well being of the strategist.

The stratagems are:
(I) **Cast a brick to attract a piece of jade.** (One of the classical 36 Stratagems).
(II) **Entice snakes out of their lairs.**

Action 20: **To warn.**

This action is not directed to the opponent, but to a third party. It carries a message to warn the opponent concerned. It can also scare away the harmful elements.

The stratagem is: **Beat the grass to startle the snake.** (One of the classical 36 Stratagems).

Action 21: **To prod.**

The strategist is ready for the combat, but the opponent prefers to wait. The objective is to make the opponent excited or emotional, but on the other hand the strategist must keep cool and cautious, and to evaluate the right amount of stimulation to apply on the opponent. Prodding is usually done by the use of linguistics, such as ridicule, sarcasm, scorn and insult. This stratagem is useful especially to the opponent who cannot control his emotions, and ill-tempered by nature.

The stratagem is: **Prod somebody into action.**

Action 22: **To chart the best course for action.**

In order to isolate the opponent and to block any rescue from his allies, or to pull people to your side, you have to be tactful.

The stratagems are:
(I) **Befriend a distant state while attacking a neighbour.** (One of the classical 36 Stratagems).
(II) **Lengthwise and breadth wise, opening and closing.**
(III) **Play double-faced and attack someone from behind.**

Action 23: **To strike.**

There are two categories of stratagems.

(I) Based on six combat scenarios.

(a) When in superior position.
The stratagem is: **To win hands down.**

(b) When in defensive position.
The stratagem is: **Offend in order to defend.**

(c) When in attack.
The stratagem is: **Gain the initiative by striking first.**

(d) When in confused situation.
The stratagems is: **Work on the hearts and minds of others.**

(e) When in gaining ground.
The stratagem is: **Outwit by novelty.**

(f) When in desperate situation.
The stratagem is: **Break the cauldrons and sink the boats.**

(II) Based on other considerations.

(a) When the opponent has a lot of supporters, it is best to capture their leader so as to facilitate the conquest.

The stratagem is: **Defeat the enemy by capturing their chief.** (One of the classical 36 Stratagems).

(b) The strategist will not like other people to take copy of his plot, and he would not give the late comer a chance.

The stratagem is: **Remove the ladder after the accent.** (One of the classical 36 Stratagems).

(c) Sometimes the strategist has to make use of a springboard to launch the strike. The strategist can also consider taking the springboard as an additional gain.

The stratagem is: **Borrow a safe passage to conquer Guo.** (One of the classical 36 Stratagems).

Action 24: **To block the opponent's retreat path.**

This action is to block the opponent's retreat and deal with him.

The stratagem is: **Shut the door to catch the thief.** (One of the classical 36 Stratagems).

Action 25: **To monitor.**

To monitor is to control the current situation to make sure that it stays on track towards its goals. Sun Tze said, "... and the command and control structure so that everything can be deployed to the best advantage." (*The Art of War,* Chapter I).

The stratagem is: **Not to be bound by fixed rules, but vary the plan according to the situation of the enemy.**

2.1.7 Actions 26-28 are all negative actions, indicating the strategist is in an unfavourable position, so he would like to avoid something, to reverse the situation or to use some special stratagems to help.

Action 26: **To avoid.**

In the course of combat, the strategist may find that the scenario has changed, and the opponent is on the favoured side. Now, he tries his best to avoid the adverse consequences. In the case of indictment for a crime, the accused keeps silent about major charges while admitting minor ones, or to dwell on other issues to distract attention.

The stratagems are:
(I) **Avoid the important and dwell on the trivial.**
(II) **Aim at swift victory and avoid prolonged campaign.**

Action 27: **To reverse.**

The best defence is to offend. The strategist tries to reverse the prevailing conditions. When it is not possible to offend by the conventional means, one can do it by other means.

The stratagem is: **Turn the guest into the host.** (One of the classical 36 Stratagems).

Action 28: **To use stratagems.**

The stratagems available to reverse the unfavourable scenario are to use beauty traps, to sow distrust among the opponents, to inflict injuries on oneself to win the confidence of the opponent, to put a job into the hands of another person without letting him know and to plot a set of interlocking stratagems to change the prevailing conditions.

The stratagems are:
(I) **The beauty trap.** (One of the classical 36 Stratagems).
(II) **Let the enemy's own spy sow discord in the enemy's camp.** (One of the classical 36 Stratagems).
(III) **Inflict injury on one's self to win the enemy's trust.** (One of the classical 36 Stratagems).
(IV) **The Stratagem with a set of interlocking stratagems.** (One of the classical 36 Stratagems).

2.1.8 Actions 29-30 include to abandon and to extricate oneself from the scenario.

Action 29: **To abandon.**

(I) A good strategist must be able to trim his sail according to the direction of the wind. In an unsuccessful engagement, he is prepared to give up the less important in order to protect the more important.

The stratagem is: **The plum tree dies for the peach tree.** (One of the classical 36 Stratagems).

(II) Sometimes, it is easier to win by leaving the opponent for the moment. Things will be better when they are at their worst. The action is to allow the opponent more latitude first to keep a tighter rein on him afterwards.

The stratagem is: **In order to capture, one must let loose.** (One of the classical 36 Stratagems).

Action 30: **To run away.**

When the scenario is deteriorating for the strategist; he has to find a way out to save himself by running away. He may find it difficult to extricate from the scenario, unless he does this in a delicate and tactful way.

The stratagems are:

(I) **The cicada sheds its shells.** (One of the classical 36 Stratagems).
(II) **Retreat is the best option.** (One of the classical 36 Stratagems).

2.3   A flexible and variable system.

We adopt the classification system based on basic behaviors because it provides more perspective to the strategic acts. Moreover, it is an open system. Though we have identified thirty basic behaviours, yet the list can be amended by expansion or compression. Likewise, the number of stratagems within each basic behavior can be amended. It is in line with Sun Tze's thesis, "to be flexible, variable and preferably formless".

2.4 Presentation of the stratagems in this book.

Each of these stratagems is elaborated in the following chapters. For each stratagem, first, we state its theme, relating the teachings of Sun Tze to it when it is appropriate.

Second, we state its source that is usually the exploit of some of the Chinese famous generals, statesmen and ordinary people. The source may also be folklore, myth or story.

Third, we provide two international cases for each stratagem, usually from the exploit of some of the famous generals, statesmen, businessmen, and ordinary people of the West. It may also be a folklore, myth or story. Since these stratagems offer timeless insights and without borders into the workings of human nature to maximize gain and to minimize loss, the exploits of famous strategists in other Asian countries, e.g. Japan and the Phillippines are also used to illustrate these stratagems. Finally, comments are made to highlight the key issues of each stratagem.

Readers should take note that for the names of the Chinese and Japanese people; it is the convention to put the family name (or last name) first, followed by the other names, e.g. <u>Chiang</u> Kaishek and <u>Matsushita</u> Konosuke. For other nationalities, the other names come first before the family name (or last name), e.g. Dwight D. <u>Eisenhower</u>.

Synopses of the stratagems are presented in Appendix C.

At the end of Chapters 3-13, exercises are provided to help the readers to enhance their understanding of the materials covered in the chapter. Answers to odd-numbered exercises are in Appendix D.   However, if the reader thinks his or hers is a better solution than the one suggested, please take our hearty congratulations.

Two indexes have been provided for easy references. Index A lists the strategies and the basic behaviours. Index B lists the names of people mentioned in this book.

Chapter 3.

To watch, to find out, to plan, to await and to take advantage of.

3.0 Introduction.

Actions 1-5 stress on patient but alert waiting, careful observation and investigation of the scenario, and quick grasp of the opportunity when it is available.

3.1 Action 1: To watch.

In view of a possible confrontation, it is always safer to watch, preferably from a distance, before getting involved in the matter. One should be observant and avoid getting any involvement if the scenario is not clear, or it does absolutely no good to be involved.

3.1.1 The stratagems are:
   (I)   **Watch the fire across the river.** (One of the classical 36 Stratagems).
   (II) **A straw will show which way the wind blows.**

(I) **Watch the fire across the river.**

3.1.1.1 Theme.

> Sun Tze said, "When there are apparent disorders within the enemies, it is best to wait and watch." (*The Art of War*, Chapter VII). Even when there is disquiet among the enemies, it may not be the best time for us to strike. Your interception can alarm the enemies, causing them to unite, or to join forces with their allies for defense.
>
> Delay entering the battlefield until all other players has become exhausted fighting among them. As for you, observe closely and be prepared for any advantages that may come from it. Sun Tze began his Chapter IX of *The Art of War* with "In the following we deal with the question of deploying the army and observing the enemy."
>
> People watch in safety while others fight, and then reap the spoils when the combatants are exhausted. Two dogs fight for a bone, and a third runs away with it.

3.1.1.2 Source.

Cao Cao watched the fight between General Gongsun Kang and the Yuan brothers. In 207, Cao Cao (155-220) the Prime Minister of the Eastern Han Dynasty defeated the two sons of General Yuan Shao, Yuan Xhang and Yuan Xi who fled to Liaodong located in the eastern part of the Chinese mainland. General Gongsun Kang ruled this part of China. Since his territory was far away from the scope of influence of Cao Cao, he paid little respect to Cao Cao.

Lately, Cao Cao conquered Wuhuan, a nomadic people who inhabited northern China. Cao Cao had always been advised by his counselors to attacl Gongsun to bring him under control. At this moment, since the Yuan brothers had sought refuge in Liaodong, it would be the best time to do both things together: to bring the Gongsun under control and to capture the Yuan brothers.

Cao Cao knew quite well about the personalities of these people, and said, "We do not have to do anything now. Gongsun will kill the Yuan brothers, and he will come to surrender to me." Things did work out in this way.

Cao Cao's staffs were curious to know the reasons. Cao Cao said, "General Gongsun had been suspicious of the Yuan brothers. These people do not trust each other. If I wage war on them, they will join hands together against me. If I do not do anything, Gongsun will think that Yuan brothers have come to espy him. Gongsun is always suspicious that the Yuan brothers will do something to destroy him. So, I am leaving them to fight against each other. Now, since I have conquered Wuhuan, Gongsun thinks he should take the opportunity to please me by killing the Yuan brothers. So he comes here to surrender to me."

Cao Cao accomplished his objectives by keeping himself away from the fire lines. His patience was rewarded.

This story is from *History of the Three Kingdoms* by Chen Shou (233-297).

3.1.1.3 Illustrations.

(1) ***Winston Churchill would like to watch Adolf Hitler and Josef Stalin exhaust each other.*** The British Prime Minister Winston Churchill (in office: 1940-1945) and the General Secretary of the Central Committee of the Communist Party of the Soviet Union, Josef Stalin (in office: 1922-1957) were political adversaries from the start.

The Communist creed represented the very antithesis to Churchill's value, monarchical stability verses revolutionary upheaval, parliamentary democracy against dictatorship of the proletariat, and free trade capitalism to collectivist and state control.

Nazi Germany's attack on Soviet Union on June 22, 1941 brought Stalin into the Allies camp. Stalin urged his allies to launch attack on Western Europe to divert the Germans in Soviet Union by fighting them on another front.

However, Churchill took Stalin's regime equally repulsive as Hitler's, and was content to sit back to watch the two dictators' forces exhaust each other.

In May 1942, Stalin sent his Foreign Minister Vyacheslav Molotov to London, urging Churchill to open a second front. On August 13, Stalin wrote a memorandum to U.S. President Franklin D. Roosevelt (in office: 1932-1945) and Churchill contrasting their decision not to invade Western Europe by that time.

In the Casablanca Conference (June 14-23, 1943), the Allies postponed the cross-channel invasion until 1944, but organised a combined staff to plan for it. For the immediate future, they would continue the Mediterranean campaigns with an invasion of Sicily. As a result of the German invasion, the Soviet Union armies were defeated. Moreover, during the German occupation and through the expulsion of Soviet citizens to German slave labour camps, Soviet Union lost about twenty million people.

(2) *2006 Lebanon War (July 12 – August 14, 2006).* In January 2006, Hamas or "Islamic Resistance Movement" won a surprise victory in the Palestinian parlimentary election. Hamas was listed as a torrorist organization by the U.S. and a few Western countries. In fact, since the death of Palestine Liberation organizer Yasser Arafat, Hamas had won some local elections in Gaza and some West Bank cities.

The 2006 Lebanon War began when Hezbollah militants fired rockets at Israeli border towns as a diversion for anti-tank missile attack on two armored High Mobility Multipurpose Wheeled Vehicles patrolling on the Israeli side of the border. Two Israeli soldiers were captured, and five more were killed in a failed rescue attempt. Israel reacted with massive air raids and artillery fire on Lebanon public and civilian infrastructure. The Hezbollah in Lebanon first emerged as a militia in response to the Israeli invasion of Lebanon in 1982. Its main objective was to resist the Israeli occupation.

Meanwhile, the Palestine Liberation Organization launched cross-border attacks from Southern Lebanon into Israeli territories to help the Hezbollah. Israel held the Lebanonese government responsible for the Hezbollah attacks due to its failure to disarm the Hezbollah. The Lebanonese government disavowed the raids, but criticised Israeli attacks. It was supportive of Hezbollah which aimed at ending Israeli previous occupation of southern Lebanon. It issued a statement to call on President George W. Bush (in office: 2001- 2009) to exert his influence on Israel to stop the attacks on Lebanon, and to reach a ceasefire. The 34-day military conflict continued until a United Nations brokered ceasefire went into effect on August 14, 2006.

Apparently, the U. S. chose not to intervene because Israel was clearing or alleviating the anti-U.S. forces, such as the Hezbollah and the Hamas in this region.

3.1.1.3 Comments.

Another name for this stratagem is "Sit on top of the mountain to watch the tigers fight." Sun Tze said, "Whether one wages war or not, it should be decided by the consideration of possible gain." (*The Art of War,* Chapter XII).

By watching a fire across the river does not mean one has nothing to do. In daily routine matters, it is to take a careless attitude. But in war, one has to follow the development of the scenario closely.

If the enemy is egotistical or somebody who tries to gain by abusing others, the wise strategist should wait to let his aggressive enemy alienate from those around him. When things work out, the in-fighting that a manipulative, cruel or controlling leader creates will eat up his energy and resources. Now, the strategist has the advantage over this enemy.

In some organizations, there may be two or more groups of people wrestling for power. As a member of the organization, each group tries to persuade you to be on its side. Without showing your choice, you may not be able to survive. By showing your selection, there is the danger that you might make the wrong choice. The wrong choice will be hazardous to your career.

(II)   A straw will show which way the wind blows.

3.1.2.1 Theme.

> Sun Tze proposed that it is important to interpret the various signs, symptoms and behaviors of the enemy. The adepts in warfare are able to concentrate their forces against the enemy and judge their moves accurately so as to beat them.
>
> Sun advocated thirty-two methods to observe the enemy and to draw deductions for each case. (*The Art of War*, Chapter IX). Broadly speaking, there methods fall into two categories:
>
> (a) Natural and artificial vegetation, animal behaviors and changes of natural scenes, such as clouds of dust.
>
> (b) Attitude and behaviors of the enemy's envoys and soldiers.

3.1.2.2 Source.

Sun Tze, *Art of War,* refer to 3.1.2.1.

3.1.2.3 Illustrations.

(1) *A Persian cat revealed a military secret.* On May 10, 1940, the Nazi Germany armed forces invaded France through the heavily wooded and semi-mountainous area of the Ardennes to north of the Maginot Line. Both the German and the French tried their best to locate their enemy's command and control centres and to destroy them.

One morning, a German officer observed the battlefields ahead with binoculars. It was a large cemetery. To his surprise, he saw a Persian cat lying on the ground to enjoy the sunbath. For a consecutive few days, between 8 and 9 in the morning, the cat was present, and it disappeared for the rest of the day. The German officer tried to reason. Persian cat was an expensive pet, not likely to be owned by the villagers. In the army, soldiers of medium and low ranking were not allowed to keep pets. It must belong to a high ranking official. Since the cat disappeared so fast, there must be a concealed bunker in the cemetery.

Based on these analyses, he reported his speculation to his seniors, and they immediately brought into six companies of soldiers with heavy artilleries to bomb the area. The German officer's guesswork was right. For the French official, he never knew that it was the Persian cat that betrayed him.

(2) ***Mud and snow could also be tell-tale signs.*** In April 1944, the Soviets began an attack on the Kerch Penninsula (Crimea). The Germans held the Crimea, even though their military position became untenable. The 4th Ukrainian Front had the mission to take the Isthum of Perekop which was the narrow three-to-four-mile-wide strip of land that connected the Crimea Peninsula to the continent.

On the night of April 6, it snowed in Perekop. Early next morning, as a Soviet soldier came into the bunker, his commander noticed that the thin layer of snow on his coat thawed. In order to keep the bunker dry, soldiers usually dug out the mud and snow and threw them outside the trenches or the bunkers. The Soviet commander called his senior to send in an airplane to take pictures of the Axis defence ground. With these photos, the commander was able to locate the heaps of mud and snow which their enemies shovelled out of their shelters. The commander ordered artilleries to bomb the Axis defence lines more precisely, and to crush the Germans. In eight days, the Soviets liberated the Crimea, capturing 38,000 Axis soldiers.

3.1.2.4 Comments.

Sun Tze said it is important to know how to interpret the very signs, symptoms and behaviours of the enemy relative to oneself. He analysed the dust formations because they provided tell-tales signs of troop's movement. The German officer and the Soviet commander watched the situations, thought about them, and conceived of the secrets behind. They were brilliant watchers and thinkers. Perhaps, thawing snow should be added to Sun's watch list of natural scenes.

3.2 Action 2: To find out.

This is a fact finding technique in which inquiry or investigation of the scenario is conducted on the opponent's situation and intention.

3.2.1 The stratagem is: **Find the way in the dark by throwing a stone**.

3.2.1.1 Theme.

> You can gather information about the enemy's situation and intention by this handy and inexpensive method. Politicians call it "releasing the balloons" to attract comments before the launch of new laws or actions.
>
> "Scheme to discover their plans and plots...use tactics to ascertain their strength and weakness, and by contact one will know the areas of their strengths and weaknesses." (*The Art of War*, Chapter VI).
>
> The purpose of these acts is to probe, and not to go for a direct confrontation against the enemy. Sun Tze said, "If one knows the enemy and knows himself, his victory will not stand in doubt. If he has a thorough knowledge of the earth and heaven (i.e. the circumstantial factors), he is sure to win." (*The Art of War*, Chapter X).

3.2.1.2 Source.

Cao Cao invited Liu Bei to have wine and to talk about the heroes of the present day. Before the Three Kingdoms Period (220-280), in 196, Cao Cao proclaimed himself the Prime Minister and made the puppet Emperor his trump card. After several decisive battles with the warlords in the north, he unified the region north of the Yellow River. Liu Bei, a descendant of a Prince of the Emperor Han's house, had the ambition to restore the Emperor's rule. However, at that moment he was in Xu Chang, the Capital of the State, under the control of Cao Cao. He was a partisan of Cao Cao, taking up a post in the court. In order to waive Cao Cao's suspicion on him, he spent his spare time in the farm.

One day, Cao Cao invited Liu to have wine with him. Cao Cao said, "You, General, have been to many lakes and rivers. You must know who are the heroes of the present day, and I wish you would say who they are."

Liu said, "I am just a common dullard. How can I know such things?" But Cao Cao kept on pressing for answers. Liu mentioned Yuan Shu, Yuan Shao, Liu Biao, Sun Ce, Liu Zhang, Zhang Xiu and some other leaders. Cao Cao rebutted these people as heroes one by one. Finally, he pointed his finger first at his guest and then at him, saying, "The only heroes in the world are you and me."

Liu Bei gasped, and the spoon and chopsticks rattled to the floor. Now just at that moment the storm burst with a tremendous peal of thunder and rush of rain. Liu Bei stooped down to recover the fallen articles, saying, "What a shock! And it was quite close."

"What? Are you afraid of thunder?" said Cao Cao.

Liu replied, "The Sage One (i.e. Confucius) paled at a sudden peal of thunder or fierce gust of wind. Why should one not fear?" Thus he glossed over the real fact that it was the words he had heard that had so startled him. In fact, Cao Cao would like to find out how ambitious Liu was, and what Liu thought about the other competitors.

This story is from *Romance of Three Kingdoms* by Luo Guanzhong (c. 1330-1400).

3.2.1.3   Illustrations.

(1) ***Adolf Hitler tested the British and the French responses by breaking the Versailles Treaty.*** After Adolf Hilter became Chancellor in 1933, he ordered the army to be trebled in size from the 100,000 men by the Versailles Treaty limit to 300,000 men by October, 1934. It was done initially under the utmost secrecy. Admiral Erich Raeder, the Chief of the Navy, was ordered to construct large warships, above the maximum size decreed by the Treaty, and the construction of submarines forbidden by the Treaty.

Hermann Goering (also spelled Göring) was to train air force pilots and the design of military aircraft. In March 1935, Hilter decided to test the resolve of the U.K. and France by authorising Hermann Goering to reveal to a British official about the Luftwaffe (Air Force). Though all these were challenges to the Treaty, yet there was little reaction from these two countries.

A few days later, Hitler "threw another stone" by declaring openly the introduction of military service and the creation of an army with 36 divisions (approximately half million men).   Again the U.K. and France had a weak reaction. While Hilter was increasing the strength of the armed forces, he made speeches proclaiming a desire for peace and the folly of war. He said he had no intention of annexing Austria or re-militarising the Rhineland and he would respect all the territorial clauses of the Treaty.

On March 7, 1936, a small troop of German soldiers marched across the Rhine bridges into the demilitarised areas of Germany. Again neither the U.K. or the French condemned this outrageous act. The lack of French reaction was beyond imagination due to the fact that this small German force was vastly outnumbered by the French army near the border.

During the period of 1934-1939, the U.K. and France adopted the controversial policy of appeasement. Hitler continued to test the limits of this policy by breaking the Treaty on one hand and negotiating new non-aggression pacts with several European countries on the other hand. Eventually, Hitler invaded Poland, and this last straw broke the camel's back, prompting the outbreak of the WWII on Sept. 1, 1939.

(2) *The Bush administration lobbied for support to U.S. attack on Iraq, 2002.* The events of September 11, 2001 served as the catalyst for the assault on Afghanistan to destroy Osama Bin Laden's Al Qaeda organization and to topple the Taliban regime. By December 22, 2001, a new government was installed in Kabul. Hamid Karzai was first named interim leader of the country for six months after the fall of the Taliban. In June 2002, he was elected to a two-year term by the "grand council", a classical gathering of Afghanistan's tribal leaders to resolve issues of national importance.

In the winter 2002, the Bush administration of the U.S. claimed to hold information that President Saddam Hussein of Iraq had close links with Al Qaeda, and the latter had posed an unacceptable threat to the world by developing nuclear weapons. President George W. Bush (in office: 2000-2008) would like to test the support of the Senate and the Congress and also the responses from other countries of the Security Council of the U.N. on his proposal to attack Iraq.

The first issue was that the U.N. weapons inspectors must be allowed to return to Iraq. Vice President Richard Cheney gave two speeches in late August 2002 in which he said inspections should not be the primary goal of U.S. policy towards Iraq because it would not work. He said that the key issue was Hussein's drive to acquire nuclear weapon, and that the return of inspectors who left Iraq in 1998, would provide no assurance.

On the other hand, the Secretary of State Colin Powell inclined to emphasise that he also believed inspections would not stop Hussein's drive to acquire weapons of mass destruction. But he believed the administration should go through the U.N. process as a way to build international support for any U.S. attack on Iraq. In fact, the Bush administration was in the process of consultation and reflection about the appropriate courses of action against Hussein.

Then, the Iraqi Deputy Prime Minister Tareq Aziz said Baghdad was ready to seek an overall solution to its confrontation with Washington as long as U.S. concerns about weapons programs were not just a pretext to attack. He repeated an invitation for U.S. politicians to visit Iraq and check for weapons of mass destruction. This suggestion ridiculed in the West as a ploy to avoid the return of weapons inspectors who left in 1998 and had not been allowed to return.

3.2.1.4 Comments.

It is common sense when a burglar wants to break in a house, he may throw in a stone first and to observe the responses of the people and the dogs if there are any, before making another move. In the politicial or military context, the action of throwing a stone will be in the form of verbal announcements or sending out scouts.

Adolf Hilter attempted to test the limits of the British and French policy of appeasement. Before U.S. launched its "Operation Iraqi Freedom" on March 20, 2003, Saddam Hussein also tested the responses of the U.N. towards his weapons developing activities. Looking at the other side of the coin, one should deliver clear responses to those who release the balloons, not to let them misunderstand.

3.3 Action 3: To plan.

Sun Tze emphasized the need of careful planning because "The general who is able to make careful deliberations beforehand can win." (*The Art of War,* Chapter I). According to Sun, there are eight factors for consideration in the planning for war.

(a) The moral cause of the sovereign and his policies.
(b) The leadership of the commanders.
(c) The weather.
(d) The characteristics of the terrain.
(e) The effective implementation of order and discipline.
(f) The numerical strength of the army.
(g) The quality of training of officers and men.
(h) The system of rewards and punishments.

Sun also advocated a very profound four-stage planning in dealing with the enemy. (*The Art of War,* Chapter III). They are:

(a) To conquer the enemy by strategy.
(b) To disrupt the enemy form forming strategic alliances with his allies.
(c) To attack the enemy in the battlefield.
(d) To besieged a walled city trying to overcome it. This option should be avoided.

3.3.1 The stratagems are:
   (I) **Take counsel in one's temple.**
   (II) **To win hands down.**

(I) **Take counsel in one's temple.**

3.3.1.1   Theme.

It is similar to an English idiom "Take counsel of one's pillow", meaning one has to weigh and consider the matter, preferably with others. We modify it to "Take counsel in one's temple", because Sun Tze said, "Those who carry out

41

planning in the temple beforehand will win if the plans are thorough and detailed." (*The Art of War,* Chapter I).

The gathering at the temple had the following aims.
(a) The temple was a place where offerings and prayers were made to the ancestors, seeking divine protection.

(b) The gathering served to unite the goals and aspirations of all those attending the meeting.

(c) The temple was a place of sacredness. It would deter anyone betraying the cause.

(d) The temple was a private and secretive place to discuss battle plans and to secure confidentiality.

3.3.1.2 Source.

Sun Tze, *Art of War,* refer to 3.3.1.1.

3.3.1.3 Illustrations.

(1) ***Japan plotted to fight Imperial Russia on another occasion.*** In Japan, the Meiji Restoration (1866-1869) was a movement towards modernization and industrialization. Japan built up a new army modelled after the Prussian force and a navy after the British. It strived to be a military power under the slogan of "National wealth and military strength".

Conflict of interests in Korea between the Qing Dynasty of China and Japan led to the Sino-Japanese War in 1894-95. Japan defeated China utterly. Mutsu Munemitsu (1844-1897) was the lead Japanese negotiator in the Treaty of Shimonoseki, 1885, which was in favour of Japan in the following terms:

(a) Recognised Korean independence.
(b) Chinese indemnity: 200 million of silver (150% of Japan's war expenses).
(c) Japan's equality with West at Chinese treaty ports.

(d) Japanese factories in treaty ports.

(e) Cession of Taiwan and Liaodong to Japan.

On April 23, 1895, six days after the negotiation, Russia, Germany and France voiced their disagreement, and requested Japan to return Liaodong (a peninsula adjacent to the Korean Peninsula) to China based on the balance of power and conflict to their interests in the region. It was called the Triple Intervention. The three countries sent their respective fleets to the region. Meanwhile, the U.K. and the U.S. declared neutral on this matter.

Ito Hirobumi (2nd term in office: 1892-1896), Japanese Prime Minister consulted his ministers in the Supreme War Council on this matter. The Council was structured according to a German style general staff system with a Chief of Staff who had direct access to the Emperor. The Emperor could operate independently of the army members and civilian officials.

After evaluation of both the favourable and unfavourable factors, Prince Yamagata Aritomo, the War Minister and Commander said, "Our army and navy are not ready to confront the joint forces of these three countries."

Despite protest by Japan to the Triple Intervention, Japan had to return Liaodong to China for an additional indemnity of 30 million of silver. The Japanese public took it as a national humiliation. Meanwhile, Japan intensified its army and navy, preparing for the event to beat its arch enemy, Russia, some other time. It happened in the Russo-Japanese War in 1904-05. After that war, Japan earned the international esteem as a military power.

(2) ***The Gulf War (August 2, 1990-February 28, 1991).*** It was an outcome of Iraq's invasion of Kuwait on August 2, 1990. Iraq annexed Kuwait which it had long claimed to be a part of its territories since its independence in 1921. In early 1990, Iraqi President Saddam Hussein denounced the Gulf States for their low oil prices conspiracy which rendered Iraq impossible to repay the debts of the Iran-Iraq war (September 22, 1980-August 20, 1988). In

addition, Iraq accused Kuwait of illegally slant-drilling petroleum across the border between the two countries.

On November 29, the U.N. set Jan 15, 1991 as the deadline for withdrawal of Iraqi troops from Kuwait. When Hussein refused to comply, Operation Desert Storm was launched on Jan 18, by the coalition of 34 nations under the leadership of U.S. General Norman Schwarzkopf. The coalition conducted a massive air attack to destroy Iraqi forces, military and civil infrastructure. Iraq called for terrorist attacks against the coalition and launched Scud missiles at Israel and Saudi Arabia to widen the war.

When the U.S. President George H. W. Bush (in office: 1989-1993) declared a cease-fire on February 28, most of the Iraqi troops in Kuwait had either surrendered or fled. The cease-fire agreements were inconclusive and vague. They called on the Iraqi government to allow U.N. weapons inspectors to search for prohibited weapons in Iraq, and the coalition allies to enforce the "No-Fly Zones" over northern and southern Iraq. The latter was a measure to prevent Hussein's regime from using military aircraft to attack the Kurds and Shiite Muslims residing in these areas respectively.

During the War, the U.S. military distributed the English version of Sun Tze's *The Art of War* to their officers in the combat zones, while the Russian military advisors also lectured the Iraqi troops on Sun Tze's teachings. The Iraqi troops put into practice what they learned in their flight for survival when the coalition forces made their raids.

3.3.1.4 Comments.

Sun Tze placed a lot of emphasis on the need of detailed planning. "The wise strategist will always weigh and consider the favourable and unfavourable factors. On the basis of the favourable factors he plans how to pursue his objective, and on the basis of the unfavourable factor, he plans how to avoid them." (*The Art of War*, Chapter VIII).

Ito Hirobumi and his ministers took prudence as gold, and stooped to conquer. Forty-six years later, on September 6, 1941, the Imperial Conference met to consider the policy that if negotiations with the U.S. (on various issues including withdrawal from occupied territories in China, and the oil embargo against Japan) failed by October, Japan would wage war against the U.S., the Netherlands and Great Britain. Prime Minister Konoe Fumimaro realized that he had lost the struggle with the adamant Army. He knew that many officials in the Navy were convinced that war with the U.S. would end in disaster. But he was unable to obtain enough support to negotiate with the militarists.

In October, after negotiation with the U.S. became deadlock, the Supreme War Council discussed the waging war issue. Oikawa Koshiro, the Navy minister evaded the question by saying, "The Navy does not want to wage war, but as it has been decided by the Imperial Conference, even if we disagree, it will proceed as planned." Konoe and his ministers failed to act responsibly in the evaluation and the choice of action. The attack on Pearl Harbour was the outcome, prompting U.S. military involvement in the Pacific.

On January 15, 1991, Saddam Hussein could avoid the blunder of confronting a coalition of 34 nations, if he and his ministers deliberated the eight factors proposed by Sun Tze (Refer to 4.2) in the planning for war.

William II (or Wilhelm II), the last German Emperor and King of Prussia (1859-1941) was the key figure on German policy leading to the First World War. He was described as aggressive, tactless and headstrong. After 1918, he was exiled in the municipality of Doorn, the Netherlands.

Legend has it that when he was reading the German version of Sun Tze's *The Art of War*, and came across the paragraph, "For an angry man may change and become pleased; a grieved man may change and become contented. Whereas a State that is once destroyed cannot be restored; a man that is once killed cannot be resurrected," (*The Art of War*, Chapter XII), he wept. He said, "If I was able to read this book twenty years ago, the German Empire would not be destroyed."

(II) To win hands down.

3.3.2.1 Theme.

> To win hands down is to win without striking a blow. To Sun Tze, winning is not only about destroying the enemy, it is about getting stronger. The ideal scenario is one can win without having to fight.
>
> Sun said, "To win every battle by actual fighting before a war is won, it is not the most desirable. To conquer the enemy without resorting to war is the most desirable." (*The Art of War,* Chapter III).
>
> Thus, Sun focused on the detailed planning and strategising, the use of diplomacy, psychological operations and the use of sheer demonstration of supremacy.

3.3.2.2 Source.

Hann Xin annexed the Yan State by winning hands down. In 205 BC, during the struggle of the Liu Bang, the King of Han and Xiang Yu, the King of Chu for the throne, General Hann Xin of the Han State would like to attack the Yan State to the north and the Qi State to the east. These states were established by the descendents of the noble families of the respective states after the fall of the Qin Dynasty. Hann sought the advice of Li Tsochun, Lord of Guang Wu, on this matter.

Li said, "General, you have just crashed the 200,000-strong Zhao army, and killed Chen Yu, Lord of Cheng An, by your 10,000-strong army, your power and authority are frightening. However, it is no good to engage in war for a long time, as stated in the war strategy books. As time wears on, the spirit of your army flags, and the supplies and provisions run short. The Yan and Qi States may know about these, and they will unite together to fight against you."

Hann was pleased with this analysis, and asked for a strategy. Li said, "Make no move at the moment. Be kind to the people of the Zhao State. You are going to reward your soldiers with good meals and wine frequently. Then, send someone able to speak and know how to say it properly to deliver your message to the Yan State. The Yans will submit to your request for annexing. Meanwhile, send another messenger to the Qi State to tell their people about the current situation. The counsellors of the Qi State will find it difficult to ally with the Yans against you."

Hann thanked Li for his proposal and acted accordingly. The Yan State was overawed and it pleaded for submission. Hann was able to annex the Yan State without military actions.

This story is from *Records of the Historian* by Sima Qian (145-86 BC). This is China's first history book writtten in a series of biographies.

3.3.2.3 Illustrations.

(1) ***Napoleon Bonaparte's confrontation with Michel Ney at Laffrey.*** In 1814, Napoleon Bonaparte (1769-1821) was forced to abdicate, and was in exile in the Island of Elba. On February 25, 1815, he escaped from Elba and landed near Cannes on March 1. He had 700 men with him. In spite of keeping things in secret, the French people knew about this and they gathered around Bonaparte.

Louis XVIII sent the 5th Regiment of the Line led by Marshal Michel Ney to arrest Bonaparte. In fact, Ney previously served under Bonaparte in Russia. He promised to bring Bonaparte back in iron cage.

On March 7, Ney met Bonaparte at Laffrey. Bonaparte walked towards the regiment alone, dismounted from his horse. When he was within ear-shot of Ney's men, he shouted, "Soldiers of the 5th Ligne, do you recognize me? If there is one among you who wishes to kill his General, here I am."

There was a brief silence, and then the soldiers roared "Vive L'Empereur!" They marched with Bonaparte to Paris; and the Bonaparte's ephemeral rule of the Hundred Days (March 20-June 28, 1815) began. Upon Bonaparte's return, Ney helped Louis XVIII to flee from France, but he did not join Bonaparte's camp despite of the latter's invitation.

(2) **The Cuban Missile Crisis (October 16–28, 1962).** In May 1962, Premier Nikita S. Khrushchev of the Soviet Union decided to install intermediate range missiles in Cuba as a means of countering an emerging lead of the U.S in installing missiles in Turkey and Italy.

The Cuban Missile Crisis began on October 16, when the U.S. reconnaissance data revealing Soviet nuclear missile installation in Cuba was shown to U.S. President John F. Kennedy (in office 1961-1963). On October 22 Kennedy demanded Khrushchev to remove all the missile bases and weapons in Cuba, and ordered a "defensive quarantine" of Cuba in order to prevent Soviet ships from bringing more missiles and materials to it. Khrushchev authorized the Soviet field commanders in Cuba to launch their nuclear weapons if they were attacked by the U.S. On October 23, twenty-four Soviet ships made their journey for the no-go zone.

Kennedy prepared 549 combat aircraft, 40,000 marines and 5 divisions, among which the 82nd and 10th Airborne were standby in Florida. On October 26, Khrushchev sent a letter to Kennedy suggesting that the Cuban missile sites would be dismantled if the U.S. gave its reassurance that it would not invade Cuba. Kennedy agreed to this. The crisis ended on October 28, when Khrushchev announced he had ordered the removal of Soviet missiles in Cuba, and the Soviet ships turned back.

3.3.2.4 Comments.

Cowing the enemy into submission by making a big display of your strength is the best, while attacking the military force is an unwise move.

Napoleon Bonaparte had less than eleven hundred men when confronted by the 5th Regiment which was sent to arrest him. In no way he could contest the captors. But he knew that Louis' efforts to reverse the results of the French Revolution made the Bourbon monarchy unpopular. Bonaparte was able to overawe the 5th Regiment, as he had the moral cause, and the respect of the soldiers.

President John F. Kennedy was determined to keep the U.S. free of the threats of Soviet missiles in Cuba by taking aggressive disposition. Later, in 1964, Premier Nikita Khrushchev lost his office because the Soviet Communist Party thought he had committed errors to back down to Kennedy over the placement of Soviet missiles in Cuba.

3.4 Action 4: To await.

One has to keep track of the changing internal and external conditions of a scenario. He has to take action when the right moment comes. Premature or delayed action can ruin the chance.

3.4.1 The stratagem is: **Wait at one's ease for an exhausted enemy.** (One of the classical 36 Stratagems).

3.4.1.1 Theme.

Tire your enemy by carrying out an active defense, in doing so, his strength will be reduced. Keep evading him and force him to come to you from far away, while you stand your ground.

Sun Tze advocated the first mover advantage concept. The army that arrived early at the battlefield would have enough time to rest and prepare for the enemy. Once the ground had been occupied, it would pose tremendous danger to others trying to take it. "The clever combatant always forces the enemies to traverse distances and dangers in order to meet him, while he waits for them at ease." (*The Art of War*, Chapter VI).

Food and rest are two important factors affecting the combat readiness and strength of an army. It is advantageous to use well-rested troops to fight the enemies who are weary after travelling long distance. (*The Art of War*, Chapter VII).

3.4.1.2 Source.

Plucking up courage with the first drum. In 684 BC in China, the Qi State invaded the Lu State. Duke Zhuanggong of Lu (reigned 693-662 BC) recruited a military strategist, Cao Gui, to be his consultant in the battlefield. When the two confronting armies had their formations, the Qi army was the first to beat the drums for attack. The Duke was about to sound the drums and launch the counter-attack. But Cao advised him to wait, saying "This is not the right moment, because the enemy's courage is roused and is at its highest." The Qi army's first attack failed and its soldiers became a bit weary.

Then, the Qi's army beat the drums again, but Cao still insisted to do nothing. The Qi army's attack was in vain, and the spirit of the Qi army ran out. When the Qi army beat the drums the third time, Cao said this was the right time to beat their drums for the first time to raise spirit of the Lu's army to charge forward. The Lu army launched the counter-attack during which the Qi army was routed. The Qi army fled from the battlefields.

Sun Tze had the same theory in his book: "In the early stage men's spirits are most fiery. Later they begin to flag. Towards the end they may fade out. Hence the clever combatant tries to avoid the enemy when their spirits are most fiery, and attack them when their spirits are flagging or fading out. This is the way to deal with the spirits of men." (*The Art of War,* Chapter VII).

The Duke would like to give order for the pursuit. But Cao stopped him, and jumped off the chariot to examine the tracks of wheels on the ground left by the fleeing Qi army and the banners. After inspecting the scenario, Cao said, "War is based on deception, and now I am sure that the Qi army is actually running away for life. This is the time to crush them." The Duke ordered the pursuit, and the Lu army won the battle which was named the Battle of Chang Shao.

Again, Sun Tze wrote about this in his book: "One must not try to pursue the enemy when their movements indicate perfect array. One must not pursue when the enemy simulate flight. One must not challenge the enemy at the time when their spirits are highest." (*The Art of War* , Chapter VII).

This story is from *Zuo Qiuming's Chronicles,* a classical history of the Spring and Autumn Period (770-476 BC). The author, Zuo Qiuming (c. 490 BC) of the Lu State, lived during the closing years of that period.

3.4.1.3 Illustrations.

(1) ***Maximus Fabius wanted to exhaust Barca Hannibal in a long war of attrition.*** Barca Hannibal (247-183 BC), Commander-in-Chief of the Carthaginian Empire, was one of the greatest military commander and strategist. He marched his army which included war elephants from Iberia over the Pyrenees and Alps into Northern Italy. During his invasion of Italy, he defeated the Romans in a series of battles at Trebia (218 BC), Trasimene (217 BC) and Cannae (215 BC).

In 217 BC, the Romans appointed Quintus Fabius Maximus Verrucosus (c. 275-203 BC) (Fabius was the family name) as a dictator which was the title of a magistrate in ancient Rome conferred by the Senate to rule the state in emergency times. Fabius was aware of the military superiority of the Carthaginians. He refused to meet Hannibal in a pitched battle. Instead he kept his troops close to Hannibal, hoping to exhaust him in a long war of attrition. He was able to harass the Carthaginian foraging activities, limiting Hannibal's ability to wreak destruction while conserving his own military force. The delaying tactics involved a pincer of not directly engaging Hannibal and a "scorched earth" practice to prevent Hannibal's forces from obtaining grain and other resources from their locations.

In 216 BC, the Romans were tired of Fabius' tactics and Fabius was supplanted, resulting in the rout at Cannae in 215 BC when the Roman army was badly defeated. After Cannae, the Romans resorted to use the Fabius' tactic of attrition again.

(2) **Napoleon Bonaparte's invasion of Russia.** In June 22, 1812, Napoleon Bonaparte began his fatal Russian campaign with about 600,000 men and over 50,000 horses. Virtually all of continental Europe was under his control, and the invasion of Russia was an attempt to force Tsar Alexander I to submit once again to the terms of the Treaty of Tilsit that Bonaparte had imposed upon him in 1808.

Bonaparte's plan was to bring the war to a conclusion within twenty days by forcing the Russians to fight a major battle. Just in case his plans were off, he had his supply wagons carry 30 days of food. But in reality, things were different. Bonaparte found, as the Germans found in 1941, that Russia had a very poor road network.

The Russian army under Marshal Kutuzov could not hope to defeat the French in a direct confrontation. Instead, they began a defensive campaign of strategic retreat, adopting a scorched earth policy of destroying everything possible as they retreated before the French. As the summer wore on, Bonaparte's massive supply lines were stretched ever thinner, and his forces began to decline. By September, without having engaged in a single battle, the French army had been reduced by more than two thirds from fatigue, hunger, desertion and raids by the Russian forces.

It was clear that unless the Russians engaged the French army in a major battle, Moscow would be Bonaparte's in a matter of weeks. The Tsar insisted upon a combat confrontation, and on September 7, with winter closing in and the French army only 70 miles from the city, the two armies met at Borodino Field. The Russian army had the advantage to wait at ease for the exhausted enemies.

By the end of the day, 108,000 soldiers had died, but neither side had gained a decisive victory. Kutuzov realised that any further defence of the city would be useless, and he withdrew his forces, prompting the people of Moscow to begin a massive exodus. When the French army arrived on September 14, they found a city depopulated and bereaved of supplies.

After waiting in vain for the Tsar to negotiate, Bonaparte ordered his troops to begin marching home. Because Kutuzov's forces blocked the route south, and the French were in no shape for a battle, the retreat retraced the long, devastated route of the invasion. Having waited until mid-October to depart, the exhausted French army soon found itself in the midst of winter. Temperatures soon dropped well below freezing, the Cossacks attacked stragglers and isolated units, food was almost non-existent, and the march was five hundred miles. Ten thousand men survived.

The campaign ensured Bonaparte's downfall and Russia's status as a leading power in post-Napoleonic Europe.

3.4.1.4 Comments.

No doubt, Barca Hannibal was a great commander and strategist; even his greatest enemy, the Romans, came to adopt elements of Hannibal's military tactics in their own strategic canon.

Equally important, Fabius' tactic of exhausting enemy in a long war of attrition impressed the modern world strategists, for instance, Tsar Alexander I in the Napoleonic War, Josef Stalin in WWII, and the Vietnam War in the 1960s and 1970s. General Norman Schwarzkopf, the Allied Commander of the Gulf War, 1991 commented that the technology of war might change, the sophistication of the weapons certainly have changed, but those same principles of war that applied to the days of Hannibal, did apply in present situations.

3.5 Action 5: To take advantage of.

As a result of Action 4, when the right moment comes, one has to take action without hesitation.

3.5.1 The stratagems are:
- (I) **Loot a burning house.** (One of the classical 36 Stratagems).
- (II) **Take away a goat in passing.** (One of the classical 36 Stratagems).

(I) **Loot a burning house.**

3.5.1.1 Theme.

> Use the misery and distress of your enemy to gain something for yourself. "When the army's ardour and morale is dampened, when the fighting strength is exhausted, and when the state treasury is spent, it will be an opportunity for the other state sovereigns to spring up and take advantage." (*The Art of War,* Chapter II).

3.5.1.2 Source.

Goujian was patient enough to wait for the chance to recover his state. In the Spring and Autumn Period (770-476 BC), the Wu State devoured the Yue State in 493 BC. Goujian, the King of Yue (reigned 498-465 BC) became a captive, and he had to serve Fuchai, the King of Wu, (reigned 495-473BC) assuring that he would be a subordinate of the Wu State.

Goujian spent ten years in preparation for the come back. Then, the Wu State suffered famine due to the destruction caused by locusts, and Fuchai himself was engaged in warfare in the far north. There were not many soldiers on guard in the Capital of the Wu State which became chaotic due to the shortage of food. Goujian knew that it was a golden chance to wage war, killing Fuchai and recovering his State in 473 BC.

This story is from *Records of the Historian* by Sima Qian (145-86 BC).

3.5.1.3 Illustrations.

(1) ***Japan got its opportunity to seize Chinese territories when China was in chaos.*** Yuan Shikai was a Chinese military leader and statesman in the last years of the Qing Empire. He served as viceroy of Chihli (now Hebei) Province from 1901 to 1907. He gathered much power in his hands. In 1911, the new China Republic was formed. In 1912, Yuan was appointed Premier and authorised to form a republican government and in 1913 he was elected President. After assuming dictatorial control, Yuan proclaimed himself Emperor in 1913. With opposition at every quarter and the nation breaking up into warlord factions, Yuan died of natural causes in June 1916, deserted by his lieutenants.

The Japanese threatened from the nation without. When World War I broke out in 1914, Japan fought on the Allied side and seized German holdings in Shandong Province, China. In 1915 the Japanese set before the warlord government under Yuan in Beijing the so-called "Twenty-one Demands", which would have made China a Japanese protectorate.

Yuan rejected some of these demands but yielded to the Japanese insistence on keeping the Shandong territory already in its possession. Yuan also recognised Tokyo's authority over southern Manchuria and eastern Inner Mongolia. After Yuan's death, shifting alliances of regional warlords fought for control of the Chineses government. In 1917, in secret communiqués, the U.K., France and Italy assented to the Japanese claim in exchange for the Japan's naval action against Germany.

(2) ***Soviet Union declared war on Japan after the first atomic bomb was dropped.*** On August 6, 1945, an U.S. bomber dropped the first atomic bomb on Hiroshima. On August 8, the Soviet Union ignored the Neutrality Pact that was valid between Japan and the Soviet Union and declared war on Japan. On August 9, another U.S. bomber dropped the second atomic bomb to Nagasaki. After Japan had accepted the terms of the Potsdam Declaration on August 14, Soviet forces occupied all of the four Northern Islands on August 28. These four islands are located off the Northeast coast of the Nemuro Peninsula of Hokkaido. They are: Habomai, Shikotan, Kunashiri and Etorofu.

On August 8, the Soviet troops landed in Port Arthur and Dairen in the Kwantung Peninsular in China. They seized the supplies of the Japanese army, packed up all valuable materials to send to the Soviet Union, and gave the Japanese weapons to the Chinese Communists.

When the Japanese house was on fire, the Soviet Union was quick to loot as quickly as possible.

3.5.1.4 Comments.

Sun Tze said, "... what makes conquest of the enemy profitable is loot." (*The Art of War,* Chapter II). Disorders and chaos are moments of uncertainty. In riots, the mobs always loot for personal gain. In chaotic times, plenty of new opportunities will be open to those who are ambitious and intelligent. New leaders emerge and old leaders lose credibility during times of upheaval when new orders are created out of chaos.

Rudolph Guilliani was declining in prestige as Mayor of New York when the attack on the World Trade Center took place on September 11, 2001. He instantly became the man on the scene: compassionate, organized, generous, courageous, and articulate. Meanwhile, U.S. President George W. Bush was being whisked around the country to be protected, and U.S. Vice President Richard Cheney was deliberately hidden from the public, Guillianti proved himself to be an able and popular leader whose decision and command of the situation were comparable to those of Winston Churchill during the bombing of U.K. in WWII.

(II) **Take away a goat in passing.**

3.5.2.1 Theme.

> Any negligence of the enemy can be turned into a benefit for you. One is able to take advantage of the enemy's faults, loopholes or negligence whenever and wherever available. For example, "When the army is beset with disorder and lack of faith, the other state sovereigns are sure to take advantage and cause troubles." (*The Art of War*, Chapter III).
>
> A strategist always makes his plans flexible enough to take advantage of any opportunity available, so as to maximize his gain however small. Hoist your sail when the wind is fair.

3.5.2.2 Source.

"I picked up the string only." While walking on the countryside, a man saw a goat gazing on the pasture. It had a piece of string tied round its neck. Since there was nobody around, he pulled the goat by its string and walked home.

After a few days, the owner of the goat was informed that the man got his missing goat. He called the government officers to arrest the man.

When the officers arrived at the man's house, the man said, "I did not steal the goat. When I was walking along, I saw a piece of string. I picked up the string only. But the goat came by itself."

This is a popular Chinese folklore from ancient times.

3.5.2.3 Illustrations.

(1) ***The adventure at Vigo Bay, 1702.*** In the summer of 1702, an Anglo-Dutch fleet commanded by Admiral Sir George Rooke with Lieutenant Admiral Philip van Almonde commanding the Dutch squadron was sent to capture Cadiz in Spain. A combined French and Spanish fleet defended Cadiz and overwhelmed the invaders. In fact, Rooke committed errors in misjudging the timing for the attacks.

On September 23, 1702, Rooke decided to retreat as his supplies were running out. On September 29, the returning fleet was on its journey when Rooke learned that the Spanish treasure fleet, one of the richest ever assembled set sailed on July 24, 1702 from Havana Cuba to Spain, had been diverted from Cadiz to Vigo which was not far away from where he was.

Rooke immediately set out for Vigo where he found the treasure fleet escorted by a Franco-Spanish fleet of about 30 vessels. The harbour had been fortified by the French and the Spanish. On October 23, Rooke attacked and destroyed the enemy's fleet in the harbour at the Battle of Vigo. He sent soldiers to capture the forts for a complete victory. He was able to take away silver and precious treasure to the value of one million pounds. When the Anglo-Dutch fleet returned to England, Rooke was then able to boost his success at Vigo Bay, despite of his defeat at Cadiz.

(2) ***The Soviets annexed the Baltic States in 1940.*** On August 23 1939, the Soviet Union, who had joined other nations in condemning Germany's aggressive policy towards its neighbours for several years, signed a Nazi-Soviet Non-Aggression Pact (Molotov-Ribbentrop Pact). The two countries promised not to attack each other in the event of

war. Then, the Soviets forced the Baltic Nations (Lithuania, Latvia, Estonia and Finland) to sign individual Pacts of Defense and Mutual Assistance with each government. The Pacts allowed garrisons of Soviet troops into the Baltic countries while they maintained their autonomy. The Soviet Union had always hoped to control the Baltic Sea to build a buffer between itself and Germany.

With no fear of retaliation by great power of the east, Germany could safely extend its aggression to Poland. At dawn on September 1, 1939, Germany made a massive invasion of Poland. The Poles resisted bravely but they were outnumbered, and the Germans possessed far superior war weapons through years of building up its armaments. On September 3, the U.K. and France who had mutual aid agreements with Poland, together with Australia and New Zealand declared war on Germany. The World War II began.

After a surprise Polish manoeuvre inflicted heavy casualties, the Germans rallied and took 100,000 prisoners. By September 16, German artillery ringed Warsaw, and the Nazis gave the Poles an ultimatum: surrender or face bombardment. On September 17, the Soviets invaded Poland from the east. On September 27, Warsaw surrendered to the Nazi. On September 29, Germany and the Soviet Union divided Poland in accordance with their August 23 Pact. The Soviets annexed the easern part of Poland, which was less wealthy and less populated in comparison to the German's share of the western part of Poland.

In early 1940, Nazi Germany invaded Norway, Denmark, France and the Low Countries in Western Europe. On June 14, 1940, Paris, the French Capital, at last fell to the Germans. The Soviets issued ultimatums that the Baltic nations set up pro-Soviet governments and used the presence of the military to force the action. The Soviets quickly set up People's Governments in each of the Baltic nations. Realising the time was ripe; on June 18, the Soviets attacked the Baltic States, i.e. Lithuania, Latvia and Estonia); followed by their annexation on July 23.

3.5.2.4 Comments.

It is human nature to wait for gains without pains. When the gains can be obtained by making little pains, why not? Looking at this from the other side of the coin, if we are careful enough not to have faults, loopholes and negligence, it would be difficult for our enemy to lead off our goats.

George Rooke failed in his mission to capture Cadiz, but he was fortunate enough to be in the right place and right time to loot the treasure fleet returning from the New World. On September 29, 1939, Nazi Germany and the Soviet Union divided Poland among themselves. Being able to expand into Poland, the Soviets were able to expand their influence in the Baltic States, i.e. Lithuania, Latvia and Estonia by one more move. These states were annexed by the Soviet Union in July 1940.

Many times when we are working on something, there are side issues to come across. If we explore these side issues, they may open up new opportunities yielding unforeseeable benefits. Sugar refining factories can easily expand their business into the production of beverages, alcohol and food seasoning. Now, by the synergy principle, they make the best use of their garbage for the production of fertilizers, papers, pharmaceuticals and building materials. The production of sugar is the lead or the string, while the other products are the goats to come along with it.

Exercises

1.   In 1583, General Toyotomi Hideyoshi in his effort to unify Japan positioned his forces against Akechi Mitsuhide in what would be known as the Battle of Yamazaki. Tsetsui Junkeian, an ally of Akechi arrived at the battlefield shortly after the battle had begun. Tsetsui discovered that Toyotomi's forces were much more superior to that of his ally.

Tsetsui had the second thought of not to attack, but instead ordered his soldiers to line up in battle formation on a hill above the Hora-ga-toge pass. Here, he could watch the battle, and to evaluate which side he should take for his own benefit.   As Toyotomi was winning the battle, Tsetsui betrayed his ally and switched his troops over to Toyotomi's side.

This incident has been so remarkable that the Japanese coined it "To wait at Hor-ga-toge".

What stratagem best describes the scheme used by Tsetsui Junkeian?
(a) Find the way in the dark by throwing a stone.
(b) Loot a burning house.
(c) Take away a goat in passing.
(d) Watch the fire across the river.

2. The eighteen months between July 1940 and December 1941 were known to the German submarine force as "the happy time."

However, one day in 1941, as a Soviet naval officer strolled around on the front of a Baltic port, he noticed a swarm of seagulls was flying towards the port. The birds were busy picking up fishes and shrimps on the water surface.

The officer thought for a while and picked up a phone to call for the Navy Command Unit. He talked about what he saw and drew the conclusion that there must be something underneath the water with moving parts driving the fishes and the shrimps up to the surface. He would like to alert all Soviet submarines to leave the port, and call in torpedo boats to take actions.

His speculations were right. Later, four Soviet torpedo boats were able to track down a German U-boat and destroy it.

Which of the following stratagems best describes this case?
(a) A straw will show which way the wind blows.
(b) Watch the fire across the river.
(c) Find the way in the dark by throwing a stone.
(d) Take away a goat in passing.

3.   It happened in the 1980's, an American businessman Mr. Smith (fictitious name) was on his first trip to Tokyo to negotiate for a billion dollar contract. He had prepared well for the bargain and was confident to strike a favourable deal.

The Japanese Company had two senior managers to greet him in the airport, escorting him to a luxurious hotel. In the limousine, they asked Smith politely whether he could speak colloquial Japanese. Smith admitted that it was his first trip to Japan, and he carried with him an English-Japanese pocket dictionary. Smith said he had to return to New York fifteen days later for his Company's Annual Stockholders Meeting.

The Japanese said their language was easy to learn, and advised Smith cordially that he might take up some sightseeing of the Imperial Palace and other scenic spots. "Fifteen days were quite long; we all wish you can enjoy your stay in Tokyo."

In the next morning, the Company sent in an U.S. born Japanese charming girl to teach Smith Japanese. After lunch, two delightful Japanese female tour escorts accompanied Smith for local tours. In the evening a banquet was held in honour of the guest by the Company. For the next twelve days, Smith's schedule was filled with all these activities: learning Japanese, sight-seeing tours, fine wine and cuisines, and splendid night lives. Whenever Smith asked for the business meeting, their reply was, "Sir, still plenty of time, and we will tell our Chairman about your request."

When it was the thirteenth morning, a business meeting was held in the boardroom of the Company. The Japanese executives split hairs in the contract, and engaged Smith in elaborations of the terms. In the afternoon, Smith had to present trophies to winners of the Company's Sports Meet.

On the fourteenth morning, the business meeting resumed. But the meeting was cut short, because the Company was to hold a farewell banquet in honour of their distinguished guest. On the fifteenth morning, in the meeting they finally came to the important items: price and the financial terms. Then, the Company's limousine was at the door. Smith was escorted by the Company Chairman to the limousine, and hundreds of Company's staff lined up to bow politely to see Smith off and yelled "Sayonara, sayonara!!"

Finally, inside the limousine Smith had to sign the contract according to the Japanese terms.

(i) Which of the following stratagems best described the scheme used by the Japanese Company?
(a) Find the way in the dark by throwing a stone.
(b) Watch the fire across the river.
(c) Wait at one's ease for an exhausted enemy.
(d) Take way a goat in passing.

(ii) If you were Mr. Smith, what could you do to avoid being manipulated?

4. The Citizen Watch Company was founded in Japan in 1924. Introduced in 1956, Parashock was the first shock resistant watch made by a Japanese manufacturer. In 1959, Parawater was hailed as Japanese first water resistant watch.

Citizen Watch Australia was established in May, 1965 with its head office in Brookvale, New South Wales. However, the Australians were not familiar with Citizen Watches, and the sales were slack. The Company thought of a promotion scheme. It was announced through the news media that on a certain day and at a certain time, a batch of Citizen Watches would be dropped from the airplane to an open space of a shopping plaza. One could keep the watch if he/she picked it up. As the watches were equipped with Parashock, they were not damaged by being dropped from the sky. It impressed the Australians on the quality of the watches, and the Citizen Watches became popular in Australia.

What was the stratagem used by Citizen Watch Company in the promotion of its watches to the Australians?

5. Sun Tze said, "The wise general makes it possible for the army to forage on the enemy. One measure of provision or provender seized from the enemy is worth twenty times his own." (*The Art of War,* Chapter II).

(i) Which of the following stratagems best describes this scenario?
(a) Watch the fire across the river.
(b) Wait at one's ease for an exhausted enemy.
(c) Find the way in the dark by throwing a stone.
(d) Loot a burning house.

(ii) What kind of forage can be most valuable to his opponent in to-day's scenario?

6. The following scenario repeats itself throughout history.

"Country A is in the midst of devastating economic crisis and large-scale civil uprising against the repressive government. The military government decides to play off long-standing feelings of nationalism by invading the country's arch-enemy, or the enemy occupying the territories under dispute with it. By doing so, it will divert public attention from the internal problems and to restore the long lost popularity and prestige of the government."

The Falkland War (March 19, 1982 – June 14, 1982) plotted by the Argentine military headed by General Leopoldo Galtieri to invade the Falkland Islands was one of such cases. "Galtieri and his staff never thought that the United Kingdom would respond."

Assume you were Galtieri's aid, investigate the eight factors proposed by Sun Tze in the planning of war, and present your arguments whether to wage war on the British.

7. On February 11, 1938, Adolf Hitler summoned the Austrian Chancellor Dr. Kurt von Schuschnigg to Berchtesgaden, Bavaria. When Schuschnigg arrived, he was treated to a two hour rant by Hitler about the perfidious behavior of Austria. He was not allowed to drink or to smoke.

Over the next few hours, he was browbeaten into accepting an agreement which allowed the Nazi party in Austria full freedom together with a guaranteed role in developing economics and military collaboration between the two countries. He was forced to take the Austrian Nazi leader Artur Seyss-Inquart into his cabinet.

The meeting lasted for about twelve hours. Schuschnigg intended to complain to Hitler about the plans for a Nazi revolt which had been discovered in Austria. Hitler did not wish to listen to his complaints and demanded, in a most aggressive tone, the complete subjugation of Austria to Germany's policies.

Finally, Schuschnigg agreed to Hitler's demands. But on his return to Vienna he restated his vow to preserve Austria's independence. On March 9, he called for a public vote on March 13 to decide if the country should remain independent or join Germany. Hitler demanded the plebiscite's delay and ordered troops to Austria's border on Schuschnigg's refusal. Scheuschnigg then resigned, and he was succeeded by Seyss-Inquart who called German troops into the country. Schuschnigg was imprisoned by the Nazi Government until he was liberated by American troops in 1945.

What was the stratagem used by Adolf Hitler to bring Kurt von Schuschnigg to the Nazi terms in Berchtesgaden, Bavaria?
(a) Take counsel in one's temple.
(b) To win hands down.
(c) Find the way in the dark by throwing a stone.
(d) Take away a goat in passing.

8. In the United Kingdom, Dennis Yates Wheatly (1897-1977) served in the British military in the WWI. Since 1931, he demonstrated his literary talents by writing novels and adventure stories. During the WWII, he worked as a planning staff in the War Office of the United Kingdom. He published many papers for the War Office, including drawing up suggestions for dealing with a German invasion of Britain, entitled *Stranger than Fiction* and the *Total War*. The latter was submitted to the Joint Planning Staff of the war cabinet.

He conceived himself as one of the Nazi invaders to the United Kingdom and designed a draft for the invasion, with all the terrorists' and brutal tactics to subjugate the British. Then, he schemed out all the counter tactics to redresss the malicious actions. Some of his ideas were adopted by the War Office. He participated in advanced planning for the Normandy Operation.

Which of the following Sun Tze's theses best describes Dennis Yates Wheatly's contribution to the Allies?

(a) "The winner is one who always ensures that it will win before going into battle. The loser is one who engages in battle first and then looks for victory."

(b) "One must not begin war unless there is something definite to gain."

(c) "If the enemies want to rest, one must try to weary them to travel long distance."

(d) "When the army's ardor and morale are dampened, when the fighting strength is exhausted, and when the state treasury is spent, it will be an opportunity for the other state sovereigns to spring up and take advantage."

9. In the 1960s, a French photofilming laboratory invented a chemical which was able to develop color films efficiently and effectively. A certain Asian photofilming company was interested in this product. It proposed to collaborate in the research and marketing of the chemical. A delegation was sent to negotiate with the French company, and the delegation requested a vistation of the laboratory.

Jean (fictitious name) who was the director of the laboratory thought that the visitation might be a ruse. On the day of the visitation, the visitors dressed formally with ties. Jean was vigilant and he noticed that one of the visitors had a long tie. This man was very interested in inspecting the equipment. He moved up and down to see how the equipment worked. For a moment his tie soaked the chemical solution.

Jean told his secretary to take a company tie and talk to the visitor. "We are sorry that your tie is wet. We would like to present you with our Company's tie." Immediately she helped the visitor to change the tie. The man was speechless and watched the lady to take the soiled tie away. At the end of the visitation, Jean gave every visitor a company tie as souvenirs.

(i) Which of the following stratagems best described the scheme used by the delegation to take a sample of the chemcial?

(a) Find the way in the dark by throwing a stone.
(b) Loot a burning house.
(c) Wait at one's ease for an exhausted enemy.
(d) Take way a goat in passing.

(ii) Why did Jean give every visitor a company tie as souvenirs?

Chapter 4.

To pretend to be ignorant, to feint and to deceive.

4.0 Introduction.

Actions 6-11 have feint as its theme, because "war is primarily a game of deception." (*The Art of War,* Chapter I). We shall cover Actions 6-8 in this chapter, and Actions 9-11 in Chapter 5.

4.1 Action 6: To pretend to be ignorant.

When the right moment has not come, one has to keep a stolid look so as not to arouse the opponent.

4.1.1 The stratagems are:
   (I) **Play dumb.** (One of the classical 36 Stratagems).
   (II) **Hide one's light under a bushel.**

(I) **Play dumb.**

4.1.1.1 Theme.

> At times, it is better to pretend to be foolish and do nothing than to be reckoned intelligent and act recklessly. Sun Tze said, "When one is active, he must feign inactive." (*The Art of War,* Chapter I)
>
> The strategists do not look crafty or intrepid before their attacks. They might even appear as idiotic, sick, deaf, dumb, drunken, insane or deceased. As the enemies are lured into misestimating the strategists' abilities, they relax their vigilance.

4.1.1.2 Source.

Sima Yi feinted to be ill. In the Three Kingdoms Period (220-280) in China, during the reign of King Cao Fang (240-253) of the State of Wei, General Sima Yi was stripped of his military power. Cao Shuang being a member of the Cao's family was in control of the army. Sima pretended to be ill and confined himself to his residence. When Cao Shuang's subordinates paid a visit to Sima's home, Sima looked very ill. Cao relaxed his vigilance on Sima. Later, in 239, when King Cao Fang was on the trip to worship his ancestors, Sima gathered his troops, ambushed Cao Shuang's army and executed Cao Shuang later.

Sima Yi's grandson founded the new Jin Dynasty (265-420) that eventually took over the three Kingdoms: Wei, Shu and Wu during the period 265-280. Sima Yi was honored with a posthumous title Xuandi of the Jin Dynasty.

This story is from *History of the Three Kingdoms,* by Chen Shou (233-297).

4.1.1.3 Illustrations.

(1) **Josef Stalin played cool to take Harry Truman's message.** The Potsdam Conference was held

from July 12 to August 2, 1945. Among the attendance, there were Communist Party General Secretary Josef Stalin of the Soviet Union, British Prime Minister Winston Churchill and later Clement Attlee, and U.S. President Harry S. Truman.

While at the Conference, Truman received news that the test of the atomic bomb at Alamogordo had been successful. On July 24, at around 7:30 p.m. after one of the sessions of the Conference, Truman got up and sauntered around to Stalin, leaving behind his interpreter, and relied on Stalin's interpreter – signifying that he had nothing important to say, just chit-chat, to tell Stalin about U.S. had an unspecified "powerful new weapon". Stalin, who knew its existence by placing agents inside U.S. mainland, showed no special interest. All he said was that he was glad to hear it, and hoped its usage would hasten the end of the war against the Japanese.

According to Marshall Georgi K. Zhukov, Commander of the Soviet zone of occupation in Germany, Stalin returned from the Conference and told Vyacheslav Molotov about Truman's message. Molotov reacted immediately, saying that he would talk to Igor Kurchatov, the scientific head of the Soviet atomic bomb project, to tell him to speed things up by producing a bomb by 1948.

(2) *Feigned deafness could be used as a sale promotional tactic.* In a small town in Ontario, David (fictitious name) and Stanlea (fictitious name) were two brothers operating a men's clothing retail. Stanlea, the young brother greeted customers with smiles in front of their shop, and David, the elder brother served the customers when they came in. Many people in town knew that these two brothers, especially David, had some hearing deficiency.

Sometimes, when a customer came in for a browse, he might causally look at a piece of outfit, and asked the price of it. David put his hand behind his ear and said, "What did you say?" The customer repeated his question, "How much is this?"

David said, "You asked the price of this one. (Pointing to the outfit, and raising his voice). Let me ask the boss... Boss, how much is this one?"

Stanlea turned round and looked at the outfit at a distance, and said, "Sixty ninety-nine!"

David asked for the price again. Stanlea said, "Sixty ninety-nine!"

David turned to the customer and said, "Yes, forty ninety-nine."

The customer was impressed by the "mishearing", and paid cash to take away the outfit. In fact, the two brothers did not have any hearing problems. They made use of their fake hearing deficiency to promote the sale.

4.1.1.4   Comments.

Throughout history, many people escaped from their dangerous predicaments by feinting to be idiotic, sick, deaf, dumb, drunken, insane, or deceased.

The Soviet atomic bomb project remained a relatively low priority until information from Klaus Fuchs and later the destruction of Hiroshima and Nagasaki goaded Josef Stalin to action. Fuchs was a physicist at Los Alamos National Laboratory. He supplied information on the British and American atomic bomb research to the Soviets during and shortly after WWII.

In 1950, he was convicted, and was sentenced to 14 years in prison, the maximum possible for passing military secrets to a friendly nation. Josef Stalin was calm when Harry Truman informed him about U. S. success in testing the bomb. Some people even doubted about Stalin's hearing capability. In fact, Stalin played it cool only.

(II) Hide one's light under a bushel.

4.1.2.1 Theme.

> When one is capable, he must feign incapable. "At the beginning one may appear as shy as a young maiden when he tries to entice the enemy to war. Afterwards, he must act as fast as a fleeing hare when he wants to catch the enemy unprepared." (*The Art of War,* Chapter XI). He must frequently alter his schemes so that no one can be sure of his intentions.

4.1.2.2   Source.

Sun Tze, *Art of War,* refer to 4.1.2.1.

4.1.2.3   Illustrations.

(1) ***Anwar El Sadat ascended to the presidency of Egypt in 1970.***   The 1967 Arab-Israeli War (June 5 - June 10, 1967) was fought between Israel and its Arab neighbours of Egypt, Jordon, Syria, with Iraq, Saudi Arabia, Kuwait, and Algeria contributing troops and arms to help. The humiliating defeat was so devastating that it compelled a domestic political reaction in Egypt. Gamal Abdel Nasser (in office: April 1954-September 28, 1970) was President of Egypt at the time, with Zakaria Mohiedin as Vice President.

Anwar El Sadat survived the turmoil of Nasser's time by loyal obedience to the latter and kept his profile low. In 1969, after holding many positions in the Egyptian government, Sadat was chosen to be Vice President by Nasser. Nasser died of a heart attack on September 28, 1970.

Sadat ascended to the presidency because Nasser's other colleagues considered him a puppet of Nasser, and that he could be easily manipulated. For months, Sadat was known as the donkey as he learned to control the levers of power. Nasser's past supporters were well satisfied for six months until Sadat installed what the state-owned media called "The Corrective Revolution" during which Sadat purged Egypt of most its leaders and other elements loyal to Nasser.

(2) ***Taking a low profile could help to win a business deal.*** In the 1970s, a British auto company solicited bids for heating and air conditioning auto parts. A short list of three suppliers was prepared, and each supplier was asked to make presentation before the company's decision makers on a certain day.

The chief executive officer of supplier C, called Bryan (fictitious name) knew that the products of the competitors were similar. Bryan held a Ph.D. degree in mechanical engineering from a well known British University. His company did not want to cut prices to get the contract. Then, he thought of a scheme.

On the day of presentation, Bryan went into the conference room with all the details of the auto parts. He approached the President of the Auto Company, and the latter chaired the committee for negotiations. He talked softly that he apologized not able to speak, because he got a soar throat. He bade the President to present the case for him.

The President turned to the presentation kit, and presented the case accordingly. The committee members asked questions, and the President tried his way to answer. Bryan did not do any talking, except to smile, to nod and to make some gestures. Finally, Bryan won the contract which amounted to one hundred thousand pounds. The moral of the story was that if you want people to do things according to your wish, take a low profile and listen, and let them talk more.

4.1.2.4   Comments.

It is always safe to conceal one's intention or ambition before the time is ripe. Apparently, many Chinese political leaders are knowledgeable of this stratagem. It helps them to watch the scenario more clearly, and not to provoke their competitors too soon.

Deng Xiaoping (1904-1997) was a leader in the Communist Party of China. He never held office as the Head of State, but served as the de facto leader of the People's Republic of China from late 1970s to early 1990s. He had gone through three ascensions and three purges in his political career. When he was not in power, he kept a very low profile of himself.

4.2 Action 7: To feint by misleading.

This action is a deliberate feint that serves as a cover for the other actions to follow.

Sun Tze said, "Strength and weakness is a matter of disposition." (*The Art of War,* Chapter V). When one is capable, he should feign incapable, and vice versa. When one makes it impossible for the enemy to determine his strategic power, he has the advantage already. If he wants the enemy to engage his stronger, more numerous troops in battle, he should feign fear and weakness to entice them, and to defeat them later. If the enemy is stronger, one can set out numerous banners, double the number of cookfires and display strength by various means. Meanwhile he leaves the scene with his army rapidly, planning to fight on another occasion.

4.2.1 The stratagems are:
  (I) **Make a feint to the east and attack the west.**
      (One of the classical 36 Stratagems).
  (II) **Pretend to advance along one path while secretly going along another.** (One of the classical 36 Stratagems).
  (III) **Point at the mulberry only to curse the locust.**
      (One of the classical 36 Stratagems).

(I) Make a feint to the east and attack the west.

4.2.1.1 Theme.

> Spread misleading information about your intention in order to induce your enemy to concentrate his defense on one front and thereby leave another front vulnerable to attack. "One who is skilful to weary the enemy on the move maintains deceitful appearance." (*The Art of War,* Chapter V).
>
> The words "east" and "west" in the label of this stratagem stand not only for the two different directions, but also two contrasting conditions, such as "strong" and "weak". When one is strong, he can feint to be weak, and vice versa.

4.2.1.2 Source.

General Zhu Jiun made a feint in his attack on the Yellow Turbans. Towards the end of the Later Han Dynasty (25-220), General Zhu Jiun tried to suppress the rebellion of the Yellow Turbans by besieging the City of Yuen. Zhu made a big display of the troops at the south-eastern part of the city, sending his men to prepare trenches. The Yellow Turbans gathered their troops in this part of the city for the defense.

Zhu organized a division of five thousand soldiers, and launched a surprise attack at the north-eastern part of the city. They broke into the city and defeated the Yellow Turbans.

This story is from *Hou Hanshu (History of Later Han Dynasty)* by Fan Ye (389-445).

4.2.1.3 Illustrations.

(1) **Napoleon Bonaparte's invasion of Egypt.** In 1798, France wanted to launch an invasion of the British Isles by appointing Napoleon Bonaparte to command the army along the English Channel. After an inspection in February 1798, Bonaparte realised that the operation could

not be undertaken until France had command of the sea. Instead, he suggested that France should strike at the sources of Britain's wealth by occupying Egypt, threatening the route to India.

By this time, the British Navy's presence in the Mediterranean was intended less as a fighting force than as a measure of encouragement to convince States like Sicily to form a coalition against the French who were undefeated on the Continent and with whom the Spanish had recently allied themselves.

News in 1798 that Bonaparte was organising an immense expedition in the Mediterranean port of Toulon worried the other European powers. Rumors spread that the candidates for invasion included Ireland where a revolt against the British was in progress, Portugal, Sicily, and even Brazil. However, Bonaparte's secret objective was to attack and occupy Egypt.

Rear Admiral Horatio Nelson thought it was strategic to direct his main navy force from the Mediterranean Sea to Gibraltar where the French fleet had to pass in order to reach Ireland. He believed that if the French sailed past Sicily, the target must be Egypt. His theory was right, and he missed the confrontation with Bonaparte's fleet in this round. In July 1798, after a rough six-week trip, nearly 400 transport ships landed some 34,000 French troops near Alexandria to attack Egypt.

(2) ***Deceptive tactics in the North African Campaign, 1942.*** In May 1942, German General Erwin Rommel, already famed as the "Desert Fox", launched a campaign against the British forces defending the road to Alexandria, the Suez Canal and the oil-rich Middle East. The target was Tobruk, the most important port along the Libyan coast east of Tripoli. Possession of this fortress would give the German Afrika Korps a secure base of supply almost a thousand miles closer to the Egyptian border.

At Gazala, Rommel's strategy was to attach bundles of wood and bushes on long ropes to all the supply trucks and some Italian light tanks. The Italian light tanks drove in the first line, one after the other, behind them all the supply trucks. The attached bundles of wood and bushes made an immense cloud of dust. For the British, it looked like the real full-scale attack. Then, they withdrew, and turned their delaying forces in the wrong direction. At the same time, Rommel attacked from the other direction with his German Panzer Division. The British were completely outwitted and defeated.

Likewise in October 1942, in the Battle of El Alamein British General Bernard L. Montgomery, known as "Monty" played deception too. A dummy pipeline was built, the construction of which would mislead the Axis to believe that the attack would occur much latter than it in fact did, and much further south. Dummy tanks consisting of plywood frames were put over jeeps in the south. In a reverse feint, the tanks to be used for the attack in the north were disguised as supply trucks by putting plywood superstructures over them.

4.2.1.4 Comments.

Sun Tze had always stressed war was primarily a game of deception. The effectiveness of this stratagem depends on whether the enemy's will power is strong enough not be confused. If he can be distracted, victory is on our side. If the enemy is able to stabilize himself not to be distracted, we will be at risk ourselves.

"One must deliberate and balance all possibilities before he makes a move. One who has learned the artifice of deviation will have the chance to win. Such is the art of manoeuvring." (*The Art of War,* Chapter VII). This is a dangerous stratagem to use, because if the enemy can see through the ploy, the strategist is at risk himself.

(II) Pretend to advance along one path while secretly going along another.

4.2.2.1 Theme.

> Set up a false front deliberately, and then penetrate your enemy's territory on other fronts to make a surprise attack.
>
> Sun Tze said, "When one is near, he must feign that he is far away. When one is far away, he must feign that he is near... One should attack the enemy where they are least prepared and when he is least expected." (*The Art of War*, Chapter I).

4.2.2.2 Source.

Liu Bang attained his ploy by clandestine means.
After the overthrown of the Qin Dynasty in 207 BC, Generals Xiang Yu, Liu Bang and others divided Qin's territories. Xiang, being the strongest, seized the fertile land along the middle and lower parts of the Yangsze River and the Huaihe River Valley. The three remote prefectures in the west, today's Sichuan and the southern part of Shaanxi were given to Liu. The fertile land separating Xiang and Liu, named Guanzhong (Central Shaanxi) were divided into three parts and given to three Qin generals who had surrendered. By doing this, a buffer was created for Xiang from Liu.

Liu was unhappy about this arrangement, but he could do nothing due to Xiang's great military strength at that time. When Liu withdrew to the west, in order to defend himself and to put Xiang off his guard, he burned the plank path along the dangerous cliffs. This action made the gesture that he would not come back.

After settling in his territories for a few years, Liu planned to fight against Xiang. He recruited General Hann Xin as his chief military staff. Hann thought the first step was to seize Guanzhong. He sent a few hundred soldiers to repair the plank path feigning that Liu would attack from there. In fact, Liu led the main force stealthily through Chencang (to the east of today's Baoji City in Shaanxi) and occupied the Guanzhong area quickly. After being successful in this ploy, Liu speeded up his campaign for the throne.

This story is from *Records of the Historian* by Sima Qian (145-86 BC).

4.2.2.3 Illustrations.

(1) ***The Trojan Horse.*** Round about 1200 BC, Paris who was the son of Priam took Helen to the City of Troy. Priam was the King of Troy. But Helen was married to King Menelaus of Sparta (Greece). Enraged, the Greek King launched a fleet of one thousand ships to go to Troy and to retrieve Helen. For ten years, the Greeks besieged Troy without success of getting into it or with getting Helen back.

The Trojans, led by Hector, began to repel the Greeks. Eventually the Greeks were driven back to their own ships. Achilles rejoined the battle, and killed Hector to avenge a good friend's death. Greek morale shot through the sky.

The Greeks devised a ploy. Odysseus (some say with the aid of Athena) ordered a large wooden horse to be built. Its insides were to be hollow so that soldiers could hide within. Meanwhile, the rest of the Greek Army piled into their ships and sailed away. One man, Sinon, was left behind. When the Trojans came to marvel at the huge creation, Sinon pretended to be angry with the Greeks because they deserted him. He assured the Trojans that the wooden horse was safe and would bring luck to the Trojans.

The Trojans, despite the warnings of Laocoon, moved the horse inside the city as an offering of peace. Then they decided to celebrate. By nightfall the whole city was in a drunken uproar far into the night. In the small hours of the morning, while everyone was drunk or asleep, the Greeks unsealed the belly of the horse and climbed down from it. Silently, they killed the Trojan sentries at all the city gates and opened the gates to the bulk of the Greek Army who had returned.

Now, the Greeks were finally inside the city after ten years of useless battles. By daylight, everyone in Troy was either dead or made captive.

(2) **Dwight D. Eisenhower feigned to invade Calais.** In determining the location to launch a large-scale invasion of the continent of Europe in 1944, General Dwight D. Eisenhower had at least three choices.

They were the Calais regions, closest to British Isles, the Cotentin Peninsula, and the Caen region at Lower Normandy. Eisenhower used this stratagem by bringing in a lot of supplies to the British shore opposite to Calais, conducting air raids on Calais, and spreading the news that General George S. Patton would be the Chief Commander of this area. Meanwhile, a Commander Headquarters was set up on the east coast of the British Isles, sending out and receiving a lot of telegrams. Its volume exceeded all other headquarters. On the other hand, there were not many activities in other sites.

On the days before the D-day, the British aircraft dropped a great deal of aluminum sheets on the British Channel. It created the illusion to the German radars that a fleet was speeding to Calais. On the D-day, the invasion was in Lower Normandy that was less fortified than those in Pas de Calais, contrary to what the Germans had expected, and giving the Allies the advantage of surprise.

Sun Tze was an advocate of this strategy: "One should attack the enemies where they are least prepared and when he is least expected." (*The Art of War,* Chapter I).

4.2.2.4 Comments.

This stratagem looks similar to that of "Make a feint to the east and attack the west", in hiding the genuine by showing the fake. However, there are two differences. The "Pretend" stratagem conceals the route of attack; while the "Make" stratagem conceals the point of attack. The "Pretend" stratagem arrests the enemy's attention in his surveillance on our activities, so as to launch a surprise strike elsewhere. The "Make" stratagem is to conduct a show to draw the enemies' attention to a certain location, prompting them to send their men and causing chaos. In the chaotic situation, one strikes the enemies from another location.

For a person to go secretly along another path, it may mean that he withdraws himself from publicity. He may go through some training to upgrade his capabilities, and to make all preparations before another undertaking.

(III) **Point at the mulberry only to curse the locust.**

4.2.3.1 Theme.

> Mulberry and locust are two different types of trees. To point at the mulberry but curse the locust is sarcasm. When it was used to describe a stratagem, the coercive warning has been incorporated into its context.
>
> To discipline, control or warn others whose status excludes them from direct confrontation by analogy and innuendo. The oriental culture does not encourage direct confrontations during disputes. It is especially true in the case of subordinates to voice their discontents to their supervisors. The subordinates have to take a circuitous route in stating their opinions through the use of analogy and innuendo.

Likewise, to be a successful commander, "he must have the whole-hearted support of all ranks of his army." (*The Art of War*, Chapter III).

When the soldiers do not follow orders, it is no good to tempt them by monetary gains, because they will become suspicious, and it would not improve the matter. The best strategy is to wait for catching their mistakes. With these, the commander can punish the wrong doers, and to warn all others about the importance of taking orders.

4.2.3.2 Source.

Sun Tze's repeated orders and injunctions. Round about 510 BC, Sun Tze (540-485 BC) was given an audience in the State of Wu. Having read the thirteen chapters of Sun's *The Art of War*, King Helu of the Wu State (reigned around 514-496 BC) invited Sun to demonstrate the drilling of troops with his 180 women. Sun divided them into two groups headed by two of the King's favourite concubines as the left and right officers respectively.

Sun explained to the women in detail the requirements and methods of training, repeatedly telling them that they must obey orders. When the drum signals were given, the women burst out laughing. Sun said that if the orders were not clear and the signals not explained well, the general was at fault. He explained the various commands several times to make sure that the women understood. But when the orders were given again, the women responded by laughing again. Being certain that the orders were clear but not followed, the officers were at fault. Sun ordered the left and right officers to be executed.

King Helu learned about this, and sent a messenger to stop the executions, but Sun disregarded the King's command. After the two officers (the King's favourite concubines) were executed, Sun appointed two new officers. All the women obeyed the orders with serious precision. Convinced that Sun was an excellent military leader versed in the art of war, the King appointed him as Grand General.

This story is from *Records of the Historian* by Sima Qian (145-86 BC).

4.2.3.3 Illustrations.

(1) ***Franklin D. Roosevelt changed his attitude on the research of atomic bomb.*** On August 2, 1939, Albert Einstein wrote to President Franklin D. Roosevelt (in office: 1933-1948) about Nazi Germany actively conducting research on building an atomic bomb. Alexander Sachs, a friend and unofficial advisor to Roosevelt was tapped to deliver Einstein's letter. However, for a vairety of reasons, Sachs was not able to see Roosevelt and deliver the leter until October 11, 1939.

After reading the letter, Roosevelt was not enthusiastic about it and blamed Sachs to bother him with the scientist's guess. On the next morning, Roosevelt invited Sachs to have breadfast together, apologising to be a bit rude to Sachs. Sachs took the opportunity to tell Roosevelt a story about Napoleon Bonaparte. Bonaparte was very successful in his army combats, but not so much with his naval wars. One day, an American named Fulton came to see the Emperor. He advised the French fleet to take off their masts and to install steam engines, and to replace the decks with steel plates. Bonaparte thought ships without masts could not sail, and steel plates could sink the ships. Fulton was turned away as the Emperor thought his ideas were crazy. But hindsight showed that if Bonaparte adopted Fulton's ideas, the French naval power would be invincible.

Roosevelt became serious after listening to the story. He thought for a while, and said, "Sachs, you win."

On October 19, Roosevelt wrote Einstein back and informed him that he had set up a committee consisting of Sachs and representatives from the Army and Navy to study uranium. Roosevelt changed his attitude because now he held the belief that the U.S. could not take the risk to allow Adolf Hitler to achieve unilateral possession of the powerful bombs. Consequently, the Manhattan Project was expedited to produce a viable atomic bomb as soon as possible.

(2) ***A satirical comment deserved another satirical remark.*** Yuri (fictitious name) was a Russian clown and circus artist. He fooled other people and was teased himself. He performed as a clown, a mime, tightrope walker and a juggler.

Once he was invited to perform in Western Europe. A man coming to the show asked, "Mr. Clown, is it necessary to have a stupid and ugly face like yours to be welcome by the audience?"

Without hesitation, Yuri replied, "Yes, if I got a face as what you describe, I am sure to get double pay." Sullenly, the man disappeared among the crowd very soon. He made himself look more foolish.

4.2.3.4 Comments.

In the case of the seniors to subordinates, even though the seniors have much authority over their subordinates, they prefer to voice their complaints in a polite way, saving the faces of their subordinates. Unless it is absolutely necessary, the complaints will not be delivered in the blunt manner. The seniors practise both the strict order instruction and the tenderhearted gentleness to raise the morale of his subordinates.

4.3 Action 8: To deceive.

This action is to deceive the opponent by passing off something as something else.

4.3.1 The stratagems are:
(I) **Cross the sea by deceiving the heaven**. (One of the classical 36 Stratagems).
(II) **Retreat in order to go forward.**

(I) **Cross the sea by deceiving the heaven**.

4.3.1.1 Theme.

> To create a front that eventually becomes imbued with the impression of familiarity, within which you may manoeuvre unseen while all eyes are trained to see obvious familiarities. Sun Tze said, "Order the officers and soldiers to carry out tasks, but do not inform them of the reason or intention. Order them to go after advantages and gains, but do not divulge the dangers involved." (*The Art of War*, Chapter XI). By keeping the true intent of the mission hidden from your subordinates, you can release them from their mental pressure.

4.3.1.2 Source.

How General Ho Yewbei and his army crossed the river. In 589, the army of the Sui State of China invaded the Chen State. General Ho Yewbei of Sui stationed his troops in the riverbank on the boundary between the two States. One day, he moved his troops to a nearby city called Lick. But he made a big show of this by beating the drums and waving the banners.

The Chen State was alarmed, thinking that Ho was launching an attack. It gathered all its soldiers on the other side of the river for defense. Then, they found out that Ho was only moving their camps to Lick. The Chen State dispatched its troops to go home.

Repeatedly, Ho did these several times, moving the troops back and forth from the riverbank to the city, making a big show of this every time. The Chen State became accustomed to this, and paid no more attention to the movements. Then, Ho seized an opportunity to move his troops across the river when the Chen State was totally unprepared, and the latter was defeated.

4.3.1.3 Illustrations.

(1) **A Japanese samurai story.** Once upon a time, there was a Japanese samurai (Japanese army officer) whose house was plagued by a large and clever rat. The samurai would like to get rid of the rat. He bought a cat from the pet vendor to bring home. The cat looked trim and fit. But it was no match for the rat.

The samurai returned the cat to the vendor and explained to the latter that the cat could not catch the rat. Now, the vendor gave the samurai a large and grizzled cat which was the best in his store, and guaranteed that the cat would accomplish its mission. But the rat evaded the cat by coming out when the cat slept. The samurai had to return the cat to the vendor who apologised not being able to help.

Then, the samurai came across a monk to talk about his problem. The monk offered him the service of the cat which lived in the temple. The cat was old and fat. The samurai was doubtful about its ability, but nevertheless he brought it home to try his luck.

For two weeks, the cat did little more than sleep all day and night, while the rat ran round the house delightfully. The samurai was disappointed and he would like to return the cat to the monk. But, the monk told him to be patient for a few days more. The rat grew accustomed to the presence of the lazy old cat and came into close range to where the cat slept. Then one day, when the rat was close to the cat, the latter swiftly struck out it paws and killed the rat.

(2) **Henry Kissinger's secret trip to China.** In 1971, Henry Kissinger served as U.S. President Richard Nixon's National Security Adviser. He paved the way to formalize the relations between U.S. and the People's Republic of China, ending 23 years of diplomatic isolation and mutual hostility.

On June 30, 1971, Kissinger flew to Vietnam to update himself with the current situation. He moved from Saigon to Thailand, to India, and to Pakistan. As he made his journey, there were fewer and fewer reporters following him. They felt that they had little to write about. Kissinger arrived at Islamabad in the afternoon of July 8. After a 90-minutes chat with President Agha Mohammed Yahya Khan, he changed his schedule, saying that he was going to the mountain resort of Nathia Gali for a brief working holiday. Yahya was apparently involved in the scheme. In fact, he was told to establish secret link between U.S. and the Communist China some time before.

On July 9, the Pakistan Government announced that Kissinger stayed in Nathia Gali for another day due to a slight indisposition – stomach ailment. A U.S. embassy official said that a doctor had been sent to examine Kissinger.

Instead of going to the mountain, Kissinger went to the airport in Rawalpindi, seven miles from Islamabad. There, he boarded a Pakistan International Airline Boeing 707, with two assistants to Beijing. They could easily pass through as some British businessmen. Pakistan Airline had been carrying passengers and freight between these two Capitals on both regular and unscheduled flights. Thus, Kissinger's trip to China and back was not known to the world at that time.

4.3.1.4 Comments.

This tactic is to keep things in the normal manner, not to stir attention, meanwhile something is being done. The cat from the temple was able to kill the rat because the latter relaxed its vigilance. In Henry Kissinger's case, from the moment of departure from Saigon, his itinerary was understated and routinely casual that the press and all observers were all but lulled to sleep.

Politicians like to use this stratagem, because it takes time to negotiate a deal. It is certainly not advisable to leak any information before the concerned parties have any consensus. It seems that Kissinger liked this stratagem very much. He had used it before when he engaged the

Vietnamese diplomat Le Duc Tho in secret talks from February to April 1971, leading to a cease fire agreement in the Paris Peace Accords of January 27, 1973.

(II) Retreat in order to go forward.

4.3.2.1 Theme.

> If the enemies are far superior in numbers and training, it is best to avoid them at the moment. One has to retreat for the moment, waiting for the opportune time to leap back and go forward. "When the envoy of the enemy speaks humbly while preparations are being intensified, it indicates that they are about to advance." (*The Art of War*, Chapter IX).

4.3.2.2 Source.

Sun Tze, *The Art of War*, refer to 4.3.2.1.

4.3.2.3 Illustrations.

(1) *How the Russian delegation got its diplomatic status.* In 1921, Vladimir Lenin instituted the New Economic Policy in Russia. He would like to ease Soviet's tension with the West by establishing foreign trade relationships, and to revive the Soviet Union economy. Meanwhile, the Italian government under the Giovanni Geolitti was pressed by the industrialists to boost trade so as to win ballots in election. In May, Lenin sent a delegation headed by the diplomat Christian Rakousky to Rome to negotiate on trade matters.

On his arrival at Rome, Rakousky went to see Carlo Sforza, the Italian Minister of Foreign Affairs demanding diplomatic status for the delegation. Meanwhile, there were anti-communist sentiments in Italy, and the delegation was often harassed by the Italian police. The Italian government refused to grant the diplomatic status to the delegation, saying that the latter represented a private organization.

On May 23, the delegation made its protest to Sforza, refusing to negotiate trade, and prepared for its home journey. Three days later, Sforza talked to Rakousky that the granting of diplomatic rights to the delegation could be considered if the latter was not to leave. On May 29, Sforza presented a letter to the Russian delegation conferring its diplomatic rights, and requested it to work with the Italian officials on the Russo-Italian Trade Pact.

(2) ***Harold Wilson's ploy on the Soviets did not work.*** In 1947, Harold Wilson was appointed Secretary for Overseas Trade in the Government of United Kingdom. In this capacity he made several trips to the Soviet Union to negotiate supply contracts. During one of these trips, he had to deal with a delegation led by Vladimir Mikhailovich Vinogradov who was to become a famous Soviet diplomat in the period 1950-1990.

In order to bring the Soviets to concession, Wilson tried to find faults with minute matters. The negotiations dragged to late evenings. Vinogradov had no comments on the long working hours. Wilson pretended to be very frustrated and would like to quit negotiation anytime. He told his delegates to pack up their luggage and to leave the hotel.

Vinogradov saw through Wilson's ploy and made no stir. Eventually, Wilson ordered his pilot to prepare taking off, so as to bring Vinogradov to his terms. Vinogradov refused. Then, Wilson had to go home sullenly.

4.3.2.4 Comments.

Vladimir Lenin, first Head of the Soviet Union (in office: 1919-1924) wrote an essay on "Retreat one step so as to advance two steps." To retreat is not to compromise, but to prepare to advance when the opportunity is available. It is different from the appeasement policy practiced by France and the U.K. on Nazi Germany in mid-1930s to bring temporary relieves with no long-term prospective.

Whether this stratagem will work is dependent on the personality and wisdom of the people involved. If the enemy can see through the ploy as Vinogradov did, then Harold Wilson failed in his tactic. On the other hand, Christian Rakousky succeeded in getting the diplomatic rights for the delegation, because he knew that the Italian government was keen to establish trade relationship with the Soviets.

Exercises

1.   One day, an American antique merchant called Sam (fictitious name) strolled along a village near Paris. He happened to notice a cat eating its meal from an exquisite bowl, dated the Seventeenth Century. Sam thought he was lucky, and schemed to get the bowl without having to pay much.

Sam looked at the cat and said to its owner, "Madam, your cat is cute, and would you mind to let me has it?" The owner said, "May be, if you can make an attractive offer."

Sam said, "How about twenty dollars U.S.? I like its colour."

The owner was delighted, and said, "It is a deal." She packed the cat in a box with perforated lids. Sam gave the money, and was ready to leave, but he looked as if he forgot something, "Madam, would you mind me to take its feeding bow, as as to make it feel at home all the time?"

The owner said something. Eventually, Sam did not get the bowl, but apparently he felt not too bad.

(i) What was the stratagem used by Sam to get the exquisite bowl?
(a) Play dumb.
(b) Hide one's light under a bushel.
(c) Cross the sea by deceiving the heaven.
(d) Retreat in order to go forward.

(ii) Guess what the owner said to Sam.

2. The Korea War originated in the division of Korea into South Korea (Republic of Korea, ROK) and North Korea (NK) after WWII. Efforts to reunify the country failed. In June 1950, after the surprise attack by the North Korean army

across the boundary between the North and South Korea, the North Korean army crushed the unprepared ROK army.

On June 27, the U.N. Security Council voted to repel the North Korean invasion. In July, General Douglas MacArthur (1880-1964) was placed in command of U.N. forces in Korea. At first MacArthur wanted only a regimental combat team. Soon, he was aware of the critical situation and asked for a minimum of 30,000 U.S. combat soldiers in the form of four infantry divisions, three tank battalions and assorted artilleries. By the end of July, North Korean forces occupied 90 percent of South Korea, leaving the south-eastern most part of the Korean Peninsula-the Pusan Perimeter- held by the U.S. and the ROK forces.

MacArthur felt that he could turn the tide if he could make a decisive troop movement behind enemy lines. He proposed a daring amphibious operation to land on Inchon on the west coast of the Peninsula. Though strategically tempting, Inchon was a tactically challenging amphibious target, with long shallow channels, poor beaches and a tidal range that restricted landing operations to a few hours a day. It took all of MacArthur's unparalleled powers of persuasion to sell his idea to the doubting Army, Navy and Marine Corps commanders. He said that, due to the presence of all natural and geographic handicaps, the enemies would not expect an attack there. Moreover, Inchon was close to Seoul, the Capital and a vital supply source. This operation was then approved by Washington, D.C.

During the amphibious operation (Sept. 15-28) U.N. forces consisting of 70,000 strong X Corps and a fleet of 230 vessels were mobilized in lightning speed. They secured Inchon, and broke North Korean control of the Pusan region through a series of landings in the enemy's territories. The U.N. ground forces were predominately U.S. marines. The Battle of Inchon ended a series of victories by the invading NK Peoples' Army and began a counterattack by the U.N. forces that led to the recapture of Seoul on Sept. 29, 1950.

However, in October 1949, General Omar N. Bradley, U.S. President Harry S. Truman's Chairman of the Joint Chiefs of Staff, made the following statement, "I predict that large-scale amphibious operations (i.e. landing in Lower Normandy in 1944) will never occur again."

What was the stratagem used by General Douglas MacAuthur in the landing at Inchon?
(a) Make a feint to the east and attack the west.
(b) Point at the mulberry only to curse the locust.
(c) Cross the sea by deceiving the heaven.
(d) Retreat in order to go forward.

3. Once there was a man, Henry (fictitious name) was on his journey. Then, he decided to stay in an inn for a few days to take a break. The front part of the inn where he stayed was an eatery. Across the street was a shop that sold expensive jewellery.

Henry sat at a table near the front window in the eatery most of the time, watching the people on the street. One day, he observed that several suspicious men on the scene. They peeped into the jewellery shop and loitered around. One of them came up to Henry and whispered, "We are here to steal some jewellery. Since you are watching us, can I ask you not to raise the alarm?" He threw down two packets of cigarettes as a bribe.

Henry said, "Your business has nothing to do with me." The thief thanked him and left to join his gang.

Henry was curious how these people steal the jewellery shop, and he stayed in the eatery and watched. The gang walked back and forth in front of the jewellery shop, some of them disappeared for the moment, and appeared later. After sun set, the jewellery shop closed. The gang left and was not seen any more. Henry was disappointed not to see the action, and he went to his room to take a bath. Then, he discovered that all his belongings were gone.

(i)   Which of the following stratagems best describes the tactic used by the gang of thieves?
(a) Retreat in order to go forward.
(b) Hide one's light under a bushel.
(c)   Cross the sea by deceiving the heaven.
(d) Pretend to advance along one path while secretly going along another.

(ii) This story brings out another issue. When someone invites a person to be a collaborator of crime, or even be an onlooker, many times it ends up being that person is the target of victimization. What makes him/her vulnerable to this ploy as Henry was?

4.   It happened in the Muromachi Period (1336-1573) in Japan. In 1560, Oda Nobunaga was a minor Commander, leading a force of 2,000 men to fight against a rival warlord Imagawa Yoshimoto who had an army of 25,000 men.

Oda knew that a frontal assault would be his own disaster. His scouts discovered that Imagawa encamped in a narrow wooded gorge that Oda knew would be ideal for a surprise attack. Moreover, Imagawa's men were celebrating their previous victories. Oda thought of a plot. He left a small force and set up dummies at his camp in a temple to attract the attention of his enemies. Meanwhile, his troops made a journey in a wide circle to come up behind Imagawa's encampment. Weather favoured Oda's scheme because late in the day there was a heavy downpour. Taking advantage of the foul weather, his troops launched a sudden attack on the enemies without being noticed.

Imagawa was beheaded when two of Oda's samurai (Japanese army officers) jumped upon him suddenly, and his army dispersed. The battle, called Battle of Okehazamal, lasted only a few minutes but Oda gained his reputation. Oda quickly emerged as one of the prominent warlords.

What was the stratagem used by Oda Nobunaga in fighting against a powerful warlord Imagawa Yoshimoto?

5.   On November 19 1941, Japan sent the codes to its intelligence agency in Washington D.C., U.S. regarding the broadcast of a special message in an emergency. "In case of emergency (danger of cutting off our diplomatic relations), and the cutting off of international communications, the following warning will be added in the middle of the daily Japanese language short-wave news broadcast:

(a) In case of Japan-U.S. relations in danger: Higashi No Kaze Ame ("east wind rain").
(b) Japan-U.S.S.R. relation: Kita No Kaze Kumori ("north wind cloudy").
(c) Japan-British relations: Nishi No Kaze Hare ("west wind clear").

The signal will be given in the middle and at the end as a weather forecast and each sentence will be repeated twice. When this is heard please destroy all code papers, etc. This is as yet to be a completely secret arrangement."

Which of the following stratagems was used by the Japanese intelligence agency in this case?

(a) Pretend to advance along one path while secretly going along another.
(b) Cross the sea by deceiving the heaven.
(c) Play dumb.
(d) Make a feint to the east and attack the west.

6.   In 1921, Nikita Khrushchev became active as a political organzer. Shortly thereafter, his rapid rose in power began. During the WWII, he had a close connection to Soviet leader Josef Stalin, and after Stalin's death in 1953, Khrushchev emerged as the new leader.

At the Twentieth Congress of the Communist Party of the Soviet Union 1956, Khrushchev testified about Stalin's crimes, and denounced him. Many delegates had the same question in mind, "As one of Stalin's followers, Khrushchev must be aware of Stalin's mistakes and errors, why

Khrushchev didn't make them clear to Stalin. Is Khrushchev responsible for these mistakes and errors also?"

When Khrushchev was delivering his speech about Stalin and how to rectify his mistakes, a piece of paper was delivered to him from the audience. It read, "Where were you at that time?"

Khrushchev paused for a while. He said, "Now, someone has this question for me, 'Where were you at that time?' " He pounded his hands on the table and asked "Who wrote this question? Please stand up and come to the stage!"

Everybody kept silent, and there was no stir. All delegates held their breath. Khrushchev did not lose his temper, and said gently, "I tell you, I was sitting as you are sitting here now. We have the same situation." Khrushchev would like to simulate the scenario for his audience to experience.

What was Nikita Khrushchev's tactic in addressing the question, "Where were you at that time?"?

7.   In the late 1800s, the U.S.Customs imposed very heavy duties on importing French gloves. However, there was a high demand for these gloves, and the profit margin was substantial if the duties could be reduced.

A salesman Mr. Lawrence (fictitious name) came up with a scheme. He went to France and bought ten thousand pairs of elegant French gloves. He packed up all the right-hand gloves and shipped to a storage location in his home city. According to the customs practice at that time, for goods not claimed within six months, these goods would be sold at auction. Since all the gloves are right handed, Mr. Lawrence was able to buy the whole log at an incredible low price.

The Chief Customs officer had a hunch, and cautioned the Customs Department to watch out for the import of the left handed gloves from France, especially to

Mr. Lawrence In the ensuing months, Mr. Lawrence received several shipments of French gloves amounting to five thousand pairs, and he paid the duties. There had never been any marked "left-handed gloves only" imported.

(i) Mr. Lawrence was successful in his scheme; can you figure out what was happening?

(ii) It is human nature to assure that when two gloves are packed together, it will be a pair. In fact, if the customs officers had been a little bit careful to examine the gloves inside a package, it would have foiled Mr. Lawrence's scheme. What stratagem was used by Mr. Lawrence in this case?

8. In 1952, Matsushita Konosuke negotiated for technical cooperation provided by Netherlands' Philips Electric Company to Matsushita Electric Company. Philips asked for technical support fee of 7 percent of Matsushita's sale. Later, Philips made the concession to reduce it to 4.5 percent. But as to the transfer of copyrights, Matsushita had to pay twenty million yens at the start.

At that time, the capital of Matsushita Electric Company was around fifty million yens. It posted a financial problem to Matsushita. After thorough investigation, Matsushita found out that Philips employed over 3,000 research and development staff working on innovative technologies. If Matsushita was to do this himself, he had to spend over several hundred million yens and to wait for many years. Matsushita sought financial support from the banks, even pledging with his own assets to raise the funds for the deal. He had never ventured to put his company in such high debt leverage position before.

What was the stratagem used by Matsushita Konosuke to work out the deal with Philips Electric Company?

Chapter 5.

To bluff, to substitute
and to conceal.

5.0 Introduction.

Actions 6-11 have feint as their theme, becasue "war is primarily a game of deception." (*The Art of War,* Chapter I). We shall cover Actions 9-11 in this chapter.

5.1 Action 9: To bluff.

5.1.1 The stratagem is: **Empty castle ploy.** (One of the classical 36 Stratagems).

If the opponent is on the favored side, but he does not have much information on our side, we can bluff him away.

5.1.1.1 Theme.

> When the enemy is superior and your situation is such that you expect to be overrun at any moment, then deliberately make your defensive line defenceless to confuse the enemy. "If we do not wish to fight... all we need do is to throw something odd and unaccountable in his way." (*The*

Art of War, Chapter VI). Unless the enemy has an accurate description of one's situation, these unusual behaviors will cause suspicion of ruses.

5.1.1.2   Source.

The empty castle ruse and the empty camps ruse.

After the death of Wenwang (reigned 689-677 BC) Duke of Chu in China, his younger brother Marquis Yuen, also the Prime Minister of the Chu State would like to win the affection of his sister-in-law, Sik Wei, by launching an invasion against the Zheng State to show his abilities. Sik was famous for her beauty.

The Zheng State was in no match with the Chu State in military power. As the Chu army was advancing towards the capital of Zheng, its Duke, Wengong (reigned 672-628 BC) was very worried. Though some ministers favoured to surrender to the Chu State, yet Suk Jim, one of the ministers suggested to seek rescue from the States of Qi, Sung and Lu that allied with the Zheng State and to use the Empty Castle Ruse. Suk understood the motive for the Marquis to wage war on the Zheng State. If the Marquis would rest on his laurels, the crisis would be over soon.

Wengong adopted Suk's ploy. Suk gave order to open all the city gates. All business activities were as usual. However, some troops were hidden in the sheltered corners. The scouts of the Marquis came, and they spotted the hidden troops. They reported to the Marquis about the possibility of ambushes when the Chu army entered the city. Meanwhile, the armies of the Alliance from the States of Qi, Sung and Lu were on the way to the Zheng State.

The Marquis evaluated the pros and cons of attacking the State of Zheng's Capital. The wise move was to withdraw the troops, claiming the victory of having defeated the Zheng's army in several battles to win the affection of Sik. In fact, it would be tough to confront the Alliance armies. The Marquis evacuated his troops in one night, leaving the camps and all banners behind to feign their presence, and to avoid the pursuit by the Zheng army. Thus, Suk played the empty castle ruse, and the Marquis played the empty camps ruse in this military combat.

This story is from *Records of the Historian* by Sima Qian (145-86 BC).

5.1.1.3 Illutstrations.

(1) ***The adventures of Ian Robert Maxwell.*** Robert Maxwell was born in Czechoslovakia in 1923 as Jan Ludwik Hoch. He moved to the U.K. in 1940 and fought for the British during the Second World War, changing his name at that time. During the occupation of Germany he became the sole U.K. and U.S. distributor for the Springer scientific publications.

Maxwell was elected to the U.K. Parliament in 1964 as a Labour member. In 1969, he was severely censured by the English High Court as unfit to run a public company after a failed attempt to sell Pergamon to a U.S. finance group called Leasco. He did not stand at the next election and he lost control of Pergamon. But he was able to borrow enough money to repurchase Pergamon in 1974.

In 1980, using borrowed funds he acquired the British Printing Corporation, (BPC) subsequently renamed Maxwell Communications Corporation. In 1984, he bought Mirror Group Newspapers (MGN) - owner of the tabloid *Daily Mirror* - from International, taking them downmarket in an unsuccessful war with Murdoch's News group.

In 1988, he bought the U.S. book publishing company Macmillan (independent of the U.K. Macmillan). His BPC and MGN holdings consisted of the Mirror group of national and regional newspapers, 50% of MTV in Europe, 20% of U.K. Central TV and Maxwell Entertainment, etc.

In October 1990, Maxwell's businesses were alleged to manipulate their pension schemes. Despite complaints from the scheme members, there was no action by the U.K. or the

U.S. financial regulators. In May 1991, Maxwell companies and pension schemes failed to meet statutory reporting obligations. Again there was no action by the U.K. or the U.S. financial regulators.

In 1991, Maxwell disappeared while cruising off the Canary Islands, presumably a suicide. Then, it was discovered that hundreds of millions of dollars had been looted from the group to finance Maxwell's lavish lifestyle and corporate expansion. In 1992, Maxwell's companies filed for bankruptcy protection. In 1995, his two sons and two former Maxwell Company's directors were on trial in the U.K.'s largest fraud cases.

(2) ***Matsushita Konosuke was "the god of management"***. In the mid 1950s, after the Korean War, Japanese economy slipped down for a while. Many organizations had to close to cut costs. Matsushita Electric Company was also in difficulty, and its suppliers and creditors watched the situation carefully.

Meanwhile Matsushita Konosuke, founder of the Company, was stricken by illness. Rumors spread that the Company would be bankrupt. Everybody inside the Company was worried. Two senior managers went to the hospital to seek the advice of Matsushitu. Then, Matsushita said, "It is my decision not to lay off one person in our Company. If we have to cut staff, suppliers and the banks will take that we are in difficulty, and they will enforce harsh terms on our credits. On the other hand, if we lay off no one, it shows that we are confident to go through the recession. As from today, our employees will work half a day, but they will get the full pay plus the regular bonus."

These two senior managers announced Matsushita's decision, and all employees of the Company were grateful to his decision. Everyone put in extra efforts to achieve perfection of his job. After two months, the demand for Matsushita's products boosted, employees had to work full time plus over-time to cope with the rising demands.

Matsushita saved his company and employees by his brilliant move during the dark hours of Japanese economy.

5.1.1.4 Comments.

The objective of this stratagem is to awe someone by assuming a bold front or bold speech. It can be useful if the opponent is very prudent. However, it is a dangerous stratagem to use for the following reasons. If the opponent is a reckless person, he will charge forward without making deliberations. Another hazard is that the opponent may be able to see through the ploy with or without scouts. Due to these dangers, this stratagem should only be considered as a last resort.

This stratagem also creates an illusion for the beholders, tempting them to put in high expectations from the illusion. The financial empire created by Ian Robert Maxwell was founded on a mirage. Politicians also make vague promises when they campaign for offices. They opened the gates of their undefended city to attract the votes. Later, they would find excuses not to fulfill these promises.

5.2 Action 10: To substitute.

When it is impossible to remove something undesirable, or to prevent something undesirable happening, one may try to substitute the target with another substance so that less harm is done or the outcome of the happening becomes more acceptable to him.

5.2.1 The stratagems are:
  (1) **Raise a corpse from the dead.** (One of the classical 36 Stratagems).
  (2) **Steal the beams and pillars and replace them with rotten timber.** (One of the classical 36 Stratagems).

(I) **Raise a corpse from the dead.**

5.2.1.1 Theme.

> It is something that is extinct emerges in another form. Exploit and manipulate by reviving something from the past and give it a new purpose.
>
> If one cannot make use of something existing, he can use some other things, whether a technology, a method or an institution that has been forgotten or discarded. If he can revive them from the past by giving them a new purpose or to bring to life old ideas, customs and tradition, one can make good use of them for his own purposes. Zombies are reanimated corpses; they like to gain their vitality also.

5.2.1.2 Source.

Why Li Yin crippled and looked so ugly. A Chinese myth said Li Yin, one of the eight fairies, had the power to extract his soul from the body to roam in the universe. He was a handsome man. Once, he told his disciple, Ah-Yang that he would accompany the Lord of the Universe in a trip round the universe. He instructed Ah-Yang to watch his body carefully. In seven days time, Li's soul would be back to join the body. But if his soul did not come back by the seventh day, he would be with the eternity, and Ah-Yang had to incinerate his body.

On the sixth day, Ah-Yang got the news that his own mother was going to die, and that he had to go home. Chinese virtues usually rank fidelity to parents as top priority. Ah-Yang had to leave, so he incinerated Li's body.

On the seventh day, Li's soul returned but could not find the body. Meanwhile, there was an ugly looking crippled beggar died recently on the roadside. In order to revive as a human being, Li's soul sought reincarnation in the beggar's corpse. For this reason, from that time onwards Li looked ugly. Though the beggar's corpse had no value, yet in this case, it helped Li to resume the form of a human being.

5.2.1.3 Illustrations.

(1) *A mysterious Anti-Nazi resistance leader in the Netherlands during WWII.* The Netherlands fell to Nazi Germany on May 9, 1940. A Dutch girl called Anne and her brother were the only survivers when the Nazi Germans attacked the village where their family lived.

Some Dutch organized active or passive resistance against the German occupiers. Resistance took the form of small scale, decentralized cells engaged in independent activities. These groups produced forged ration cards and counterfeit moeny, published underground newspapers, sabotaged phone lines and railways, prepared maps and distributed food and goods to the needy countrymen. They had a system of hiding people to protect downed Allied airmen.

One day, in her backyard, Anne found a British pilot with the name Johnny Stedfast whose plane had been shot down. Not soon later, Stedfast died. Anne and her brother buried Stedfast.

Anne hatched a plot. They organized an Anti Nazi resistance unit with the British Royal Air Force Pilot Johnny Stedfast as the leader. Anne and her brother acted as liasons to other Dutch resistance groups. Orders from Stedfast dispatched only through Anne and her brother; nobody had ever seen Stedfast. "Johnny Stedfast" organized counter intelligence, domestic sabotage and communication network to aid the Allies force from 1942 and through the liberation of the Netherlands.

After the war, the Allies would like to thank Johnny Stedfast and to award him with a medal. Anne and her brother had to reveal the truth.

(2) ***Corazon Aquino carried on her husband's mission.*** In early 1970s, the criticisms of President Ferdinand Marcos of the Philippines grew from the dishonesty of his 1969 campaign and his failure to curb the bribery and corruption in government. There was also a more general discontent due to the increase of greater poverty and violence. Meanwhile, the popularity of Senator Benigno Aquino and the Liberal Party were growing rapidly. Marcos blamed the communists for the suspicious Plaza Miranda bombing of a Liberal Party rally on August 21, 1971. A staged assassination attempt on the Defense Secretary, Juan Ponce Enrile, brought in the declaration of martial law on September 21, 1972. Aquino was amongst the 30,000 opposition politicians, journalists, critics and activists detained under martial law.

After five years in detention, a military court found Aquino guilty of subversion in November 1977 and sentenced him to death. Aquino was too well known and prominent to execute. But he developed heart disease in prison and in May 1980 he was released for treatment and exile in the U.S. In 1983, he decided to return to the Philippines. On his arrival at Manila International Airport on August 21, he was shot dead. His death resulted in widespread antigovernment demonstrations.

In February 1986, presidential elections between Marcos and Corazon Aquino, the widow of Benigno Aquino resulted in Marcos claiming victory. Corazon Aquino called on "People Power" a peaceful resistance to force Marcos from office. Marcos was subsequently forced into exile when the military backed the People Power. On February 25, 1986 Corazon Aquino was inaugurated as President (in office: 1986-1992), and in 1987 a new constitution was adopted. Even amongst her allies who had joined with her to defeat Marcos, many had doubts whether the simple housewife had the political acumen for the enormous task of national reconstruction that her administration faced. She was able to be in this position because her husband had been regarded as a martyr of democracy.

5.2.1.4 Comments.

The influence of the deceased organisations or people can be revived for new missions. Corazon Aquino possessed unique background for the gravitation of her followers. It is a persuasive measure for acceptance of new mission under old banners.

When a person encounters defeat or failure, it is worthy to step back and think. With enhanced spirit and accumulated experiences, one can come back. He may pursue a different career for success. On the other hand, there are people who are so fond of olden concepts and rotten rules that they would like to impose on others. The Teliban rule of Afghanistan forbade their women to go to schools is one example of this kind of tragedies.

(II) **Steal the beams and pillars and replace them with rotten timber.**

5.2.2.1 Theme.

> Replace the enemy's strength with weakness. It is possible to give the enemies the weakness that they do not recognize by infiltrating one's own personnel to take the key roles in the enemy's camp.
>
> "One may advance and may be absolutely irresistible if he makes for the enemy's weak points." (*The Art of War,* Chapter VI). But it is less risky and less costly to cause the enemy to turn away his own best people (the beams and pillars) and replace them with inferior staff (the rotten timber).

5.2.2.2 Classic.

Tyrant Jie and King Zhow were Hercules. According to the legend, the Tyrant Jie of the Xia Dynastry (last depraved ruler, c. 1765 BC.) and King Zhow (also called Dixin) of the Shang Dynasty, (last depraved king, c. 1121

BC.) were despots. But they were as strong as Hercules. They could pull nine cows in a row, and change the beams and pillars by themselves. The original context was used to describe the mighty strength that those two kings possessed. Later, it was taken to mean "substituting the real things with fakes."

5.2.2.3   Illustrations.

(1) **Marshal Tukhachevsky was set up by the Germans.** In 1936, Adolf Hitler knew that Marshal Tukhachevsky and his subordinates in the Soviet Union would be his chief obstacle when he wanted to expand the territories eastwards into the Soviet Union. Meanwhile, Josef Stalin, due to his paranoia, had always feared of military coups.

Hitler told his intelligent agents to fabricate letters of correspondence between Tukhachevsky and the German military officers, money vouchers possibly hinting to information espionage, and other confidential memos of Tukhachevsky. These fabricated materials were revealed "accidentally" to the agents working for the Soviet Union.

In 1937, Josef Stalin led his purge of the Red Army, Tukhachevsky and ninety percent of generals plus half of the officer corps was eliminated. After taking away of its best generals, the Russian Army filled these slots with inexperienced commanders. The Russians replaced their own beams and pillars with rotten timber. It was one of the reasons for the spectacular Nazi success in the early months of the German invasion of the Soviet Union in 1941.

Only after the World War II, the German survivors claimed that Hitler and his team framed Tukhachevsky.

(2) **Adolf Hitler, Josef Stalin and Saddam Hussein all had their doubles.** Joseph Paul Goebbels, the German Nazi Propaganda Minister (in office: 1933-1945) arranged six doubles) "droppelgangers" or body look alike for Adolf Hitler for the purposes of security and public appearance.

(Newsweek March 13, 1939 issue). In order to avoid being discovered as doubles, these doubles would be good for public appearance, parties, meetings or briefings where the real Hitler was not expected to have that much interaction with their underlings. Because of this, there was the rumor that the dead body as photographed inside the bunker before Hitler's corpse was burned with gasoline in the Chancellery garden belonged to someone else. Josef Stalin told U. S. President Harry S. Truman (in office: 1945-1953) during lunch in Potsdom on July 17, 1944 that Hitler did not commit suicide, but had probably escaped.

Josef Stalin was said to have at least a double that was almost his identical twin. The man lived to 93 years old, his first name was Rashid. Alexei Dikiy, an actor who played Stalin in films coached Rashid so that the latter could better portray Stalin in real life. No one knows for sure how many doubles Stalin had.

Likewise, Saddam Hussein had several doubles. One of them actually defected to the U.S. because he could not take the strain of worrying about being killed any time.

5.2.2.4 Comments.

This stratagem aims at disrupting the enemy's camp, removing their strength by substituting weakness that the enemy is not aware of. Adolf Hilter was able to remove Marshal Tukhachevshy and his term by a plot so as to weaken the Soviet's military strength.

Many dictators have the fear of being assassinated. They would like to have their doubles as substitutes in many occasions. The double is supposedly going to die a martyr's death on the battlefield so that the real person can either live on or in the case of Hitler, glorified without dying.

5.3 Action 11: To conceal.

One may conceal a hostile scheme or aggressive intention with a smile.

5.3.1 The stratagem is: **Hide a dagger in a smile.** (One of the classical 36 Stratagems).

5.3.1.1 Theme.

> Charm and ingratiate yourself to your enemy. When you have his confidence, you move against him in secret. "When without warning of distress the enemy suddenly sues for peace, it indicates a plot." (*The Art of War,* Chapter IX).

5.3.1.2 Source.

Honey in mouth but dagger in heart. During the reign of Emperor Xuanzong (712-755) of the Tang Dynasty (618-907), there was a Prime Minister called Li Linfu. Li was a crafty person who knew how to curry favor with those people whose ranks were above his. He was very jealous of those who were talented and prestigious. He would try his best to elbow them aside and to eliminate them. He bribed the influential eunuchs to give praises to him for good work being done. Thus, he won the trust of the Emperor, holding the highest official post for a consecutive seventeen years.

Li always feigned smiling face, kindness, humbleness, and he spoke cajolingly. However, he was very wicked, and he never hesitated to harm people whom he did not like. Soon, all people knew his hypocrisy. They said, "Li has honey in his mouth, but dagger in his heart."

This story is from *History as a Mirror*, written in the annalistic style. It recorded the events from 403 BC to 959 AD, (from the Warring States Period to the Five Dynasties). Its chief compiler was Sima Guang (1019-1086) of the Northern Song Dynasty.

5.3.1.3 Illustrations.

(1) ***"Speak softly and carry a big stick".*** U.S. President Theodore Roosevelt (in office: 1901-1909) articulated this slogan at the Minnesota State Fair on September 2, 1901. "Essentially it is necessary to be respectful towards all people to refrain from wronging them, while at the same time keeping ourselves in conditions to prevent wrong being done to us. However, we have to speak softly. If a nation does not speak softly, then sooner or later the policy of the big stick is certain to bring war." This thinking led to expansion of the U.S. Navy and greater involvement of U.S. in world affairs.

Weeks after the start of the World War I (1911-1914) when Germany invaded Belgium, Roosevelt chided President Woodrow Wilson (in office: 1913-1921) for his stubborn neutrality by verbalizing this slogan again. China was taken as an example. In spite of speaking softly time after time for quarter of a century before 1914, China was not able to save herself from being bullied by the Western colonial powers and Japan, as she did not have a big stick to defend herself.

(2) ***Japanese diplomatic talks before Pearl Harbor attack.*** In the several months before December 7, 1941, the Japanese envoys and the representatives of the Government of the United States carried on informal and exploratory conversations. Its purpose was to arrive at a settlement if possible of questions relating to the entire Pacific area based upon the principles of peace, law and order, and fair dealing among nations.

These principles included:
(a) the principle of inviolability of territorial integrity and sovereignty of each and all nations;
(b) the principle of non-interference in the internal affairs of other countries;
(c) the principle of equality, including equality of commercial opportunity and treatment; and
(d) the principle of reliance upon international cooperation and conciliation for the prevention and pacific settlement

of controversies and for improvement of international conditions by peaceful methods and processes. (United States Notes to Japan, November 26, 1941.)

All these principles aimed at securing the peace of the Pacific area and thereby contributed toward the realization of world peace.

On December 1, 1941, Japan's militarist government decided to use the stratagem "Gain the initiative by striking first." In order to distract the U.S. government while secretly positioning a powerful aircraft carrier strike force for a surprise attack on the U.S. Pacific Fleet at its Pearl Harbor base in Hawaii, the Japanese government had ordered its envoys in Washington D.C. to engage the Americans in intensive diplomatic negotiations for cooperation and for peace. The Pearl Harbor was attacked in the morning of December 7, 1941.

5.3.1.4 Comments.

One should take extra caution if his enemies put on smiling faces with no signs of hostility. Possibly they are waiting for the moment to pick up the dagger to strike. If one is careful enough, he may be able to detect the flaws. One should be aware of flattering also.

However, it is not necessary for all smiling faces to be bad. When we confront tough competitors on difficult problems, smiles and good attitude convey sincerity to resolve the conflicts. With tolerance and compromises, mutually acceptable solutions for a "win win" situation could be worked out.

Theodore Roosevelt's Big Stick Policy has helped to formulate U.S. national diplomatic objectives up to now. It stressed that both talking softly and carrying a big stick were important at the same time.

Exercises

1.   In the Wild West, legend has it that a commander of a cavalry stockade had almost run out of his supplies. Meanwhile, the Indians gathered their forces that far out-numbered what the commander had, and they would attack the stockade soon. The commander told his men to open the gates and sweep the entryway to the stockade. The Indians were so puzzled by this scenario and they decided not to attack and withdrew the forces.

(i) What is the stratagem used by this commander?

(ii) What circumstance is best for the strategist to use this stratagem?

(iii) Assuming you belong to the Indians camp, what would be the best move in this scenario?

2.   Today in some countries ruled by aristocrats, the people in power always propagate doctrines such as "national pride and glory" and "glorious classical values" as a means of gaining credibility and justification for power plays.

        What of the following stratagems do these aritocrats use?
(a) Raise a corpse from the dead.
(b) Pretend to advance along one path while secretly going along another.
(c) Point at the mulberry only to curse the locust.
(d) Steal the beams and pillars and replace them with rotten timber.

3.   Lieutenant M. E. Clifton James fought in the trenches during the WWI. He was a peacetime actor who bore an extraordinary close physical resemblance to General Bernard L. Montgomery. Montgomery or Monty was the

victor of El Alamein and the Commander-in-chief of all ground forces for the Normandy landings of 1944.

The British Secret Service hatched a plot which involved using James to impersonate Monty. Monty's double was then to be dispatched to Gibraltar and North Africa in order to delude the Axis that Monty was going to lead an invasion from southern France, rather than from Normandy.

For a few months, James was posted as a Sergeant of the Intelligence Corps to Monty's staff so that he could study the general's voice, gestures and mannerisms. As an actor, James had little difficulty in mastering Monty's every movement, but he was more worried about his ability to capture Monty's personality.

On May 15, 1944, James flew as Monty on Winston Churchill's plane to Gibraltar, where he was greeted by the British Governor and introduced – as if by chance – to several of Hitler's known secret agents. A similar show took place in Algiers, where he was cheered by the British army. The Axis transferred some of their armies from the Normandy area to Southern France to reinforce its defence.

James' performance was described as "one of the greatest plans of deception that has ever been attempted."

Which of the following stratagems best describes the ploy made by the British Secret Service?
(a) Raise a corpse from the dead.
(b) Pretend to advance along one path while secretly going along another.
(c) Point at the mulberry only to curse the locust.
(d) Steal the beams and pillars and replace them with rotten timber.

4.   It happened in the 1990's, an American businessman Mr. Jones (fictitious name) and his associates were on their business trip to Shanghai to negotiate. He learned about Mr. Smith's story in his trip to Tokyo (refer to Question 3 in

Exercises of Chapter 3), so he stressed on holding the meeting the day after his arrival at Shanghai.

The Chinese Company had several senior managers to greet them in the airport, escorting them to a luxurious hotel. That evening, the Company held a reception dinner in honour of their guests. During the banquet, fine cuisines and Maotai were served. In 1972, Mao Zedong entertained Richard Nixon with Maotai during the state banquet in the U.S. presidential visit to China. Maotai has an alcohol content ranging from 53% by volume down to 35%. Rounds and rounds of ganbeis (cheers) were toasted to the guests by all those present. Eventually, all the guests had to be helped to their rooms.

The meeting was scheduled next morning at 10:00 a.m. Mr. Jones and his associates suffered from hangover symptoms. Though they managed to attend the meeting at 10.40 a.m. they bargained far worse that they could do.

What was the stratagem deployed by the Chinese Company?
(a) Empty castle ploy.
(b) Hide a dagger in a smile.
(c) Steal the beams and pillars and replace them with rotten timber.
(d) Raise a corpse from the dead.

5. U.S. President Theodore Roosevelt gave the order to the Great White Fleet to complete a circumnavigation of the globe from December 16, 1907 to February 22, 1909. The fleet consisted of four squadrons of four battleships each, with their escorts. The hulls of these ships were painted mostly in white color. It took place at a time when tension was slowly growing between the U.S. and Japan. The latter had recently showed its navy's competence in defeating the Russian Baltic Fleet in the Battle of Tsushima, 1905.

When the fleet sailed into Yokohoma, the Japanese went to extraordinary lengths to show that Japan desired peace with the U.S. Thousands of Japanese school children waved American flags to greet the U.S. Navy officials as they came ashore.

The campaign was an outcome of Roosevelt's foreign policy, often referred to as the "Big Stick". Roosevelt wanted to demonstrate to his country and the world that the U.S. Navy was capable of operating in global theatre, particularly in the Pacific.

(i) What was the stratagem used by both the U.S. and Japan in the Yokohoma scenario?

(ii) What was another spin off from the show of the Great White Fleet? (Hint: It had to do with the U.S. and Japan naval confrontation thirty years latter.)

6.   After WWII, General Douglas MacArthur became Supreme Commander of the Allied Powers (September, 1945-April 1951) in the Pacific region. At first, he was not so certain where the Japanese Emperor Hirohito would be put on trial for alleged war crimes.

On November 26, 1945, MacArthur thought the Emperor's abdication would not be necessary, and he ignored the advices of many memebers of the Japanese intellectuals. His staff drafted a new constitution which renounced war and reduced the Emperor to a figurehead.

On January 1, 1946, Emperor Hirohito publicly renounced his divinity and began a serious of goodwill touring of his country. MacArther exonerated the Emperor and all members of the imperial family implicated in the war for criminal prosecutions. He decided it was necessary for the recovery of the Japanese nation to maintain continuity with the Emperor as the figurehead. It had the far-reaching influence on the strategic position of having Japan on the front line against the communist bloc in the Pacific Rim.

What was the stratagem used by General Douglas MacArthur to influence the Japanese and to rebuild Japan?

Chapter 6.

To be circuitous, to make use of, to borrow and to shift off.

6.0 Introduction.

In Actions 12-15, a third party or object is involved in all actions.

6.1 Action 12: To be circuitous.

This action does not aim at the primary target due to the presence of many difficulties. Instead it is carried out on a secondary target first. After achieving success, it will help to attain the original objective.

6.1.1. The stratagem is: **Besiege Wei to rescue Zhao.** (One of the classical 36 Stratagems).

6.1.1.1 Theme.

Let the enemy fully commit himself against his prey, and then instead of rushing to the rescue, attack something he holds dear. The art of manoeuvring is to take a circuitous route in order to reach the destination, and to turn disastrous circumstances into advantageous situations.

> "If one wants to engage the enemies in battle and if the enemies seek refuge behind inaccessible shelter, he can draw them out by attacking some places which they will be obliged to rescue." (*The Art of War*, Chapter VI).

6.1.1.2   Source.

To save Zhao by attacking Wei. In 353 BC, the Wei State was very strong. King Huiwang (reigned 379-335 BC) of the Wei State sent General Pong Quen to attack the State of Zhao. (Refer to Appendix B for map). The Zhao State was defeated, and finally its Capital, Handan was besieged by the troops of Pong.

The Zhao State was at its critical moment, and its King sent his envoys to King Weiwang of the Qi State (reigned 378-343 BC) for rescue. King Weiwang assigned General Tien Ji as the Commander, and Sun Bin (c. 380-320 BC, the descendant of Sun Tze) as Chief of Staff to lead an army to rescue the Zhao State. The size of Qi army was relatively much smaller than that of Wei.

On Sun Bin's recommendation, the Qi army instead of going to Handan which was farther away went to besiege Da Liang, the Capital of the Wei State. A few soldiers guarded Da Liang, because Pong had picked the best and the available ones to go with him to attack the Zhao State. In addition, it took less time to reach Da Liang than Handan from the Qi State. Learning that Da Liang was in critical condition, Pong had to withdraw his troops back to the Wei State. On his way back, the Qi Army ambushed Pong's troops.

Sun Bin was a master of strategies. The Qi army did not have to go to Handen, which was much farther away; and despite of its size, it defeated the stronger Wei army.

Pong and Sun learned the art of war together under the same master, Gui Gu Zi. His real name was Wang Yu, and he got his name by living in seclusion in the vicinity of the Ghost Valley. The strategists, Su Qin and Zhang Yi were his students also. Later, King Huiwang of Wei recruited Pong to be a Commander taking charge of his army. Pong realized that Sun could be the toughest competitor to his career. He tricked Sun to go to the Wei State, and set Sun up with a crime. Sun was convicted and was punished by amputation. At last Sun was able to devise this stratagem to save the Zhao State, and to take vengeance on Pong.

This story is from *Records of the Historian* by Sima Qian (145-86 BC).

6.1.1.3 Illustrations.

(1) ***The tales of one thousand and one nights.*** In ancient Arabia, King Shahriyar had become disgruntled with the unfaithfulness of his wife. In revenge, he vowed to have a new bride each night. Each was to be put to death the following morning. Over hundreds of women were killed.

The daughter of the Prime Minister was called Shahrazad, and she had a clever plot when her turn to serve the King came. She asked the King's permission to allow her sister Dunyzad to come into their room to listen to Shahrazad telling a story. The King became so entranced by Shahrazad's story and it reached its climax when dawn came. The King would like to hear the conclusion of the story, so he spared Shahrazad for one day.

Night after night Shahrazad would leave the King in suspense at dawn. This lasted for another thousand days. Finally, the King spared Shahrazad's life, and abandoned his dreadful habit.

(2) ***The Battle of Tsushima (May 27-28, 1905).*** The Russo-Japanese War (1904-5) was the outcome of coflict of interests between Russia and Japan for the domaiance in Korea and Manchuria. Though Russia had built the Trans-Siberia Railroad (1891-1904), it lacked the facilities to reinforce its military strength in the Far East region. By contrast, Japan had steadily expanded its control over there since its war with China in 1894.

119

The War began on February 8, 1904, when the Japanese fleet launched a surprise attack and laid siege at Port Arthur which was leased to Russia by China. The Russians and the Japanese fought land battles in the Liaodong Peninsula and naval battles at Port Arthur. The Russians had to retreat to Mukden. Port Arthur was besieged for a long period of time by the Japanese, and fell to the enemy on January 2, 1905.

During the War, Japan was aware that it could not secure the complete command of the sea on which their land campaign depended. Meanwhile, Russia would like to reinforce its Pacific Fleet by sending the Baltic Fleet under the command of Admiral Z. P. Rozhestvensky to sail around the world from Baltic Sea via the Cape of Good Hope to China. It sailed in October 1904, and would reach the Far East in May 1905.

In order to win the land battles, Japan thought that it had to destroy the Baltic Fleet. Admiral Togo Heihachiro decided to play deception, disguising the Japanese merchant ships with structures to look like battleships. The fake fleet appeared in the sea north of the Taiwan Island. It looked as if the Japanese Combined Fleet was to attack the Baltic Fleet overthere.

Rozhestvensky avoided the Japanese "Combined Fleet", but it was lured to pass through the Tsushima Strait on its way to Vladivostok, because Port Arthur had fallen to the Japanese. In the Battle of Tsushima, Rozhestvensky was taken by surprise; and Russia was annihilated, losing eight battleships, numerous small vessels and more than 5,000 men. After the Battle, Japanese army occupied the entire Sakhalin Islands so as to force the Russians to sue for peace.

By winning this Battle, Japan compelled Russia to abandon its expansionist policy in the Far East, being the first Asian power in modern times to defeat a European power.

6.1.1.4 Comments.

The stratagem aims at changing the rules of game, reversing the enemy from the offensive to the defensive role. It is most effective to attack the place that the enemy values most. "If one is on the defensive all the time, he finds his forces insufficient. If one is on the offensive, he finds his forces sufficient all the time." (*The Art of War*, Chapter VI).

Shahrazad saved her life and hundreds of other women (to rescue Zhao) by tempting the King to indulge in stories (besiege Wei). Likewise, Admiral Togo Heihachiro thought it was necessary to destroy the Russian Baltic Fleet so as to control the sea as a prior to win the land battles. Even though the enemy is strong, yet if you are observant you may be able to locate a gap in his armour, a weakness that can be attacked instead.

6.2 Action 12: To make use of.

This action refers to the way with which one can win by making use of the thrust from his opponent. It is derived from the Chinese martial arts in which one can knock down his opponent by making use of the force put forward by the opponent. One can also win by exploiting the momentum of the battle situations and conditions.

6.2.1 The stratagems are:
  (I)   **Beat somebody at his own game.**
  (II) **Push the boat along with the current.**

(I) **Beat somebody at his own game.**

6.2.1.1 Theme.

Devise a ploy to take the bait as offered by the enemy and beat him with some other ruses afterwards. In order to do this, the strategist must have a thorough knowledge of his own conditions as well as the enemy's conditions, so as to see through the whole scheme. "By holding out baits one can make the enemy go to places where he wants them to go." (*The Art of War,* Chapter VI). But for the expert strategist, he would devise a ploy to take the bait as offered by the enemy and beat the latter with some other ruses afterwards.

When agents are involved, one must ferret the enemy's agents and "use incentives to bribe them and treat them well so that they may become double spies to work against their former masters." (*The Art of War,* Chapter XIII).

6.2.1.2 Source.

The river god would like to take a bride every year. In the Spring and Autumn Period in China, during the reign of Duke Wenhou, (424-387 BC) of the Wei State, Ximen Pau was appointed as the Magistrate of the City of Ip. Ximen made a tour of the region under his jurisdiction. He found out that the population of the city had decreased tremendously in recent years. It was because the nearby River Zhang flooded every year. A gang of crooks claimed that the river god requested a bride every year to pacify.

The gang solicited money to hold the ceremony of offering the bride to the river god. The crooks approached the families with maidens, saying that these maidens could be the brides of the river god this year unless they were paid to go away. Thus, many families moved away from the city. In fact, the gang had the support of the corrupted officers sharing the profits from this venture.

Eventually in the ceremony they managed to find a miserable maiden tied to a raft and send the raft with the bride to the bottom of the river.

Ximen as the new Magistrate said he would like to attend the ceremony. It was a great show on the day when the river god took its bride. Thousands of people gathered in the ceremony. Ximen said he would like to see the bride. The gang leader and his assistants came forward with the bride. Ximen said that the bride was not pretty enough and he told the gang leader, "Why not you go to report to the river god about postponing the ceremony till we find a more beautiful bride."

He ordered his guards to tie the gang leader on a raft and send the raft to the bottom of the river. The congregation waited for some time, then Ximen said to gang, "Your leader is very slow in doing things, why not get his assistant to tell him to hurry up."

He ordered his guards to do the same thing to the first assistant as to the gang leader. Ximen waited for some more time and he got his guards to do same thing to the second assistant. Next, he suggested sending a notary public to seek the advice from the river god and did the same thing to him.

By this time, members of gang and other notary public were scared to death, and they begged for mercy. Ximen revealed the evil deeds of the gang, and banned the ceremony forever. Under Ximen's administration, the City of Ip became prosperous again.

This story is from *Records of the Historian* by Sima Qian (145-86 BC).

6.2.1.3 Illustrations.

(1) ***Franklin D. Roosevelt beat his enemy in the enemy's own game.*** Yamamoto Isoroku (1884-1943) Fleet Admiral and Commander-in-Chief of the Combined Japanese Fleet conceived of the surprise attack on the U.S. naval base at Pearl Harbour on December 7, 1941.

After this success, he devised another plan to attack Midway Islands in the hopes of luring the entire U.S. fleet into battle and use the Japanese carrier advantage to crush the U.S. naval force in the Pacific.

In fact, the U.S. naval intelligence official code name "Magic" cracked the Japanese diplomatic cipher that was produced by an encryption machine nicknamed "Purple". The Roosevelt Reich Navy broke the Japanese naval codes long before Attack on Pearl Harbour. The Japanese did not know about this. When President Franklin D. Roosevelt (in office 1933-1945) and his staff was preparing for the Midway confrontation, a Chicago newspaper published about this. Both the U.S. and the Japanese intelligence were shocked to read it.

Roosevelt deliberated if he was to charge the newspaper for leaking this top secret, it would startle the Japanese to cancel attack on the Midway Islands. Moreover, it could alert the Japanese that their codes had been deciphered, and they might change the codes. In that case, the U.S. intelligence had to spend time to crack the new codes. Roosevelt preferred to play dumb on this, and the Japanese likewise ignored about it.

In the ensuing battle on June 4-7, 1942, U.S. navy sank all four Japanese carriers. Only one U.S. carrier was lost. This battle helped turn the tide of the Pacific war against the Japanese.

(2) *A make up artist tricked the fugitive.* In Hollywood, there was a professional make up artist with the name of Betty (fictitious name). She was well known for her masquerading skills. One day, a male courier knocked the door in her home. She opened it; but it happened to be a young fugitive running away from a police precinct.

The fugitive threatened Betty with a knife to change his look, so as to run away from California as safe as possible. Betty asked the fugitive what he would like to look. She asked, "How about a woman?"

He declined this suggestion, because he had to coordinate this with his manners. Betty asked, "How about a middle-aged man?"

The fugitive agreed to this suggestion, and Betty did accordingly. After it was done, he looked at the mirror, and he could not recognise himself. Then, he ran away.

Very soon, he was arrested by the police. It was because a few days ago, Betty saw the picture of a wanted criminal in the malls and in the shopping plazes, and she masqueraded the fugitive to look exactly like the wanted criminal.

6.2.1.4 Comments.

The art of warfare is to pretend to accommodate the motives and desires of the enemy. (*The Art of War,* Chapter XI). To be successful in deploying this stratagem, one must have a thorough knowledge both of his enemy and himself. The state of mind is critical. When there is bait held out by the enemy, one is going to get the bait and to come out as a final winner of the game.

President Franklin Roosevelt was fully aware of Admiral Isoroku Yamamoto's scheme, but his team pretended not to know the ruse of the enemy, and managed to outwit the enemy by changing the entire scenario adverse to them. Betty did according to the fugitive's instruction and the latter fell into her trap.

(II) **Push the boat along with the current.**

6.2.2.1 Theme.

Sun Tze said, "The adept in warfare is able to push his army in a manner comparable to the onrush of stones falling from the great heights of mountain - due to momentum." (*The Art of War,* Chapter V). It is the sudden push that enables rushing torrents strong enough even to move stones. By making use of the momentum of the scenario, one can accomplish tasks more efficiently and effectively.

6.2.2.2 Source.

Sun Tze, *Art of War,* refer to 6.2.2.1.

6.2.2.3 Illustrations.

(1) ***The Suez War of 1956.*** In the early 1950s, Palestinian Arab Fedayeen launched infiltration and attacked Israeli civilian centers and military outposts from Egypt, Jordan and Syria. Arab infiltration and Israeli retaliation characterized the Arab-Israel relations. In 1955 Egyptian President Gamal Abdel Nasser began to import arms from the Soviet bloc to build his arsenal for the confrontation with Israel.

In September 1955, in violation of international agreements and in what amounted to an act of war, Egypt blockaded the Straits of Tiran. It stopped Israel's sea trade with Africa and the Far East. On July 26, 1956, Nasser nationalized the Suez Canal. Most of the shares of the Suez Canal Company were held by the British and the French. On October 25, Egypt signed a tripartite agreement with Syria and Jordan placing Nasser in command of all three armies.

With diplomacy failing to reverse Nasser's decision, the U.K. and France embarked on preparations to regain control of the Suez Canal and on October 29, together with Israel launched a military operation in the Sinai Peninsula. On October 31, the U.K. and France conducted air and naval attacks against Egyptian airfields and cities. By November 5, Israel had achieved its immediate goals of destroying Egyptian Sinai positions.

U.S. pressure resulted in Israelis withdrawing from the areas it had captured. However, Israel elicited a promise that U.S. would maintain its freedom of navigation in the waterway, and a resolution creating U.N. emergency force to supervise the territories vacated by the Israeli forces.

(2) *Johann Strauss II and his orchestra avoided prolonged performance.* Johann Strauss II (1825-1899) was an Austrian composer, known as "the waltz king". He was the most famous member of the Strauss family. He visited Russia, Britain, France, Italy and the U.S. to perform.

In 1872, Strauss and his orchestra performed in Boston, U.S. The audience was very much fascinated, and rounds of encores were applauded after the scheduled time. Strauss was happy but worried. He felt that his musicians and he were tired. He had to do something to redress the situation, but he did not want to disappoint his audience.

Over one night, Strauss composed a polka which was fast and lively dance music. On the next performance, after finishing the scheduled program, the audience applauded for encore. His orchestra played this newly composed polka, and the audience was enthralled.

Then, when the trumpets were playing, and at the end of a stanza, Strauss pointed his baton to the cello musicians who stood up and left. One moment later, when the violins were playing, and at the end of another stanza, Strauss signalled the metal wind instruments players to leave the stage. Then, when the clarinets were playing, the percussion team left. The momentum of the musicians leaving the stage continued until only Strauss was alone on the stage. Strauss turned round and bowed to the audience, and the curtained lowered.

The audience was amazed to see this, and they all stood up and cheered a long time. Now, everybody understood what Strauss wanted to do.

6.2.2.4 Comments.

British and French determination to reverse Egypt's naturalization of the Suez Canal provided an opportunity to Israel to launch a coordinated military campaign against Egypt. Taking advantage of the momentum, Israel occupied Sinai swiftly. It added Israeli's bargaining power for the freedom of navigation in the waterway, and security from infiltration by the Palestinian Arab Fedayeen.

Johann Strauss II created the momentum for his musicians to leave the stage so as to avoid prolonged encore requests. It was done so pleasantly that nobody was offended.

6.3   Action 14: To borrow.

One has to borrow the name, its authority and the influence of a notable third party (or object) so as to impress or to gain a favour from his opponent. He can also make the third party an instrument.

6.3.1   The stratagems are:
- (I)   **Kill with a borrowed knife.** (One of the classical 36 Stratagems).
- (II) **Turn around one thousand catties with the strength of four liangs.**
- (III) **Make a cat's paw of someone.**

(I) **Kill with a borrowed knife.**

6.3.1.1 Theme.

> This stratagem is to let somebody else do the dirty job of killing one's enemy. When the enemy has been identified, but the allies were still uncertain what to do, it is best to trick them to attack the enemy. One may also bribe the enemy's officials to turn traitor. By doing so, one can rest at ease, so as to conserve his own energy and strength.
>
> Induce others to fight your battles for you, so as to conserve your strength. This is one of the craftiest stratagems, because the schemer can hide his identity.

6.3.1.2 Source.

Duke Huangong of the Zheng State tricked the Duke of the Wee State. In the Spring and Autumn Period (770-476 BC) in China, Duke Huangong of the Zheng State (reigned 806-771 BC) would like to invade the Wee State. He compiled a list of the good ministers, clever strategists, capable generals and loyal people of the Wee State. He said that these people would be awarded a share of the Wee State when he annexed its territories. To broadcast this, he performed a great show of this by staging offerings to the Heaven, and buried the list into the altar.

The Dule of Wee State was blinded by jealousy, thinking that these people betrayed him, working for the enemy. He arrested all these people and killed them. By doing this, very soon Duke Huangong had no difficulties in annexing the Wee State.

6.3.1.3 Illustrations.

(1) **Religious doctrines could be used as knives.** On November 27, 1095, Pope Urban II gave a proclamation at the end of a church council in Clermont, France. In it he appealed for help that he had received from the Byzantine Emperor, calling upon the nobility of Western Europe and the Franks, to go to the East and assist their Christian brothers, the Byzantines, against the attacks of the Muslim Turks.

He also encouraged them to liberate Jerusalem, the most sacred and beloved city in Christendom, from the domination of Muslims who had ruled it since taking it from the Christian Byzantines in 638. As a further inducement, the Pope offered them a Papal Indulgence, which promised the immediate remission of all sins of any who participated in the expedition.

The responses to the Pope's speech were great. Large numbers of Franks, both nobles and ordinary people, responded to his call with great enthusiasm, and streamed eastwards in several waves. Beyond all reasonable expectations, they retook Jerusalem on July 15, 1099, establishing several Crusader States which lasted for almost two centuries.

Pope Urban II wanted the expedition to the East to be a military one, undertaken by soldiers and controlled by clerics. The responses to his call for the liberation of the Eastern Church were great. Soon tens of thousands of ordinary people were on the People's Crusade. Since 1095, there had been seven major Crusades lasting for one hundred and seventy years. Most of the other bands of crusaders never made it to the east.

The slogans "to liberate the Eastern Church and to liberate Jerusalem" were the knives with which the Christians and the Muslims had to fight against each other in the Middle Ages.

(2) *Let the Germans clear the way for the Communist rule in Poland.* By summer 1944, as the Soviet Union's Red Army was advancing from the east of Poland, the German occupying forces were on the defensive side. At that time, there were not many German troops in Warsaw. The Soviets encouraged the Polish Home Army, directed by the Polish Government-in-Exile in London, to wrest Warsaw from the Germans.

However, as the Soviets "liberated" Eastern Poland, they set up a pro-Communist civil authority in Lublin with the plot to establish a Communist post-war government in Poland. The Polish Home Army thought it was wise to do otherwise. They preferred to attack the Germans in Warsaw prior to the Red Army, with the understanding that the Soviet reinforcements would be available if needed.

Late in July 1944, the Red Army entered the Warsaw suburb of Praga, across the Vistula River.

On August 1, the Polish Home Army General Tadeusz Komorowski, (known as Bor-Komorwski) with a force of between thirty-five and fifty thousand partisans, attacked the Germans in Warsaw. The Polish civilians joined in the fight, and they controlled most part of the city by August 4. But the Germans obtained reinforcements: S.S. police units, a brigade of Russian ex-prisoners, and a brigade of ex-convicts, which even Adolf Hitler had previously ordered to remove from the front due to their extreme brutality. The Polish Home Army and the civilians were completely destroyed.

During the Warsaw Uprising (August 1 to October 2) the Red Army encamped within sight across the Vistula, never attempted any assistance. The Soviet's stratagem was to borrow the German hands to kill off all the Polish Home Army and the Polish civilians. They refused permission to let the Americans and the British to use their airfields to drop ammunition and relief supplies to the Poles. In September, when the Germans had the control of Warsaw, the Soviets allowed a small amount of ammunition to be dropped in, but it was useless, because they were for the Soviet armaments and they could not fit the Poles' weapons.

At last, eight-five percent of the city was razed, two hundred thousand Poles were killed and the Polish Home Army was annihilated. The Germans deported the left over population. When the Germans were finally defeated, there was no Polish Home Army left to oppose the Communist political domination in Poland.

6.3.1.4 Comments.

This is one of the dirtiest stratagems. The essence of this stratagem is to distract the victim to the scapegoat, hiding the identity of the person hatching the ploy. In reality, there are neither perpetual allies nor everlasting enemies. The ally can play the role of the enemy by the desire for gain. For instance, one may join effort with an ally to beat a common enemy who is too strong to tackle by oneself. After that, the ally may join hands with a third party to play tricks on you by the desire for gains also.

Therefore, one has to be alert of the hidden schemers through keen observation and if possible through the use of espionage. Sun Tze valued highly the importance of intelligence. "Information cannot be obtained by offering prayers to gods and spirits or by inductive thinking or by deductive calculation. It can be obtained only from men who have a thorough knowledge of the enemy's conditions." (*The Art of War,* Chapter XIII). One word of caution: intelligence however brilliant cannot provide dramatic success where strength or preparedness does not exist.

(II) **Turn around one thousand catties with the strength of four liangs.**

Note: 1,000 *catties* = 800 kg; 4 *liangs* = 0.2 Kg. To be physically valid, it should be "Turn around one thousand catties with the mass of four liangs". The units of mass are kilograms and grams.

6.3.2.1 Theme.

> In the classical Chinese martial arts, a basic tactic is to borrow strength according to the principle of leverage. Consider the lever; a small force applied over a long distance is the same amount of work as a large force applied over a small distance. The "long distance" is made available by stratagems.
>
> "Though the enemies possess a large army, they may be rendered powerless." (*The Art of War,* Chapter VI). In social and political manipulation, "borrowing strength" is always considered as an important and tactful move.

6.3.2.2 Source.

Chinese martial arts.

6.3.2.3 Illustrations.

(1) ***Leonardo da Vinci scared away the prior who houunded him.*** Leonardo da Vinci (1452-1519) was a person with broad varied knowledge and skills. He has been widely considered to be one of the greatest talented people ever to have lived. Much of his earlier working life was in the service of Ludovico Sforza, Duke of Milan (1452-1508).

He worked on *The Last Supper* in the 1490s. It was about the last meal Jesus Christ shared with his Twelve Apostles before his death. During the meal, Jesus revealed that one of his Apostles would betray him. Da Vinci told the story of the consternation that the statement caused to His Apostles.

He painted from dawn till dark without stopping, but he was idle for three to four days. He took a long time to consider how to depict the facial expressions of Jusus and the traitor Judas, and left these parts not finished for a long time.

The prior (monk whose rank next below an abbot) spied on da Vinci, and made a fuss of da Vinci's behaviours to the Duke. Da Vinci was annoyed. In order to be free from being hounded by the prior, da Vinci told the Duke that he might be obliged to use the prior as his model for Judas. The prior dared not give da Vinci any more trouble. When finished, the painting was acclaimed a masterpiece of design and characterisation.

(2) ***A strong feudal lord (daimyo) was scared away by small tricks.*** During the Warring States Period (1467-1573) of Japan, there were 260 feudal lords of families called daimyos. A daimio (daimyo) was also a large landowner. Individual daimio was frequently in armed conflict with other daimyos throughout the period.

According to legend, once the powerful Lord Yoshino launched an attack on its neighbour, the Shimoichi daimio. Since Lord Yoshino had four times the number of men than that of Lord Shimoichi, the latter was defeated thrice and it was on the verge of being subjugated.

A ninja who was a person specially trained in a vaiety of unathrodoxed arts of war to do espinonage, scouting and assassination volunteered his skills to help his master, Lord Shimoichi. One night, the ninja stole Lord Yoshino's kimono from the latter's camp. On the next day, Lord Shimoichi returned it to Lord Yoshino. That night, the ninja stole Lord Yoshino's iron helmet which was also returned on the next day.

On the third night, the ninja again stole Lord Yoshino's pillow which was returned to its owner on the fourth day. At last Lord Yoshino was scared, because he thought he might lose his head sooner or latter. He withdrew his men from Lord Shimoichi's territory that afternoon.

6.3.2.4 Comments.

When the enemy thrusts his terrific blows, one can turn them aside with a wit. The counter thrust could come from a small finger, but with the right dynamic from an ingenious mind.

Leonardo da Vinci has been widely considered to be one of the most talented people ever to have lived. By pretending to make the prior as a model for Judas, the prior stopped all his fuss.

Likewise, the ninja performed some small tricks on Lord Yoshino, even though the latter had a much more powerful army and had won three battles, yet the Lord preferred not to stay one more night in his enemy's territory.

(III) **Make a cat's paw of someone.**

6.3.3.1 Theme.

> To put a job into the hands of another without letting him know. According to Sun Tze, "the general should act like a shepherd who forces his flock of sheep to run hither and thither without their knowing the final destination." (*The Art of War,* Chapter XI).
>
> The general must keep the army in ignorance of his plans by presenting false appearances. He must frequently alter his methods and schemes so that no one can be sure of his intentions.

6.3.3.2 Source.

Sun Tze, *The Art of War,* refer to 6.3.3.1.

6.3.3.3 Illustrations.

(1) *The British agents made use of a U.S. senator to prompt Nazi Germany declaring war on U.S.* In 1939, as tension mounted in Europe, the America First Committee and U.S. senator Burton K. Wheeler (in office: 1923-1947), were keen supporters for their isolationist beliefs. After WWII had started, they continued to oppose any aid to the U.K. or any other countries overseas engaged in war.

The British was aware that if the conflict of interests between Japan and the U.S. in the Pacific escalated to war, the U.S. would divert all resources to fight in the Pacific. Subsequently the U.S. would spare nothing to aid the U.K. and other European countries. The British secret agents had a mission to change the situation.

One day, a young officer in uniform went to Wheeler's residence. He claimed he worked in the Pentagon, and he supported Wheeler's isolationist brief. He handed to Wheeler a letter marked "Confidential" and left. After reading the letter, Wheeler was furious. It was the Victory Plan that provided the rationale for U.S. to intervene the war being fought in Europe. It suggested that if U.S. and Japan were engaged in war, U.S. should declare war on Nazi Germany and crush it first before dealing with the Japanese. Once Germany was defeated, Japan would not fight.

Wheeler passed the Victory Plan to three newspapers including the Chicago Tribune that published it on December 4, 1941, three days before Japanese attack on Pearl Harbour. The German agents were interested in this piece of news. After investigation and analysis of Wheeler's background, they believed that the leaked out information was bona fide. When Adolf Hitler was informed about the Victory Plan, he was infuriated. Subsequently Germany declared war on the U.S. on December 11, 1941.

On December 7, Japan attacked Pearl Harbour causing a lot of damages, and now Germany declared war on U.S. four days later. Americans felt that the Germans "dropped stones on them when they fall into a well". They had to fight both the Japan and Nazi Germany on two fronts. Wheeler was heart-broken to see the outcome.

(2) *A recruitment program turned out to be espionage.* In 1971, a certain French chemical company invented a new type of detergent. An American, Jackson (fictitious name) who was a chemist himself thought that this new product could overwhelm the American detergent markets.

He made a recruitment advertisement for several chemical engineers and technicians to work in the U.S. with very attractive remunerations. The advertisement captured the attention of many technical staff, among which eight applicants were from the said French chemical company. These people worked respectively in the research and development laboratory, in the production lines and in the quality control laboratory.

During their individual interview, Jackson asked a lot of questions concerning their work on the pretext of verifying their credentials. After the interviews, Jackson succeeded in getting all the information he needed to produce the detergent. He left France in secret, while the applicants waited eagerly for their employment contracts.

Very soon, the detergent with similar capabilities as that produced by the French chemical company was available in the U.S. stores. It was making its way to the international markets.

6.3.3.4 Comments.

This stratagem is similar to that of "Kill with a borrowed knife." However, it emphaizes on getting things done through a third party without letting him know, and the process usually does not involve bloodshed.

The agent dressed up as a U.S. army officer claiming to work in the Pentagon tricked Senator Burton Wheeler. In fact, the Victory Plan did not come from the U.S. army. As a supporter of the America First Committee and a well-known isolationist, the British agent borrowed his hand to pass the Victory Plan to the newspapers. Due to Wheeler's special background, Nazi Germany believed it was genuine, and took the initiative to declare war on U.S. The British succeeded in this ploy, while Wheeler was not aware that he had been manipulated.

Jackson obtained the information needed to produce the new type of detergent. The technical staffs of the French Chemical Company were ignorant that they had been exploited.

6.4 Action 15: To shift off.

The aim is to find a scapegoat, and to shift something undesirable such as blame or disaster on to the scapegoat.

6.4.1 The stratagem is: **Shift the misfortune to somebody else by moving the corpse to his place.**

6.4.1.1 Theme.

> A person has killed someone. In order to cover up, he moved the corpse to another person's place so as to frame the latter. The strategist manoeuvres the victim by framing a third party for the crime. The strategist can conceal his/her identity.
>
> This tactic looks similar to "Kill with a borrowed knife". But, in that case the offense, (whether the killing or a felonious undertaking), is targeted to the person to whom the ploy is targeted.

6.4.1.2 Source.

Empress Wu Zetian's palace politics. Empress Wu Zetian was the only ruling woman in Chinese history that declared herself Empress. When she was thirteen years old, she was known for her wit, intelligence and beauty. She was recruited to the palace of Emperor Taizong who was known as Li Shimin (reigned 627-649). Soon she became his favorite concubine. But she also had eyes for Emperor Taizong's son known as Gaozong (reigned 650-683).

After Taizong died, Gaozong became the Emperor. Wu was now twenty-seven years old. Soon, she became Gaozong's favorite concubine; giving birth to the sons he wanted. As mother of the future Emperor of the Tang Dynasty, she gathered much power. However, she would like to eliminate Gaozong's consort Empress Wang.

Wu gave birth to a daughter whom Gaozong was very fond of. Once, Wang paid a visit to Wu, and played with the little girl. After Wang left, Wu strangled the girl. When Gaozong came, she behaved as usual. Gaozong asked for the girl, but he found that she was dead. Wu said Wang was there a moment ago, and she had left. Gaozong alienated from his queen consort.

Later Gaozong was sick. Wu sent her maid to hide a tiny straw human-figure tagged with Gaozong's name and birthday in a form used by witchcraft in Wang's palace. Wu told Gaozong that she had received confidential report that Wang worked voodoo on him. Gaozong ordered his guards to search Wang's palace and they found the tiny straw human-figure. He was very angry and he put Wang in life custody.

Then, Gaozong suffered a crippling stroke. Wu took over the administrative duties of the court, a position equal to the Emperor. She instituted a secret police force to crack her opposition. She would not hesitate to kill anyone who offended her. In 690, she enthroned herself by establishing a new dynasty named Zhou (690-704). After her death, the Tang Dynasty was restored.

6.4.1.3   Illustrations.

(1) ***Most favoured stratagem used by the Japanese militarists.*** With China torn by foreign countries' invasions in the late Nineteenth Century, the Japanese militarists viewed China as an obvious area for Japan to exand its territory by military force. Manchuria is a resource-rich area situated in the north-east of China. Japan and Russia struggled for control of this strategically important area for many years.

During the 1920s, the Japanese imperial government was not responsive to proposals for military aggression against China. In September 1931, conspirators in the Japanese Guandong Army (the militarists) blew up a section of railway track in the south of Manchuria. They blamed the Chinese saboteurs for the destruction. When the Japanese government was powerless to intervene, the Guandong Army mobilised, taking Mukden (now Shenyang). In January 1932, they attacked Shanghi, south of their territory in the Shandong Province. A truce was reached in March 1932. Japan established Manchukuo (1932-1945), a puppet regime led by ex-emperor Xuantong (also known as Henry Puyi) of the Qing Dynasty.

On July 7, 1937 Japan started what had been called the first battle of World War II. The Japanese Army took drills near Lugouqiao (Marco Polo bridge) a bridge across the Yongding River about ten miles west of Beijing, China. When a soldier went missing, the Japanese accused the Chinese army across the river of abducting the soldier. The soldier soon turned up, but the Japanese commander had already ordered an attack.

Within weeks, Japan controlled the east-west region from Beijing to Tianjin. President Chiang Kaishek decided to fight the Japanese this time, despite of the appeasement made early to Japan by giving up Manchuria to avoid a war. Though there were international protests, yet the ineffective League of Nations refused to mediate the undeclared war.

(2) ***Operation Himmler gave the excuse for attacking Poland in 1939.*** In 1939, after having gained both Austria and Czechoslovakia, Adolf Hitler was confident that he could again move east to annex Poland without having to fight U.K. and France. To eliminate the possibility of conflict with the Soviet Union, the Nazi-Soviet Non-Aggression Pact (Molotov-Ribbentrop Pact) was signed on August 23, 1939. It was a secret protocol dividing Eastern Europe into spheres of influence.

Hitler wanted an excuse for attacking Poland without Germany appearing to be the aggressor. Heinrich Himmler came up with an idea which was coded Operation Himmler. On the night of August 31, 1939, Nazis took an unknown prisoner from one of their concentration camps, dressed him in a Polish uniform, took him to the town of Gleiwitz, on the border between Poland and Germany, and then shot him. The staged scene with the dead prisoner dressed in a Polish uniform was taken as a Polish attack against a German radio station.

Hitler used the staged attack as the excuse to invade Poland on September 1. The speed of invasion gave it the name Blitzkrieg, or lighting war. The U.K. and France had sworn to defend Poland. Honoring these obligations, the two countries sent ultimatums to Hitler demanding his withdrawal from Poland. Hitler declined to respond. On September 3, British Prime Minister Neville Chamberlain went to the airwaves to announce that the U.K. was at war with Germany. France also declared war on Germany, followed by Australia, New Zealand and India shortly thereafter. The World War II began.

6.4.1.4 Comments.

This is another dirty tactic (the other one is "Kill with a borrowed knife"). Many times this tactic is used to create a situation for accusing the third person for the crime. The target is the third person.

There are great similarities between the Japanese conspirators and Heinrich Himmler in fabricating the scenarios, getting the excuses for the attacks. However, this is something that the victim cannot do much about, because the offender is usually powerful. The only thing the victim can do is to probe into the matter carefully and to disclose the facts.

Exercises

1. In the Presidential Elections of the U.S., when Candidate A is on the unflavored side of the pre-election poll, his aids would dick out the dirty rugs of Candidates B, C and D etc. They would say that B had an outside-marriage affair with somebody, either of the same sex or the other sex. C evaded from draft for military service twenty years ago, his daughter drinks and drives without valid license and that she is a lesbian. D is mentally retarded, because he makes a mess of the quantitative figures, and he cannot spell correctly the simple word, "potato".

All these aim at downgrading the personal integrity and the capability of the competitors so as to gets more votes for Candidate A.

What is the stratagem used by the aids of Candidate A in this case?
(a) Besiege Wei to rescue Zhao.
(b) Beat somebody at his own game.
(c) Kill with a borrowed knife.
(d) Shift the misfortune to somebody else by moving the corpse to his place.

2. In early 1942, the Japanese Fleet Admiral Yamamoto Isoroku planned to attack on Midway Islands so as to lure America's remaining carriers in the Pacific into a trap and sink them. He was not aware that the American and British cryptanalysts had broken the Japanese Naval Cipher, codenamed JN-25, and had been able to read at least 10 percent of the Japaneses Navy's radio transmissions.

The Combat Intelligence Office under Commander Joseph P. Rochefort noticed an increase in Japanese radio traffic to its fleet units. However, he had no clues to the exact target of the operation, as it was coded as "AF". Rochefort had a trick. Utilizing the underwater telephone connection with Midway, he asked that Midway transmit, via uncoded radio traffic, a message saying that the desalination plant in Midway Islands was out of order. The Japanese was tricked, and when Rochefort's men decoded another message thereafter, they were pleased to read the "AF has problesm with its de-salting plant".

Now, Admiral Chester W. Nimitz, the U.S. Pacific Fleet Commander knew that the main Japanese target was Midway, eliminating Yamamoto's deception in attacking Dutch Harbour on June 3, 1942.

What was the stratagem used by the Combat Intelligence to find out the meaning of the code "AF"?

3. In business management, there is a way to get rid of employees not belonging to one's clan. These people are transferred to head departments or branches, which are not making profits. The mission is to reorganise the structure of these units to bring in productivity and profits.

Downsizing and lay-off are usually some of these means to achieve the objectives. Discontent among the employees began to grow, and these executives had a hard time. After the re-organisation was complete, it is their turn to be laid off.

Which of the following stratagems is used in this case?
(a) Besiege Wei to rescue Zhao.
(b) Beat somebody at his own game.
(c) Make a cat's paw of someone.
(d) Turn around one thousand catties with the strength of four liangs.

4. At the turn of the Twentieth Century, Brunner Mond (founded in 1873) of the United Kingdom was the world's leading manufacturer and supplier of soda ash and associated alkaline products. It dominated the alkaline products in China.

During the WWI, Brunner Mond focused on producing war supplies and stopped its exports to China. A Chinese enterpreneur took the chance to establish a chemical company to produce alkaline products taking over Brunner Mond's markets. After the War, Brunner Mond came back to the Chinese markets, and it would like to drive out the Chinese competitor. It cut its prices by 40%.

The Chinese Company was in dilemma. It could not compete by price cutting due to its relatively weak financial strength as compared to Brunner Mond. If it did not cut the prices, it could not sell its products, and the company could not survive.

Since WWI, the Chinese Company had been selling its products in Japan, and it hatched a scheme. It contacted the Mitsue Corporation to sell its products taking advantage of the latter's network at prices lower than those of Brunner Mond, but higher than the prices it could sell in the Chinese markets.

At that moment, the market share of the Chinese Company was only 10% of that of Brunner Mond. The Chinese products quickly eroded the Brunner Mond's markets. In view of the challenge, Brunner Mond had to cut prices, and the financial consquences were large.

Since the Chinese products could be sold at higher prices in Japan than in China, the Chinese alkaline products were exported to Japan in large amount. Brunner Mond had to negotiate with the Chinese Company to stop the price war, and to restore the status quo.

What was the stratagem used by the Chinese Company in view of the challenge by Brunner Mond in the Chinese alkaline products market?

5. In 1887, Yamaha Torakusu set out to produce a high-quality reed organ, founding what would become the Yamaha Corporation. He built the very first Japanese made piano in 1900. In 1904, Yamaha pianos and organs were awarded an Honorary Grand Prize at the St. Louis World's Fair.

The century-long quest for excellence has resulted in higher standards of quality, consisting efficiency and performance throughout the piano making industry. As it grew, the company capitalised on a unique heritage of artisanship and technological expertise to diversify into an astoundingly wide range of products and services. They include musical instruments, professional/home audio video products, home furnishings, motorcycles, snow mobiles, watercrafts, computer peripherals, and music education.

Since 1954, Yamaha Music schools have been dedicated to presenting the higher quality keyboard tuitions around the world. In 1966, Yamaha established the Yamaha Music Foundation in Tokyo. Its main purpose was to stimulate interest in the playing and enjoyment of music against people from over the world.

The Yamaha Corporation claims: "True to our musical origins, no matter what business we take one, or what country we do business in, we remain perfectly attuned to a set of common values that define the World of Yamaha."

What is the stratagem used by the Yamaha Corporation in its expansion into multi-dimensional businesses?

6.   On June 8, 1934, a Japanese envoy in Nanjing disappeared. The Japanese militarists made the protest to the Nationalist Government of China about this missing envoy, claiming that he had been kidnapped and killed by the Chinese underground gangs.

The Japanese battleships sailed to Nanjing and they were ready to attack Nanjing. The Chinese government dispatched search teams consisting of thousands of people to look for this Japanese envoy.

In the morning of June 13, in Zijinshan, near the Mingxiaoling Mausoleum (the imperial tombs of the Ming Emperors), a roadside restaurant owner told the search team that he had a strange customer last night. The customer could only speak a few words of Mandarin. He ate a bowl of noodles, and left without paying the bill. Following this lead, the search team found a man in a nearby cave with self-inflicted wounds on his body.

The fact was this envoy was ordered to go to Nanjing to commit suicide. The search team found him before he took his last breath. If this ploy was not revealed, the Japanese invasion of China might have started in 1934, instead of in 1937.

What was the stratagem used by the Japanese militarists in this case? How do you compare this scheme with that of Operation Himmler?

7.   On June 22 1941, Nazi Germany invaded the Soviet Union, making the Nazi-Soviet Pact (Treaty of Non-aggression between these two countries) signed on August 23, 1939 null and void.

In December 1941, a Conference was held in Moscow between the U.K. and the Soviet Union on their alliance against the Nazis. Josef Stalin proposed to base post-war Polish western borders on the Oder-Neisse Line with Russian acquisition of the Polish territories after Nazi invasion to Poland. Anthony Eden, then the Foreign Minister of Britain demanded the Polish border in question was the 1939 line before the war. Stalin also wanted to keep the territories acquired from Finland and Romania. Eden rejected the settlement about the Polish borders as it was contrary to the terms of the Atlantic Charter. The negotiations came to a stalemate.

On their way back to the hotels, Eden and his aides felt that Stalin was a bit weary that the U.K. and the Soviet Union might not come to an agreement. Further, they were aware that eavesdroppers had been planted in the hotels where they stayed. They planned a show in the hotel by being unenthusiastic about the proposed alliance of the U.K. and the Soviet Union. They queried whether it was sagacious to give Soviet Union 500 airplanes and 500 tanks. On the next meeting between Stalin and Eden, Stalin softened his tone, and skipped the Polish border controversy as a pretext to other negotiations.

What was the stratagem used by Anthony Eden in breaking the stalemate on the Polish borders issue in his negotiation with Josef Stalin?

Chapter 7.

To procreate.

7.0 Introduction.

Action 16 is to fabricate some pre-conditions favorable to the strategists before any action is taken.

7.1 Action 16: To procreate.

This is to fabricate or to make up when there is no such thing, to stir up the matter, and to elaborate or exaggerate things even it is a very minor issue.

7.1.1 The stratagems are:
    (1) **Create something out from nothing.** (One of the classical 36 Stratagems).
    (II) **Fish in murky waters.** (One of the classical 36 Stratagems).
    (III) **Decorate the tree with bogus blossoms.** (One of the classical 36 Stratagems).

(I) Create something out from nothing.

7.1.1.1 Theme.

> Get what you need by creating a false idea in the enemy's mind and fix it in his mind as a reality. The stratagem makes use of both spurious and real things together to distract the enemy. Rumors are one of those commonly used methods to fabricate something out of nothing. However, they cannot last long if all the things are spurious.
>
> Fantasy and imagination can also make something out from nothing. They are not necessarily bad, as all innovations start with dreams of new tools and products: use of electricity, the airplanes, the computers, optical fibre communication and space travel. The use of this stratagem, like the use of explosives, can be constructive or destructive.

7.1.1.2 Source.

How General Zhang Zin got his needed arrows. In the Tang Dynasty of China, General An Lushan rebelled against Emperor Xuanzong of Tang, (reigned 712-755) during 755-763. General Zhang Zin of Tang was besieged in the City of Yungyu by An's subordinate General Linghu Chao.

Zhang had a much smaller army than that of Linghu, and he had hardly any arrow left for use. He ordered his army to make one thousand straw scarecrows. In the dark of the night, these scarecrows were lowered over the city walls by ropes, accompanied by the beating of war drums. Linghu's archers had a busy time to shoot at these scarecrows. Before dawn, Zhang's scarecrows had gathered more than one hundred thousand arrows. The next day Linghu realized that he had been tricked.

On the second night, the Tang soldiers again lowered the scarecrows, but Linghu ordered his men to ignore them believing it was the same trick to get more arrows. When Zhang saw that no archer was shooting at the scarecrows, he ordered that five hundred soldiers be lowered instead. They made a lightning raid on the Linghu's camps. Linghu's troops were caught completely by surprise and they fled away from the camps. The siege of Yungyu was lifted.

The story is from *Sin Tang Shu (New Standard History of the Tang Dynasty)* compiled by Ouyang Xiu (1007-1072) and Xong Qi (998-1061) of the Song Dynasty during the period 1044-1060.

7.1.1.3 Illustrations.

(1) ***Tsar Peter the Great tricked his enemy with his "concealed armies".*** Tsar Peter the Great of Russia (reigned 1682-1725) sought for more maritime outlets. At that time, the Baltic Sea was controlled by the Swedish King Charles XII (reigned 1697-1718). After Peter's trip to the West Europe, he declared war on Sweden which was also hated by Denmark, Norway, Saxony, and the Polish Lithuanian Commonwealth. Peter turned out to be ill-prepared to fight the Swedes, and was defeated in the Battle of Narva in 1700.

After the battle, Charles decided to deploy his armies against the Polish-Lithuanian Commonwealth, giving Peter the time to reorganize the Russian army. In 1708, Charles turned his attention back to Russia, and defeated Peter at Golovchin in July. The Swedish force under the command of General Adam Ludwig Lewenhaupt had 16,000 men, and its base was in the Baltic sea port of Riga.

Peter knew that although the Swedes were stronger, yet their King and Commanders were shilly-shally. In view of the immediate danger, Peter wrote some letters to the Russian commanders in various locations to urge them to come with their men and supplies to the Russian coastal areas. These letters were delivered by messengers who deliberately ran into Swede's occupied areas and be caught. The Swedes took the matter seriously. They believed that Peter had concealed some of the armies. Charles ordered Lewenhaupt not to occupy the Russian coastal areas, but to move southwards with most of his men to join Charles and his army of 25,000 men based in Poland.

Lewenhaupt was to bring a fresh supply of ammunition and food to Charles in preparation to attack Moscow. Peter led his armies to move quickly to intercept the Swedish forces and beat them in the Battle of Lesnaya on September 6, 1708. It was a turning point in what was known as The Great Northern War. Deprived of the supplies, Charles was forced to abandon his attack on Moscow.

(2) *A native of Formosa taught in Oxford College during 1704-06.* Around 1702, a strange man identified himself as a native of Formosa, now known as Taiwan, arrived in Holland where he met William Innes, a Scottish clergyman serving in the English army. He was blonde and fair-skinned, like a European. He spoke an unknown language, followed a foreign calendar, and worshipped the sun and the moon. At that time, Europeans knew very little about Asia. Innes gave the man a Christian name, George Psalmanazar, and converted him to Christianity.

News of the Formosan spread throughout Europe, and in 1703 the man now known as Psalmanazar accompanied Innes to England to meet the Bishop of London. In London, Psalmanazar's fame spread wider. People marvelled at his curious habits. For instance, he ate heavily spiced raw meat and slept upright in a chair with a lamp burning.

In 1704 Psalmanazar published a book titled *An Historical and Geographical Description of Formosa*. This book offered European readers an intriguing glimpse at Formosan culture. It revealed that convicted murderers in Formosa were hung upside down and shot full of arrows, that polygamy was allowed, and that every year the Formosans sacrificed 18,000 young boys to appease their gods.

After the publication of this book, Psalmanazar was recruited by the Oxford College to translate religious literature into Formosan and to lecture on Formosan culture.

Jesuit missionaries who had actually been to Formosa raised the most serious objections to Psalmanazar's identity. Jesuit Father Fontaney published a book refuting what Psalmanazar had written. The Royal Society asked Psalmanazar to defend himself against Fontaney's accusations. Psalmanazar did so by declaring that Fontaney was a Jesuit and therefore a liar, a response that the anti-Jesuit members of the Royal Society found to be acceptable.

The doubts about Psalmanazar did not subside, and in 1706 he confessed. Later, he explained that after reading Law's *Serious Call to a Devout Life,* he was sorry for his cheating. He made up the false identity as a means to attract attention and to make money while traveling. He spent the rest of his life as an editor and a writer. Before he died he wrote a long confession titled *Memoirs of ****, Commonly Known by the Name of George Psalmanazar.* This work was published posthumously in 1765, a year after his death.

7.1.1.4 Comments.

Out of nothing, one can create something as Tsar Peter the Great outwitted the Swedes by giving the latter the impression that he had more troops which could be called upon to reinforce the coastal areas. It induced the Swedes to make the wrong decision to attack Moscow instead of occupying the Russian coastal areas.

Rumours and lies are one of those commonly used methods to fabricate something out of nothing. When a rumour had been repeated several times, it could be considered as truth. George Psalmanazar made his living by a false pretension. Joseph Paul Goebbels, Adolf Hitler's propaganda minister, embraced Hitler's thesis that a big lie was often more credible than a small lie.

(II) **Fish in murky waters.**

7.1.2.1 Theme.

> Throw your enemy into chaos; exploit his weakened position to seize every advantage for you. This stratagem is similar to "Loot a burning house". However, it is more aggressive. If the water is murky, we can go ahead to take advantage of it.
>
> Sun Tze said, "When the enemies are thrown into disorder, one can crush them with ease." (*The Art of War*, Chapter I). If the water is clear, one has to stir up the water to make it murky before he can take advantage of it. Thrown in murky waters, the enemy is more vulnerable.
>
> In a chaotic scenario, there are usually new leaders emerging, challenging each other to take control of the situation. Some of the weaker ones are confused, losing their orientation and they disappear. The clever ones are sharp enough to take control of the situation to their advantage.

7.1.2.2 Source.

It could have been from *Liutao* by Lu Shang in 1100 BC. "When the army has been attacked several times, its morale may have flagged. The soldiers are scared and weary of the future attacks. They murmur about demoralisation, and whisper the rumours. Though they say nothing, yet in fact they suffer from fear. The absence of strong authority results in extreme lack of order and discipline. These are the signs of losing strength."

In this scenario, the soldiers are likened fishes in the murky water. They can be caught easily.

7.1.2.3 Illustrations.

(1) ***Otto Skorzeny was labelled "the most dangerous man of Europe".*** On September 12, 1943, Otto Skorzeny commanded a rescue mission that freed the

deposed Italian dictator, Benito Mussolini, from imprisonment at Gran Sasso in Italy. On December 16, 1944, taking advantage of the cold and fog, Nazi Germany started the Battle of the Bulge by attacking the sparsely deployed U.S. troops around Bastogne, Belgium. The objective was to advance to Antwerp in order to cut off supplies for the Allies and separate the British from the American troops.

Meanwhile, about two dozen German soldiers, most of them in captured American army Jeeps and disguised as American soldiers, penetrated American lines in the early hours of the Battle. These soldiers spoke perfect English. They sowed disorder and confusion behind the Allies lines by cutting wires, turning road signs around and damaging.

The tightened security made things harder for these German infiltrators and some of them were captured. Even during interrogation they continued to spread a rumour that Otto Skorzeny was leading a raid in Paris to kill or kidnap General Dwight D. Eisenhower. The effect of this disinformation caused Eisenhower to be confined to his headquarters for weeks. The captured infiltrators were executed by firing squad. It was the standard practice of every army at the time. Skorzeny avoided being caught and survived the war.

(2) ***Kambe made the water murky to have his way.*** After the WWII, Japan was in the process of rapid redevelopment. Hazama-Gumi was a construction company specialized in infrastructure construction such as dams, tunnels, railways, highways, subways, airport, waterways, and shipyards. At that time, there were "Big Five" construction companies: Shimizu Corporation, Taisei Corporation, Kajima Corporation, Takenaka Corporation, and Obayashi Corporation.

Kambe was the President of Hazama-Gumi which was not counted among the "Big Five". Several times, he was turned down in bidding projects because of this. He thought it would help the growth of his company if he could have his company to be listed as one of the "Big Six". His tactic was to pay large amounts of advertising fees to the influential newspapers. He requested that when the "Big Five" advertised, the newspapers would insert the advertisement of his company to make it "Big Six"; when his company advertised, they would put in the names "Big Six". In the newspapers' commentaries and reports, whenever they talked about construction companies, they would quote "Big Six" instead of "Big Five".

At first, Kambe had to bear the sneers of his competitors, because there was a substantial parity between the "Big Five" and Hazama-Gumi. Despite of these, and with much patience, he was able to have his way worked out. The public talked about the "Big Six", and the business of Hazama-Gumi grew at a fast rate. After three years, Hazama-Gumi truly attained its status among the "Big Six".

7.1.2.4 Comments.

In English, there is a saying, "It is good fishing in troubled waters." After the water has been stirred up, the fishes lose their sense of directions, failing to find places to hide. Therefore it is good time to catch fishes. To stir up means to cause disorder to the scenario, during which deceptions and thefts can be carried out under the veil of disorder. The murky water offers the best environment for the opportunists to perpetuate their ploys, and to find excuses in doing so.

Embezzlement, substitution of one thing for another and espionage of information are some of these misdemeanours. Otto Skorzeny and his men in disguised American army uniforms did a lot of damages behind the Allied lines.

Moments of uncertainty are caused by disorders. Many founders of new dynasties knew that these moments were the best times to take actions. For the ambitious and intelligent leaders, they would stir up the water to make it as murky as possible. Kambe strived to make his company ranked equal to the "Big Five" to make it "Big Six" in the Japanese construction business after WWII. He could do this, because he took action to stir up the water, making it murky first.

(III) **Decorate the tree with bogus blossoms**.

7.1.3.1 Theme.

Some trees do not bear flowers or the flowers come and go within a very short time. However, it is possible to decorate the tree, making it look as if it bears flowers all the time. Today, this can be done by tying plastic flowers or paper flowers onto the tree. It is a partially real and partially false situation, so as to deceive other people. Through the use of artifice and disguise, one can make something of no value appear valuable; of no use, being useful; and have no harm, being malicious.

When one's army is relatively weak as compared to the enemy, one should hide this fact, and strive to make his army look strong. He can ally with a third party to strengthen the force. After forming the alliance, one can put one's best troops in the formation together with those of the ally. The strength and the size of the formation will be very much reinforced. Certainly it looks more threatening to the enemy.

The origin of this saying is from *I Ching,* which is the mother of Chinese thought. Growing out of early Chinese divination, *I Ching* instructed emperors, priests and scholars on the advisability of anything from waging war to harvesting. It is a book in which divination and common wisdom is put together. The teachings of *I Ching* spread to diverse arts such as face-reading, palmistry, fortune-telling and feng shui which is the Chinese art of placement, of balancing and enhancing the environment.

The core of this stratagem is to use deceptive appearances to make one looks much more powerful than he really is. This is a temporary measure, because the enemy may discover the truth in the course of time.

7.1.3.2 Source.

Young Li Shimin won his first battle. The second Emperor of the Sui Dynasty, Emperor Yangdi (reigned 604-617) was a frivolous ruler. He was interested in expanding his territories. He attacked Koguryo situated in today's North Korea and Liaodong (North-eastern China) four times (612-614), and failed every time. In 615, the Khan of Tujue (or King of proto-Turk) took this opportunity to besiege the Emperor in the Gate of Yonge Moon.

The Emperor sent scouts for help, but these scouts could not break through the siege. The help seeking messages were carved on wood, and they were thrown into the river. At this moment, Li Yuan, one of the Emperor's generals was in Tai Yuen in the Shenxi Province. People brought him a piece of wood containing the Emperor's message. His second son was Li Shimin, aged around 16 at that time. Later he became the Second Emperor of the Tang Dynasty as Emperor Taizong (reigned 627-649).

Li Shimin analysed the case and said, "The Turks was able to besiege the Emperor, because they thought that there is no rescue coming. At this time, we do not have many soldiers, and it is difficult to break the siege. What we can do is to walk our soldiers in single file, lengthening the formation. The soldiers carried banners and beat the drums, creating the illusion that a large army is mobilizing for the rescue. If they know that we do not have many soldiers, we would be surrounded and destroyed."

Li Yuan's soldiers did accordingly. The Turks' scouts caught the sight at a distance, thinking that hundred thousands of the Chinese troops were coming for the rescue. The Khan was informed, and he immediately withdrew his troops from the Gate of Yonge Moon. Then, Emperor Yangdi was rescued.

7.1.3.3 Illustrations.

(1) ***Search lights could enhance the disposition of an army.*** Georgi K. Zhukov (in service: 1915-1957) was a Soviet military commander who led the Red Army to liberate the Axis' occupation of the Soviet Union in WWII.

After the Soviet forces captured Vienna on April 14, 1945, Josef Stalin ordered 20 armies, 8,500 aircraft, and 6,300 tanks to march towards Berlin under the commands of Zhukov and Ivan Koniev. On April 15, Zhukov's army began to shell Berliin to soften the initial German resistance. For thirty minutes he pounded the city, raining half a million shells five miles deep into the German lines. The Germans did not shoot back. A moment later, still before dawn, a single search light beam shined vertically upwards into the sky, followed by 143 other search lights. The search lights were dipped low to aim at the eyes of the German defenders as the Soviet infantry and armour charged forward.

The Germans were taken by surprise of the light beams, and thought they were Zhukov's new weapons. These search lights functioned as pyschological weapons to scare away the defenders. The Soviet artillery fired and their troops began charging forward to break the German lines. Though the Soviet troops under Zhukov and Koniev suffered large casualties, yet their generals had one thing in mind: to be the first to reach Berlin before the Allies.

(2) ***The U.S. President's comments and no comments.*** There was an American publisher with the name Roger (fictitious name). Once, he had a stockpile of books in his warehouse. He thought of a way to promote their sales. Through a friend, Roger presented a copy of the book to the U.S. President. After a month, his friend happened to have a chit-chat with the President, and asked the latter about the book.

The President casually made the comment, "It is quite good." The friend told Roger about this. Roger made a stir of the comment by advertising in the newspaper, saying "We got a book which the President said is quite good." Soon, he sold all the books.

A year later, Roger had the same problem with another book. He sent a copy to the President. The President knew Roger's trick, and when he was asked about the book, he said, "It is bad." Roger adversed in the newspaper saying, "We got a book which the President said, 'It is bad.'" Very soon, the books were sold out because people wanted to know why the book was bad.

In the third year, Roger played his trick again on another book. The President declined to make any comments on it several times. Then, Roger advertised on the newspaper, "We apologise to the President, because we had a book which the President found it difficult to make any comments." Rogers sold the inventory of that book very quickly.

7.1.3.4 Comments.

Essentially this stratagem is to borrow help from others, whether people or objects, to strengthen one's appearance. Georgi K. Zhukov knew that the Germans reinforced their defense lines close to Berlin. He pretended he had a secret weapon to browbeat the enemy. Likewise, the American publisher made use of the U.S. President's comments and no comments to promote the sale of his stocks.

Exercises

1. In the 1970s, the City of Ina in Japan would like to develop tourism. However, there were no historical landmarks or cult to attract visitors. However, the residents were familiar with the folklore of Kantaro, a warrior in the Japanese medieval time. In fact, nobody was sure whether Kantaro in any way had something to do with Ina.

Then, a gigantic statute of Kantaro was erected in front of the railway station. A memorial park was built in honour of the legendary hero. Annual parade was also organized. In the tour guides, the stories of Kantaro were elaborated, as if he was the "Robin Hood" of Japan. Souvenir stores were packed with Kantaro toys, plastic weapons and Kantaro cakes. After some time, Ina became a tourist spot in that area.

What was the stratagem used in helping to found the tourism business of Ina?

2. The story of three stonemasons gives insight to the choice of person most suitable to be manager of the respective businesses. When asked about what these men were doing, the first mason said, "I am making my living."

The second mason said, "I will get the job done."

The third mason rose his head, looked at the sky, and his eyes sparkled, saying, "I am building a cathedral."

One day, if these masons were managers, what kind of business each of them will be most suitable? Why?

3. Once in New York, there was a Mr. Johnson (fictitious name) who was in heavy equipment installation business. His projects involved a lot of technical areas, so he had to subcontract some of the jobs. When each contractor came to his office for negotiation, he would deliberately leave some

forged quotations from other contractors on his table. Then, in the middle of the conversations, he would leave his office on the pretext of going to washroom, or talking to some of his staff in another room, leaving his guest alone.

His guest would always be thrilled to get a glance of the competitors' quotations marked "Confidential", and became very confident to make the bids. In fact, the quotations were fabricated and planted in the office by Mr. Johnson himself. In this way, he was able to exploit much profit in his undertakings.

It happened some time later, a prudent contractor came into the scenario. He was thrilled at first, but became sceptical after. He examined the terms of the contract, and came to the conclusion that if he was to beat his "competitors" in pricing, he could not break even.

(i) What was the stratagem used by Mr. Johnson in his negotiations with the contractors?

(ii) Why did some of the contractors fall into Mr. Johnson's trap?

4. The theme of the story of "The fox borrows the tiger's might" is to browbeat others by flaunting one's powerful connections.

A fox was about to be devoured by a tiger, but his wit saved him. He told the tiger that he was sent to rule the animal kingdom by the Emperor of Heaven. "Want to witness my authority? Take a tour with me," the fox said to the tiger.

All the animals fled when they saw them. The tiger was fooled; he did not realize that it was he himself that the other animals were afraid of. At last the tiger said, in a much more respectful voice, "You're right. The Emperor of Heaven must have sent you." The tiger raced away quickly.

What was the stratagem schemed by the fox?
(a) Create somthing out from nothing.
(b) Fish in murky waters.
(c) Decorate the tree with bogus blossoms.
(d) Take away a goat in passing.

5.   It happened in Taiwan in the 1970s. A manufacturing company would like to order a fully automated production system from an U.S. engineering company. The latter provided a detailed price quotation, breaking into main machine parts, axillaries, optional components, installation charges, training, freight, packaging and maintenance. In fact, it went very far to detail the main machine parts with their prices and warranties in fine prints to confuse the readers. The itemized prices were inflated.

The Taiwanese company got quotations from engineering companies in Europe, and realised the trick of the U.S. engineering company. Later on, in their negotiations, it was about to bring the prices in the quotation down by 40 percent.

What was the stratagem used by the U.S. engineering company?

6.   It happened in the 1960's in Saigon, Vietnam. Some American G.I.s drove their jeeps to the bars to get a few drinks. When they came out, they found the four wheels of their jeeps were gone, and the jeeps sat on boxes. It was not very effective to report their cases to the police, nor would they like their seniors to know about this.

They found out that the most effective method was to make a phone-call to the auto junk-shops. Within an hour, people would deliver the wheels with the right specifications at a considerably high price. Obviously, some people made a living by doing this.

What was the stratagem used by the people to make their living?

7.   There is a fable about a crow. It gathers the feathers left by the peacocks, and sticks the feathers onto its body to make itself look specious. Some crows are sharp enough to see through the fake. But it is a pity that some do not.

Which of the following stratagems best describes the ruse by the crow?
(a) Fish in murky waters.
(b) Create something from nothing.
(c) Decorate the tree with bogus blossoms.
(d) Cross the sea by deceiving the heaven.

Chapter 8.

To transfer and to take away.

8.0   Introduction.

Actions 17-18 aim at the removal of the condition that favours the opponents.

8.1   Action 17: To transfer.

In actual operations, the circumstantial conditions are most important in affecting the outcome. It is one measure to create a more favorable scenario to the strategist.

8.1.1   The stratagem is: **Lure the tiger out of the mountain.** (One of the classical 36 Stratagems).

8.1.1.1 Theme.

Lure the enemy to come out from a situation that favours him to a situation that favours you. According to Sun Tze, if one wants to engage the enemies in battle and if the enemies seek refuge behind inaccessible shelter, he can draw them out by attacking some place which they will be obliged to relieve. (*The Art of War,* Chapter VI).

In order to lure the enemy, another method is to use baits. "He would make the enemies leave their positions by holding out baits so that his men could ambush them." (*The Art of War,* Chapter V).

8.1.1.2   Source.

Sun Ce tricked Liu Xun to leave his stronghold and be eliminated. During the Three Kingdoms Period in China, and in the year 199, General Sun Ce had secured his territories in the south and would like to expand his conquest to the prosperous area of Lujiang to the north. That area was under the control of Liu Xun, the Governor of Lujiang. The terrain was favorable to the defenders, because it was accessible only through a couple of easily defended passes, and Liu's army was well trained.

Liu was also ambitious to annex its neighbor, the State of Shangliao. With this in mind, Sun thought of a ploy. Sun sent an emissary laden with gifts and a letter to Liu. He praised the Liu's military skills and proposed an alliance with him to invade the Shangliao State. He claimed that for years the Shangliao State had looted his territories. If Liu was to attack the Shangliao State, Sun would launch a retaliatory raid on it also. Liu could take over the whole of Shangliao State afterwards.

Liu disregarded the advice of his counselors, and led his army to attack the Shangliao State, leaving his own capital unguarded. When Liu was busy in his battles, Sun led his army, not to assist Liu, but to take the almost undefended Lujiang and to seize its capital. Liu failed in his campaign against the Shangliao State. On his return journey, he found that his own capital fell into the hands of Sun. Sun now had the advantage of the Lujiang terrain to defend. Liu Xun and his army had to flee pell-mell.

This story is from *History of Three Kingdoms* by Chen Shou (233-297).

8.1.1.3 Illustrations.

(1) ***The founding of the German Labor Front in 1933.*** In early 1933, Adolf Hitler became Chancellor of Germany. He would like to take control of the trade unions which were very powerful within Germany. He thought of a plot. On May Day (May 1), traditionally a labour holiday, the government declared a national holiday and joined with the trade union leaders in holding a celebration.

Hitler invited the union leaders all over Germany to attend a ceremony in Berlin. It was a move to lure the trade union leaders out of their bases. On May 2, 1933, he ordered the Sturm Abteilung (SA, known as the brown-shirts) to arrest these people.

He then gave Robert Ley the task of founding the German Labour Front (DAF), the only union organisation allowed in the Third Reich. Ley confiscated union funds and used the money to fund the Strength through Joy programme. A pay freeze was introduced in 1933 and the DAF rigorously enforced it. Wages were now decided by the DAF and compulsory deductions made for income tax, and for its Strength through Joy programme.

The DAF also issued workbooks that recorded the worker's employment record and no one could be employed without one. In so doing, Hitler destroyed the trade unions and gained control of the labour force in Germany.

(2) ***Conspirators plotted to oust Premier Nikita Khrushchev during his vacation in the Black Sea.*** Nikita Sergeyevich Khrushchev was the Premier of U.S.S.R. from 1958. He lost support from the conservatives members of the Communist Party and the KGB when he denounced Josef Stalin. Though he introduced many industrial and agricultural initiatives and administrative reforms, yet the economy which worked on coercion for years was on the

decline. The Party bosses were tired of his erratic leadership and radical reforms.

When Khrushchev was on vacation in Crimea, a peninsula in Southern Ukraine in October 1964, the conspirators, led by Leonid Brezhnev, Aleksandr Shelepin and the KGB Chief Vladimir Semichastny called a special meeting of the Presidium of the Central Committee. At that time, Khrushchev's wife Nina Petrovna was in Czechoslovakia, and his son-in-law Alexei Adzhubei, Editor of daily newspaper *Izvestiya* was on a trip away from Moscow.

On October 13, when Khrushchev was brought back from his vacation, he was accused of mishandling the 1962 Cuban missile crisis, and acting with disregard for the best interests of the state and for wielding power in an arbitrary, capricious manner. The Central Committee Plenum required his resignation.

On October 14, he agreed to this and signed his resignation as First Secretary and Head of government. The next day the Presidium of the Supreme Soviet officially ended his term as Chairman of the Council of Ministers.

It happened that on Oct 12, the Soviet Union launched *Voskhod* 1 into orbit. It was the first spacecraft to carry a multi-person crew, and the two day mission was the first flight performed without space suits. The mission was probably cut short by the coup that ousted Khrushchev.

8.1.1.4 Comments.

"The highest form of military leadership is to conquer the enemies by strategy, second to prevent the joining of their forces, third to attack them in the battlefield, and the worst policy is to besiege a walled city." (*The Art of War*, Chapter III). When the enemies had their terrestrial advantages, it would be difficult to attack them.

When someone, no matter how powerful or strong he is, has been taken out of his territories (which may also mean his profession, his scope of influence etc.), he is no longer in command of the situation. The trade union leaders left their bases for Berlin where the brown-shirts could arrest them. Sun Tze said, "To secure oneself against defeat depends on one's own efforts, while the opportunity of victory must be afforded by the enemy." (*The Art of War*, Chapter IV).

Premier Nikita Sergeyevich Khrushchev could never imagine that when he was talking to the three astronauts on the *Voskhod* 1, from his resort in the Black Sea, his conversations were cut short. It was because the conspirators were plotting a coup to oust him in Moscow. Khrushchev was away from his base, and the conspirators seized the opportunity.

8.2 Action 18: To take away.

This action is to remove the means which support the opponent, and to do this thoroughly.

8.2.1 The stratagem is: **Remove the firewood under the cooking pot.** (One of the classical 36 Stratagems).

8.2.1.1 Theme.

When confronted by a powerful enemy, do not fight him head-on but weaken him by undermining his foundation and destroying the source from which he obtains his support. In English, we call it "Take away fuel, take away flame." The scenario is likened to boiling water in a pot by burning firewood underneath. When the firewood has been ignited, its combustion raises the temperature of the water. If the firewood is withdrawn, the water in the pot will cool down.

The fighting spirit and the morale of the enemy's soldiers; the judgement and decisiveness of their generals are some psychological basics. Sun Tze said, "A whole army may become demoralized just as a general may be robbed of his presence of mind." (*The Art of War*, Chapter VII).

The stratagem aims at the root cause of the situation, and to do something thoroughly by focusing the efforts on the basic and essential matter. When the adept in war is able to remove the basic support of his enemy, he can keep the latter under control.

8.2.1.2 Source.

By getting rid of Lian Po, the Qin army overwhelmed the Zhao State. It happened in 260 BC during the Warring States Period (475-221 BC) of China, when the Qin State invaded the Zhao State, the Zhao General Lian Po adopted a strategy of building strong walls of defense. The Qin army could not break the city walls. King Xiaochengwang of Zhao (reigned 265-245 BC) did not agree with Lian's war of attrition tactic, but to order Lian to attack. Lian refused to do so.

Fan Chen, the Chief Minister of the Qin State learned about this. He knew that if Lian was gone, the Zhao State would be defeated. He spread the rumor that the Qin army only feared about General Zhao Kuo. Lian was too old, and sooner or later Lian would be captured. Zhao Kuo was the son of the famous General Zhao She. Zhao Kuo had studied many books of military strategies when he was still very young. Zhao liked to talk about war tactics and the deployment of armies. Even his father could not baffle him. Many people thought he was a man of talent. But he had no experience in the real operations.

King Xiaochengwang replaced Lian with Zhao Kuo. When Zhao Kuo came to the battlefield, he slavishly followed what was written in the war strategy books, and change Lian's plan of fighting a protracted war. The Qin General, Bai Qi, was pleased with this. He played a ruse, cut off the Zhao army's supply routes and enclosed the Zhao's forces. Zhao Kuo tried to break out of the encirclement but was killed by an arrow. The 400,000 strong army of the Zhao State was destroyed in the Battle of Changping (260 BC).

This story is from *Records of the Historian,* by Sima Qian (145-86 BC.)

8.2.1.3 Illustrations.

(1) ***Attempts to break the Mitsubishi shipping monopoly in 1880.*** By 1877, 80 percent of Japanese maritime traffic was controlled by the Mitsubishi Shokai (Company) owned by Iwasaki Yataro. Operating a monopoly in maritime transportation, Mitsubishi was free to charge highly inflated rates for its services. Customers used it shipping service were obliged to store in Mitsubishi warehouses and insure their goods with the Mitsubishi Maritime Insurance Company.

The other zaibatsu (money cliques) particularly Mitsui, relied heavily on Mitsubishi for shipping and suffered greatly from its monopoly prices. Masuda Takashi of the Mitsui Corporation decided that he would no longer tolerate the monopoly practices. He proposed to Shibusawa Eiichi, an enemy of Iwasaki, and founder of the First National Bank of Japan to establish a rival shipping company called Tokyo Fuhansen.

Meanwhile, Mitsubishi realised the support of Masuda was from Shibusawa who held considerable power. Thus, Mitsubishi sought the help of Count Okuma Shigenobu, the newspaper tycoon. The newspapers began to criticize Shibusawa's financial decisions and his personal affairs to undermine Masuda's efforts.

Companies intending to join the Fuhansen withdrew their decisions. Mitsubishi took an additional measure to bribe the shareholders of the Tokyo Stock Exchange not to support the Fuhansen project. Within a year Mitsubishi succeeded in driving Fuhansen out of business.

It was only after Okuma's death in 1881, his political opponents joined hands with Iwasaki's rivals to destroy the Mitsubishi shipping monopoly.

(2) ***The Norwegian heavy water sabotage.*** Heavy water is water which contains a higher proportion than normal of the isotope deuterium. It could be used to produce nuclear weapons.

In 1934, the first commercial heavy water plant was built at Vemork, in the Telemark region of Norway, with a capacity to produce 12 tonnes of heavy water per year. From 1940 and throughout WWII, the plant was under German control and the Allies decided to demolish the plant and its heavy water to deter German development of nuclear weapons.

Between 1942 and 1944, a sequence of sabotages by the Norwegian resistance movement as well as the bombings from the Allies ensured the destruction of the plant and the heavy water produced. These operations codenamed "Freshman", "Grouse" and "Gunnerside" finally managed to put the plant out of production in early 1943, essentially ending the German research on nuclear weapons. The raids were the most successful acts of sabotage in WWII.

8.2.1.4 Comments.

If one cannot defeat his enemy by military tactics, one may be able to defeat him with non-military ways, such as to pinch off the capable staff from the enemy's camp. If circumstances allow, one can recruit these people for their services. If the enemy lives on rice, one can steal the wood for the cauldrons and the enemy will starve.

It is also strategic to find out the sources from which the enemies receive their support, and it is his advantage to cut off those sources from the enemies. Without the sources of support, the enemies will be deprived of provisions in terms of finance, manpower or materials.

Mitsubishi knew that the support of Masuda Takashi was Shibusawa Eiichi. Thus Mitsubishi sought the help of Count Okuma Shigenobu to challenge Masuda and Shibusawa. Likewise, it was only after the death of Count Okuma, Mitsui was able to revive the establishment of a rival shipping company to that operated by Mitsubishi Shokai (Company).

The raids to destroy the heavy water plants and the heavy water produced deterred German development of nuclear weapons.

Exercises

1.   In 1851, the gold rush to California was at its height. Cornelius Vanderbilt (1794-1877), an American railroad magnate arranged ship accommodation from New Orleans to Nicaragua, overland travel across the isthmus, and another ship for the voyage up the Pacific to San Francisco.   He founded the Accessory Transit Company and paid the Nicaraguan government $10,000 for a charter to cross the country. His route was 600 miles and two days shorter, and half the going price to California as compared to the route via Panama.

Vanderbilt's success in operating this profitable route caught the attention of William Walker, a famous America filibuster.   The term filibuster was used in the Nineteenth Century for private individual who settled in foreign country with the intent of eventually overthrowing the existing government and annexing the territories to the U.S. It was almost used to Anglo-American setters in Latin America. He would like to take over Vanderbilt's business. However, Vanderbilt had established strong influence in Nicaragua. Walker had a scheme.

In 1853, Walker bribed Vanderbilt's physician and the people in the social circle around Vanderbilt to say that the latter's had some health problems. Vanderbilt was convinced to take the first vacation of his life. Before going abroad to Paris, Vanderbilt resigned the presidency of the Accessory Transit Company. When Vanderbilt was away, Walker collaborated with one of the local factions in a civil war. A puppet President was installed, and the new government rescinded the Accessory Transit Company's charter so as to issue a new charter to a rival company vested with Walker's interests. In 1856, Walker declared himself Commander of the country's army and soon after President of the Republic of Nicaragua for the period July 12, 1856 to May 1, 1857.

What was the stratagem used by William Walker in taking over Vanderbilt's business in Nicaragua?

2.   During the WWII, submarine warfare was the navy major component of the Battles of the Atlantic.   Though the German U-Boats (submarines) could be useful fleet weapons against enemy naval warships, in practice they were most effectively used in the economic warfare role, enforcing a naval blockade against enemy convoys bringing supplies from North America to Europe.

Over time, the Allies developed improved defense tactics which managed to reduce the numbers of merchant ships sunk. But Nazi Germany kept up with the steady losses of U-Boats due to their simple designs allowing them to be mass-produced.   Then, Germany developed acoustic homing torpedoes, designed to run strength to an arming distance of 400 meters and to aim at the loudest noise detected.

The British Navy thought of a ploy to thwart the Nazi's efforts to recruit U-Boat crew.   Fliers were printed with U-Boats pictured as steel coffins, saying that the crew could easily end up being swallowed by fishes. They stressed the casualty of submariners was 15 times more than that of army, 8 times more than that of combat pilots, 9 times more than that of battleship crew.   These fliers were dropped into the German cities by air, and they deterred the recruitment of submariners. In fact, the German U-Boat fleet suffered extremely heavy casualties, losing 743 U-Boats and about 28,000 submariners (a 75% casualty rate).

What was the stratagem used by the British Navy to thwart the Nazi's efforts to recruit U-Boat crew?
(a) Lure the tiger out of the mountain.
(b) Remove the firewood under the cooking pot.
(c) Create something out from nothing.
(d) Fish in murky waters.

3. On August 28, 1793, the Southern French City of Toulon turned itself over to the Bourbons. A British, Spanish and Royalist French military force occupied the city. A British fleet under Admiral Lord Hood anchored in the harbour to provide the naval support. The French revolutionary government reacted quickly and besieged the city on September 7, with several attempts to recapture it. They failed through poor leadership of the revolutionary generals.

It gave a young Chef de Bataillon Napoleon Bonaparte the chance to scheme with political allies to replace their leader with General Jacques Dugommier. The new Commander agreed to plans proposed by Bonaparte to storm a key fort which would allow French artillery to open fire on the British fleet. The attack occurred on December 17, and less than a day the British fleet was compelled to sail away.

On December 19, the revolutionary troop reoccupied Toulon, with Bonaparte promoted to Brigadier General on December 22. It was Bonaparte's first great victory.

(i) Why was it a brilliant move to occupy a fort to dominate the city's harbour and bombard the British fleet, instead of attacking the city?

(ii) What was Sun Tze's teaching relating to this tactic?

4. Emperor Keiko is the twelfth Imperial Ruler of Japan to appear on the traditional list of Emperors. No firm dates can be traced to this Emperor and the historians regarded him as a "legendary Emperor". It was some time before the Fifth Century. He sent one of his children, Yamato Takeru to rid out a notorious bandit. This outlaw was an expert swordsman. He killed all those who were sent to catch him.

Yamato hid his identity so as to befriend with the outlaw. After getting familiar with each other, they went to swim regularly. When Yamato was sure that the bandit was entirely not aware of his motive, he designed a plot.

One day, Yamato brought with him a wooden sword that looked similar to the one used by the bandit. He hid it in his baggage when he went to swim with the bandit. When the bandit was in the water, Yamato went ashore and switched the bandit's sword with the wooden sword. After swim and they had gotten dressed, Yamato drew out his weapon to attack the bandit who immediately reached for his sword. Of course, the bandit's wooden sword was chopped off, and he was killed.

Identify three stratagems used by Yamato in his plot against the bandit from the followings, and explain.
(a) Cross the sea by deceiving the heaven.
(b) Point at the mulberry only to curse the locust.
(c) Steal the beams and pillars and replace them with rotten timber.
(d) Decorate the tree with bogus blossoms.
(e) Remove the firewood under the cooking pot.
(f) Lure the tiger out of the mountain.

5. In a certain Asian country, when somebody intends to run for public office, sometimes the incumbent (especially when he seeks to be re-elected) will assess the newcomer's strength. When the newcomer proves to be a very competitive candidate, the incumbent or his assistants will approach the newcomer's employer, or seniors of his kinsmen, or his college professors (teachers) or his father-in-law, to talk about the possibility of withdrawing from the election and joining the incumbent's camp.

What is the stratagem that the incumbent or his assistants use in this case?

6. In 1996, Coca-Cola outsold Pepsi in almost every market in the world. In Latin America, Venezuela was the only country in which Pepsi had outsold Coca-Cola for almost fifty years. Its sales were four times that of Coca-Cola's.

Coca-Cola's think tank was aware of the principle: "when confronted with a powerful enemy, do not fight him hand-on but try to find his weakest spot to initiate his collapse." Pepsi's relationship with its bottler was found to be tenuous. It was because Pepsi paid no attention to the bottler's request for additional investment. Thus, Pepsi held no equity in its bottler.

Coca-Cola negotiated secretly with the Pepsi's bottler to switch its allegiance. In late August 1996, Coca-Cola and the bottler arrived at an agreement under which Coca-Cola would buy 50 percent of the bottler and invest additional money into building its Venezuela business. Pepsi was completely overwhelmed to know that its only bottler, in the only Latin America in which Pepsi had a lead, had changed side. Almost over night, Coca-Cola's grew from a 10% market share to 50%, while Pepsi dropped to almost zero.

What was the stratagem used by Coca-Cola's think tank to beat Pepsi in the sale of their drink in Venezuela, 1996?

Chapter 9.

To attract, to warn, to prod, and to chart the best course for action.

9.0 Introduction.

Actions 19-24 deal with the opponents faced directly and openly. Only Actions 23-24 are real confrontation with the opponents. We cover Actions 19-22 in this chapter, and Actions 23-24 in Chapter 10.

9.1 Action 19: To attract.

To give an allurement for the sake of gaining benefits is a delicate matter. Unless the strategist has good judgement as to what and how much should be given, and when and how frequently the allurements should be made, this action may work the other way to hurt the financial well-being of the strategist.

9.1.1 The stratagems are:
(1) **Cast a brick to attract a piece of jade.** (One of the classical 36 Stratagems).
(II) **Entice snakes out of their lairs.**

(I) **Cast a brick to attract a piece of jade.**

9.1.1.1 Theme.

> To begin with, this was a Chinese idiom. It had an elegant literary origin; meaning one has to present some superficial remarks or a short essay by way of introduction so that others may come up with valuable opinions and literary work.
>
> But now, it takes up the meaning that many people have the weakness of being greedy. Use baits to entrice the other person and takes him in. By doing so, one can exploit greater advantage from that person later. Sun Tze said, "When the enemies like small gains, one should entice them by baits." (*The Art of War,* Chapter I).

9.1.1.2 Source.

Zhang Jian induced Zhao Gu to put in better stanza. In the Tang Dynasty (618-907), there was a highly accomplished poet with the name Zhao Gu. When he toured the beautiful City of Suzhou, a local poet, Zhang Jian who admired much of Zhao's talent, wrote two lines on a wall of the city's Divine Rock Monastery. Zhang did this to induce Zhao to put in lines to make a better stanza. When Zhao visited the monastery and noticed what Zhang had written down, he completed the poem by adding another two lines. (In some Chinese poems, there are four lines in a stanza.)

People referred Zhang's act as "casting a brick to attract a piece of jade", since Zhao was a famous poet.

This story is from the *Poems of Different Dynasties Reviewed* by Wu Jingxu of the Qing Dynasty (1644-1911).

9.1.1.3 Illustrations.

(1) ***Josef Stalin made use of his agreement to fight Japan as a brick to get pieces of jade.*** In the Teheran Conference, November and December 1943, Josef Stalin of the Soviet Union was promised a cross English Channel invasion from the Allies, but he had to agree to help in the fight against Japan in the Far East. However, the Soviets maintained their neutrality against the Japanese till the U.S. had dropped the first atomic bomb at Hiroshima on August 6, 1945.

At the Yalta Conference, January to February 1945, the Soviets were given a green light to jump in against Japan at the last minute to sop up the spoils. The Soviets were allowed to seize Port Arthur, Dairen, the Kurile Islands, and Outer Mongolia. During the period 1944-1945, the Soviets were furnished with over a billion dollars worth of U.S. arms and supplies in the Far East.

The U.S. dropped the first atomic bomb at Hiroshima on August 6, 1945. Then, Soviet Union declared war on Japan on August 8, 1945. Its army entered China when the Japanese armies were to lay down their weapons. They dismounted the factories and valuable goods for dispatch back to the Soviet Union.

Billions of American and confiscated Japanese arms were promptly turned over by the Soviets to the Chinese Communists, resulting in the defeat of the Guomindang (Nationalists). General Chiang Kaishek had to leave for Taiwan with his air force and gold reserves.

By his agreement to aid in the fight against the Japanese, Stalin was rewarded handsomely.

(2) ***Small gift tokens promoted sales.*** In a Chicago Exposition held in 1957, John Hegel (fictitious name) of the Hegel Company (fictitious name) in the food processing industry leased a showroom. However it was up in the mezzanine. Though the Exhibition Hall was packed with

visitors, yet very few came up to the mezzanine. John watched the situation for a day, and came up with an idea.

On the second day John was not in the showroom. He went to a token manufacturing factory to order thousands of tokens made overnight. Each token bore the words, "With this token, you can pick up a souvenir from Hegel Company up in the mezzanine." The tokens were distributed at the entrance of the Exhibition Hall. They prompted visitors to come up to Hegel's showroom in the mezzanine.

The newspapers made headlines about it. The radio journalists came for interviews. In fact, the quality of Hegel's products was good. Eventually, Hegel Company was able to make a profit of five hundred and fifty thousand dollars in this Exhibition, more than any other exhibitors.

9.1.1.4 Comments.

On the use of baits, Sun Tze said, "When the enemies like small gains, one should entice them by baits." (*The Art of War*, Chapter I). The wise man should take flattering and other baits, such as illusions of wealth, power and sex with caution.

The Allies promised Stalin to invade Nazi Germany from the English Channel, and Josef Stalin did fight against the Germans from the East. However, they expected the Soviet armies to help the U.S. and the Chinese to fight against the Japanese in the Far East. Stalin did this when he was perfectly sure that Japan was going to surrender. Stalin exploited many benefits which consisted of territories and military supplies by his agreement to help the Allies in the Far East. John Hegel promoted sales by gift tokens in spite of the poor location of his showroom.

(II) **Entice snakes out of their lairs.**

9.1.2.1 Theme.

> Use allurement to entice the conspirators or hidden objects to come forward or to reveal themselves. The allurements are the baits with hidden hooks to catch these people, so as to gain control over them or to wipe them out.
>
> Sun Tze said, "By provocation one can ascertain their mood and movement; by tactics one can ascertain the vulnerability of his enemy." (*The Art of War,* Chapter VI).

9.1.2.2 Source.

Sun Tze, *Art of War.* (Refer to 9.1.2.1).

9.1.2.3 Illustrations.

(1) *A sheriff cracked a case of theft.* In the Wild West, legend has it that a hardware store owner had a pair of new boots. He was going to change his boots in front of his store and suddenly he heard his wife calling for him from inside. He came into the shop to help his wife. Later, when he came out from the store, the pair of boots was gone. But a pair of worn boots was left behind. However, he could see a man riding on a horse racing away in the distance.

He reported the case to the sheriff. The sheriff knew that there would be a town meeting in two days. He visited every house in the neighbourhood, and invited all people to the town meeting, saying that an important announcement would be made.

During the town meeting, the sheriff said he was told by the sheriff of a neighbouring town that a man riding on a horse had been killed by the bandits. The man left behind a pair of worn boots. On showing the pair of worn boots, an old woman rushed out and cried. She said, "My son left for his father-in-laws' farm three days ago wearing this pair of boots." Very soon, the young man was arrested for the theft.

(2) ***A ploy that helped to solve a case of burglary.***
In the 1960s, a gang of burglars broke into a French museum. It must involve several people, skilled in disenabling the electronic security system, opening the locks and logistic arrangements. According to the manager of the museum, these burglars took away ten paintings and a 3-carats diamond ring. He said, "The diamond ring is most exquisite, superb in 4Cs (Cut, Color, Clarity and Carat weight), nobody will miss it." The burglars left no clues behind, and it was a challenge to the police.

The newspapers and the TV reported this case, and it became the talk of the town for a while. One day, a suspect was gunshot, and hurried to the hospital. The suspect confessed that he was one of the wanted criminals for the museum burglary. He told the police that he and his companion went into the museum to take the paintings, while other members of the gang were outside. They claimed that he had hidden away the diamond ring. Disputes among the gang ended in exchanging fires. He denied strongly that he had taken the diamond ring.

Then, the police was able to recover the paintings, and arrest all criminals. When the police talked to the museum manager about the missing diamond ring, the latter believed that the wounded suspect was telling the truth.

There was no diamond ring in the museum. It was a ploy to sow mistrust in the gang. Without this ploy, the criminals could get away with this nearly perfect burglary.

9.1.2.4 Comments.

To a certain degree, this stratagem is similar to the stratagem "Cast a brick to attract a piece of jade." The latter uses bait to lure the other person and take him in. Usually, the bait is small in cost as compared to the potential returns. However, this stratagem focuses on enticing the enemies or evil people to come forward to reveal them.

As a convention, snakes usually denote evil characters or concealed matters. The sheriff linked the pair of worn boots and being murdured together so as to prompt the people who knew the "victim" to expose themselve. Likewise, the museum manager schemed to sow distrust among the burglars by the virtual diamond ring. Internal disputes among the gang members led to their arrest.

9.2 Action 20: To warn.

This action is not directed to the opponent, but to a third party. It carries a message to warn the opponent concerned. It can also scare away the harmful elements.

9.2.1 The stratagem is: **Beat the grass to startle the snake.** (One of the classical 36 Stratagems).

9.2.1.1 Theme.

> This stratagem aims to frighten or startle the enemy to see how he reacts so as to ascertain his situation. It is a reckless act that alerts the enemy. The act of beating the grass is to frighten away the snake and to achieve the following goals.
>
> (a) To expose the enemy's identity, and to give him warning. In this respect, it is similar to **Entice snakes out of their lairs**.
> (b) To warn the other potential evildoers, making them aware that they are being hunted.
> (c) To test the enemy's response; his behavior will reveal his state of mind and his strategy.
>
> When an army finds itself in the neighborhood of dangerous passes, ponds filled with aquatic grass or woods with thick undergrowth, a most careful and thorough search is necessary. These are the places where men in ambush or insidious spies are likely to lurk. Beating the grass in these places enables one to detect the hazards.

9.2.1.2 Source.

To punish an evildoer as a warning to others of his kind. Wang Lu was a corrupt official in the Tang Dynasty (618-907), and he raked a large amount of money. His subordinates did the same, taking bribes and extracting wealth by their privileges. It caused widespread discontent among the people living in the area under Wang's jurisdiction.

One day, when going over the file of letters, Wang discovered a joint complaint against one of his subordinates who was accused of corruption and breach of law, and to a certain degree involving Wang himself.

When he read the letter, he was shocked. "I must be more careful in the future," he said to himself. "It's fortunate that this letter is in my hands." After reading the letter, he wrote on the file the following words as they came to his mind, "You may only have beaten the grass, but I have been scared as if the snake is hiding in it."

This story is from the *Anecdotes of the Kaiyuan and Tianbao Reigns,* written by Wang Renyu (907-960) of the Five Dynasties. The book told stories of the Emperor Xuanzong of the Tang Dynasty, who reigned between 712 and 756.

9.2.1.3 Illustrations.

(1) *The aftermath of the Battle of Sante Cruz, 1942.* The Battle of Sante Cruz (October 26, 1942) was a tactical victory for the Japanese Imperial Navy in terms of ships sunk. Since that Battle, quite a lot of American Navy officers and servicemen became paranoiac. They had delusions that Japanese submarines and airplanes were constantly haunting them.

The top Navy officers thought they had to redress the matter. One day, it was very gloomy with dark clouds over the sky. The siren of the U.S. fleet wailed. It was broadcast that the radar detected some unidentified objects ahead.

Some of the servicemen reacted violently, losing their senses, and gasping their breaths. After a few minutes, the emergency signals were turned off. The broadcast said that the unidentified object was a dolphin. Everybody was relieved. Those who were paranoiac felt shameful of their behaviors.

In fact, it was a ploy designed by the navy's top officials. They revised with all servicemen on the codes of disciplines and boosted their spirit.

(2) **Chrysler's CEO beat the grass by showing his convertible to capture the attention.** In 1978, Chrysler Corporation was on the verge of going out of business. Lee Iacocca joined Chrysler to rebuild the entire company from the ground by job layoffs and closing plants. Iacocca introduced his minivan project, subcompact project and the revival of convertibles.

In the 1970s, the American auto industry abandoned the convertibles due to low demand and pending crash regulations that would make the convertibles difficult to produce.

Iacocca revived the body style of Chrysler LeBaron. He drove it on busy interstate highways, to large shopping plazas and entertainment centers. The car attracted many spectators and became the talk of the town. Iacocca would like to stimulate people's interest, and to capture their attention.

Chrysler was able to sell 23,000 LeBarons in the first year of its debut. The financial situation of the Company turned round quickly and it was able to repay the loans seven years earlier than expected.

9.2.1.4 Comments.

One has to lay down a well-thought plan first. In view of dangers, it is best to remain calm and inscrutable. Startle the enemy to see how he /she reacts. When the enemy is strong, it will be useless to make threats. In this case, it is better to work on the circumstantial factors or to do something that instills the threats.

The siren was raised (to beat the grass), so as to expose those who exhibited symptoms of paranoid schizophrenia (to startle the snakes). The top officials had to give them more counsel in dealing with paranoia and contingency. By showing the revived convertible in various public locations, Lee Iacocca was able to capture the public attention and test the responses to this product.

9.3   Action 21: To prod.

The strategist is ready for the combat, but the opponent prefers to wait. The objective is to make the opponent excited or emotional, but on the other hand the strategist must keep cool and cautious. He has to calculate and balance the right amount of stimulation to apply on the opponent.

9.3.1 The stratagem is: **Prod somebody into action.**

9.3.1.1 Theme.

> Irritate the enemy to get him excited and emotional, while you keep cool and cautious. Prodding is usually done by the use of linguistics, such as ridicules, sarcasms, scorns and insults. To prod is to stimulate into action. A prod is a pointed instrument for pricking. After someone is prodded, he will feel the pain and in many cases he will respond to the prod. This tactic will only work on those people who are emotional, or who cannot control their temper. The strategist will then be able to monitor the victim's behaviours.

> Sun Tze said, "If the opponent is of choleric temper, one should seek to irritate him." (*The Art of War*, Chapter I). This stratagem can be used to incite people. In politics, it becomes instigation.

9.3.1.2   Source.

Su Qin's ploy to prod Zhang Yi. During the Warring States Period (475-221BC) of China, the century between 319 BC and the final victory of the State of Qin to unify China in 221 BC is known in history as the age of alliances and counter-alliances, hezong (vertical) and lianheng (horizontal). Hezong was the international policy of the States of Qi and Chu, meaning a north-south alliance and a co-operation of the six States, Qi, Chu, Han, Zhao, Wei, and Yan against the State of Qin. Su Qin, a political strategist, advocated it.

Lianheng was the international policy of the State of Qin, meaning the subordination of the six eastern states to the Qin State. Zhang Yi, another political strategist, promoted this policy.

Su and Zhang were fellow schoolmates under the same master Qui Gu Zi. Su, as a wandering persuader, proposed to form the alliance among the six states against the Qin State. By 319 BC, he succeeded in getting the coalition to send an alliance army to deal the Qin State a smashing blow, but the question of leadership and unified command was knotty that the alliance could in no way resolve. Su was honored as the Honorary Chief Minister of the six States. He knew all the critical problems of the alliance. In order not to disrupt the hezong, he must have somebody in the Qin's court to take charge of the state affairs.

Su had a ploy. He told his assistant to take up the identity of Jia Sheren as a rich merchant. Jia took the journey from the Zhao State to the Wei State to meet Zhang. Zhang as a wandering persuader was miserable at the moment because he could not seek a post in the court of the

Chu State. Jia met Zhang and told him that Su was now the Chief Minister of the Zhao State. Jia thought it would be a good idea for Zhang to pay a visit to Su, so as to get an appointment in the Zhao court. Zhang agreed and made the journey with Jia. When Zhang arrived at Su's court, he was not able to see Su because the latter was busy. In the next few days, Zhang did not have any luck either.

On the fifth day, Zhang was allowed to enter the court. Su was on the platform of the court busy with his councilors. At lunch time, Su bade welcome to his guest and suggested to talk to the latter after lunch. However, Zhang was told to sit in the lower court and he was given a lunch on a dish. Su enjoyed luxurious food and drinks in the high table.

Zhang felt humiliated. After the lunch, Su summoned Zhang to ask what Zhang would want from him. Zhang was unhappy with this humiliation. Su prodded Zhang that it was Zhang's lack of talent that had caused his misery.

Zhang was angry and he shouted, "May Heaven bless me, I shall never be looked down by you anymore!"

Zhang left Su's court and talked to Jia about his unpleasant experience with Su. He said he had to go to the Qin State to try his luck. If he was successful, he would lead the Qin's army to attack the Zhao State to avenge Su's insult. Jia accompanied Zhang to make the journey and paid all expenses incurred.

Zhang arrived at the Qin State, and he managed to obtain an appointment in Qin's court. Zhang worked his way up with his lianheng policy. Soon, Qin Huiwenwang (reigned 337-311 BC) appreciated Zhang's talent and made him a councilor. Then, Jia bade farewell to Zhang. Zhang was sad because Jia had helped him so much, especially when he was miserable.

Before Jia left, he disclosed the whole story to Zhang. After learning the truth, Zhang was so moved that he comforted Jia by secretly promising not to raise army against the six States as long as Su lived.

This story is from *Records of the Historian* by Sima Qian (145-86 BC).

9.3.1.3 Illustrations.

(I) ***A map to prod the U.S. public.*** In the Nineteenth Century, non-intervention was the U.S. foreign policy. In the 1930s, the Neutrality Acts were a series of laws passed by the U.S. Congress in response to the growing turmoil in Europe and Asia. They intended to aviod U.S. becoming entangled again in foreign conflicts such as those leading to the WWI. After WWII broke out on September 1, 1939, groups like the America First Committee or people like Charles Lindbergh advocated U.S. to keep out of this War.

On October 27, 1941, U.S. President Franklin D. Roosevelt (in office: 1933-1945) in his address on Navy Day said that he had in possession a secret map by the Nazi Germany under the instruction of Adolf Hitler. It recorded a new world order. It was a map of South America and a part of Central America as Hitler proposed to reorganize. All existing boundary lines among the present 14 separate countries were obliterated. South America was divided into five vassal states, bringing the whole continent under German dominance. A new puppet state called the Republic of Panama was established. It affected the U.S. life line, i.e. the Panama Canal. It was a map that showed Nazi Germany's design not only on South America, but on U.S. Overnight, the non-intervention sentiment of the American public was softened.

Regarding the map used by President Roosevelt in his speech, later on some historians found out Adolf Hitler had nothing to do with it. It was made up by the British Intelligence.

(2) *A German U-Boat officer was prodded to give information about the German acoustic torpedoes.* In 1943, U.S. Captain Daniel V. Gallery commanded an autonomous "hunter-killer" anti-submarine task group. A typical task group consisted of a number of escort vessels like Destroyers and Destroyer Escorts, which were centered on an escort carrier. Its mission was to hunt the German submarines (U-Boats) prowling off the coast of West Africa, threatening the ships of the Allies which brought supplies from North America and their convoys.

The task group had some successes. However, before the German submariners deserted their U-Boats, they were required to scuttle (sink) the boat so that the most secret technologies such as the torpedo guidance system and German command codes never fell to the Allies.

Once, a U-Boat equipped with German Navy's T5 acoustic torpedoes was sunk. Among the captives, there was a German officer with the name Hertz (fictitious name). He took charge of the operation of the acoustic torpedo system. U. S. Lieutenant-Commander Taylor, also an authority on torpedoes would like to obtain the technical information on German acoustic torpedoes from Hertz. Taylor knew that he had to handle this delicate matter with extreme care. He preferred to befriend with Hertz to cultivate a friendly relationship. After some time, Hertz was aware of his status as a prisoner of war, and he asked Taylor why he was not prosecuted. Taylor said causally, "You are a Prisoner of War only. Nobody cares much about you."

Hertz said, "I am a sophisticatedly trained torpedo officer." Taylor rebuked, "German Navy is mediocre. There is nothing special in your U-Boats." Hertz was infuriated, and said, "We have just invented the acoustic torpedoes, far more advanced than your torpedoes." Taylor smiled sarcastically, "Another gimmick? Oh, by Joe, don't bluff."

Hertz was upset with Taylor's remarks on the quality of German torpedoes. He got hold of a pencil to draw a diagram of the torpedo, illustrating its parts, and the technical innovations in its design. Taylor listened carefully, and got the necessary information. In the next year, on June 4, 1944, the task group captured U-505 before it was scuttled. Besides the U-Boat itself, the U.S. was able to get its torpedo guidance system, German command code books and the combat tactics used by U-Boats. But Taylor was able to acquire the technologies of the acoustic torpedoes months ahead.

9.3.1.4 Comments.

Many master strategists used this stratagem in their ploys to stimulate their subordinates or to aggravate their enemies. In the above cases, the stratagem worked. But for the people who can keep themselves calm despite of insults or prods, this tactic will not work.

By the "Lend-lease policy", President Franklin D. Roosevelt aided the U.K., the Soviet Union, China, France and other Allied nations with vast amount of war materials between 1941 and 1945. Before the Pearl Harbour Attack, U.S. had enforced embargo against Imperial Japan. U.S. could hardly evade the turmoil of Europe and Asia. We are not sure whether Lieutenant-Commander Taylor was familiar with the 36 stratagems, but he was definitely a master of this stratagem.

Sun Tze reminded us, "A sovereign must not embark on a military campaign simply out of anger. A general must not go into battle out of pique." (*The Art of War*, Chapter XII).

9.4 Action 22: To chart the best course for action.

In order to isolate the opponent and to block any rescue from his allies, or to pull people to your side, you have to be tactful.

9.4.1 The stratagems are:
- (I) **Befriend a distant state while attacking a neighbour.** (One of the classical 36 Stratagems).
- (II) **Lengthwise and breadthwise, opening and closing.**
- (III) **Play double-faced and attack somebody from behind.**

(I) **Befriend a distant state while attacking a neighbour.**

9.4.1.1 Theme.

It is easier to attack the nearby enemies due to logistic reasons, than those far away. Ally yourself with your distant acquaintances to prevent them from joining forces with your present enemy. It is important "to drive a wedge between the enemy's front and rear, to prevent the enemy from co-operation with his allies, reinforcement and rally among their fighting forces." (*The Art of War*, Chapter XI).

Sun Tze said, "When one orders his army to leave behind the equipment to march day and night over one hundred *lis* (one *li* is 0.5 km) to fight for some advantageous position, it is most likely to be defeated, and the generals will be captured. It is because only the strongest can arrive on time, leaving the weaker and tired behind. As a result, not more than one-tenth of the troops will be present. When the forced march covers only fifty *lis*, it is most likely that the vanguard generals will be defeated because not more than half of the troops will be present. When the forced march covers only thirty *lis*, it is most likely that not more than two-third of the troops will be present..." (*The Art of War*, Chapter VII).

Another consideration is the supply lines. It will be more expensive to transport military supplies over longer distance. Though there is no guarantee that attacking close-by states will bring in swift victory, yet it is easier to control the situation when the battlefield is not so far away.

9.4.1.2 Classic.

Unification of China, 221 BC. After the long-term wars in the Spring and Autumn Period (770-476 BC), seven major States, namely Qi, Chu, Yan, Han, Zhao, Wei and Qin, remained in the Warring States Period (475-221 BC). To expand their forces and territories, the seven States on the one hand, carried out reforms in their own State to strengthen themselves and, on the other, were scheming to annex other States. They formed and broke alliances and attacked one another.

The Qin State, situated in the remote west, was not initially considered one of the strong powers. However, the Qin State made progress after implementing its legal system and reforming its social system. For generations, the State Qin had Chief Ministers with vision.

Fan Chen, one of Qin's Chief Ministers, advocated this stratagem, ("to befriend a distant state while attacking a neighbour") after Qin's painful experience of invading the Qi State, situated in the eastern part of China near the coast. The Qin Army had to make long journey passing over the States of Han and Zhao. Thus, the Yan State in the north-east of China had been the Qin State's ally for quite a long time due to its privileged geographical location, furthermost from the Qin State. (Refer to Appendix B).

In a decade the armies of the Qin State successively destroyed the six States: Han (in 230 BC), Zhao (in 228 BC), Wei (in 225 BC), Chu (in 223 BC), Yan (in 222 BC), and Qi (in 221 BC) to establish the King of Qin, Ying Zheng, as the First Emperor called Qin Shihuangdi.

The Warring States Period was ended by the founding of a tyrannical military Empire called Qin.

This story is from *Anecdotes of the Warring States* collated by Liu Xiang (77-6 BC).

9.4.1.3 Illustrations.

(1) ***Imperial Japan attacked China but strived to befriend with the U.S. in the 1920s-1930s.*** During the 1920s, a rapidly modernizing Japan was seeking to acquire raw materials and territories from the Asian mainland. Meanwhile, the U.S. was exporting scrap metals, oil and aviation fuels to Japan. In September 1931, Japan invaded Manchuria and established the ex-Qing Emperor Xuantong as head of the puppet regime of Manchukuo.

President Herbert Hoover (in office: 1929-1933) rejected a military response to it, and refused to impose economic sanctions against Japan. He chose simply not to recognize the Manchurian regime since it was based on force. Japan perceived U.S. would not use military measures to interfere its designs in the Far East. It was only after Japanese invasion of China in 1937, the relation between U.S. and Japan began to deteriorate rapidly.

In 1940, Japan occupied northern Indochina, a step towards its goal of capturing the oil supplies in the Dutch East Indies. To check Japanese aggression, President Franklin D. Roosevelt (in office: 1933-1945) proclaimed an embargo in the export of scrap metals, rubber and oil to Japan on September 26, 1940.

(2) ***The Molotov-Ribbentrop Pact signed on August 23, 1939.*** On September 30, 1938, by the Munich Agreement, the Sudetenland district was tranferred to Nazi Germany as a result of the appeasement policy adopted by the U.K. and France.

At the end of the Conference, British Prime Minister Neville Chamberlain had Adolf Hitler sign a declaration of

Anglo-German friendship, to which Chamberlain attached great importance, but Hitler none at all. Chamberlain claimed to have secured "peace in our time".

Hitler felt that since the U.K. would ally herself with other nations, and would not stand aside to his continual ambition, the U.K. replaced the Soviet Union in his mind as the main enemy of the Reich. Moreover, the Soviet's economic and strategic centres were much further away from Germany, and it would require tremendous amount of troops to attack these places. Another reason was that Hitler did not want to fight on two fronts. Based on these reasons, Hitler thought it was crucial to seek Soviet cooperation. Meanwhile, the U.K. and France were unable to reach an agreement with the Soviet Union for an alliance against Germany. On August 23, 1939, Hitler completed a secret non-aggression pact (the Molotov-Ribbentrop Pact) with Josef Stalin, agreeing to partition Poland between them.

On September 1, Adolf Hitler launched his invasion of Poland. It happened a few months before in the Far East; there was the Nomonhan Incident in which Soviet Union clashed with Japan on border disputes. The outcome was a decisive Soviet victory. The Soviet Union and Japan signed a cease-fire agreement on September 15. Stalin, free of any worry of his Far East problems, was free to enter Poland, Latvia and Estona on September 17, as prearranged by the Molotov-Ribbentrop Pact.

9.4.1.4 Comments.

To ally with distant states can eliminate the danger of the cooperation and rally of our close-by enemy with them. The objective is to isolate the enemies, and to strike each one in turn.

Imperial Japan waged war on China in the First Sino-Japanese War (1894-1895), and the Second Sino-Japanese War (1937-1945). Due to the disputes on the sovereign of territories bordering Manchukuo, it fought against the Soviet Union in the Battle of Lake Khasan (1938) and the Battle of Halhin-Gol (1939). China and the Soviet Union are Japanese neighbours. In 1941, only after U.S. enforced the embargo of raw materials to Japan, and it was perceived as a threat to Japanese expansion in the Far East, Japan grew hostile to U.S. and attacked Pearl Harbour on December 7, 1941.

Adolf Hitler sought the co-operation of the Soviet Union in his initial conquest of the continental Europe. In order not to fight on both sides, he arranged the Molotov-Ribbentrop Pact with the Soviet Union which shared the spoils of Poland and the Baltic States.

Not to befriend with the neighbouring states does not mean that one has to attack them. Another reason is to keep one out from the matters of the neighbours. In the Spring and Autumn Period and the Warring States Period of China, the states frequently formed and broke alliances. If the neighbouring states had a grudge with some other states, the trouble could spread across one's borders. By alienating from his neighbours, one might avoid to be involved in his neighbours' problems.

(II) **Lengthwise and breadthwise, opening and closing.**

9.4.2.1 Theme.

> Be tactful in political and diplomatic situations so as to gain advantages. Tactics used include disintegrating and undermining other people's solidarity (opening) or pulling others into your side by forming alliance (closing).
>
> Many times these actions require the use of espionage. Sun Tze said, "Only the sagacious and wise can use espionage. Only the benevolent and righteous can find right men to do espionage. Only those who are thorough, sharp and ingenious can make use of the results of espionage." (*The Art of War,* Chapter XIII).

9.4.2.2   Source.

Su Qin and Zhang Yi, the master political strategists. The Warring States Period (475-221 BC) of China is known as the age of alliances and counter-alliances. Hezong (vertical) was the foreign policy of the States of Qi and Chu, meaning a north-south alliance of the six states, Qi, Chu, Yan, Han, Zhao and Wei against the State of Qin. Su Qin as a strategist advocated it.

Lianheng (horizontal) was the foreign policy of the Qin State, meaning the subordination of the six eastern states to the Qin State. Zhang Yi, another strategist, promoted this policy. The ways in which these strategists lobbied their strategies coined the name of this stratagem.

9.4.2.3   Illustration.

(1) **European powers pulled together to contend Napoleon Bonaparte, 1805.** The alliance, led by the U.K. including Russia, Prussia and Austria against France was a failure. On December 2, 1805, Napoleon Bonaparte defeated Austria at the Battle of Austerlitz. Austria had to cede all of Italy, north of Rome to Bonaparte who crowned himself as King of Italy.

On July 7, 1807, after defeating both Prussia and Russia, Bonaparte compelled these two countries to join the Continental System to ally France and to boycott all trade with Britain by the Treaty of Tilsit. This Treaty also allowed Bonaparte to keep territories seized from them. The alliance with Russia broke down very quickly, because the Russian economy depended much on exporting raw materials like grain and timber, and importing manufactured goods, especially from the U.K. Meanwhile, the British pulled over the pro-British Russian officials to caution Tsar Alexander I against Bonaparte. A major motive for Bonaparte to invade Russia in 1812 was to punish the Tsar not to keep the terms of the Treaty of Tilsit.

In 1808, however, Bonaparte invaded Spain. He wanted both Spain and Portugal to become part of the Continental System; he overthrew the King of Spain and put his brother Joseph-Napoleon Bonaparte on the throne. The Spanish resented Joseph-Napoleon's presence in Spain, his abolition of the Inquisition, and his control of the church and they began to fight back. Thus, the War of Liberation began. The war went very badly for the French; the Spanish, hopelessly outgunned, fought using guerilla tactics which the French were unaccustomed to. The war dragged on until 1813 when the Spanish, with significant help from the British under the command of Arthur Wellesley, later Duke of Wellington, drove the French back to France.

British Prime Minister William Bentinck (in office: 1807-1809) sent an emissary to the Ottoman Empire, telling the Sultan that the Treaty of Tilsit had a secret appendix which was to throw his Empire out of its European territories. When Bonaparte led his six hundred thousand troops to invade Russia, the Continental System disintegrated.

(2) *Otto von Bismarck had a master plan to build up a military strong Germany.* In 1862, Otto von Bismarck became the Chancellor of Prussia. He was in favour of uniting Germany under a Prussian king by defeating Austria. In 1863, a revolt in Russian Poland occurred. It was a possible threat to Prussia, because it might spread to Prussia's Polish subjects in Posen. Bismarck offered military help to the Tsar Alexander II amidst widespread support for the Poles by France and Austria. The Tsar refused help, but agreed that Prussia could hand over any rebels seeking refuge there. However, William I (Wihelm I) of Prussia did not ratify this move. Russian neutrality was almost guaranteed. Russia was unlikely to become involved in a Prussia-France or Prussia-Austria war.

An unexpected alliance between Austria and Prussia took place in 1864. King Christian IX of Denmark declared that the Duchy of Schleswig was a part of the Danish State. The population was predominantly German. Bismarck used this alliance to his advantage. Prussia and Austria worked together and crushed the Danes and the Treaty of Vienna ratified in October 1864, giving Prussia and Austria joint dominion over Schleswig and Holstein.

During the next two years Bismarck sought to isolate Austria by making agreements with France and Italy. France gave a vague assurance of neutrality and Italy wanted to regain Venetia from Austria concluded an alliance with Prussia. Austria was provoked to such a degree that it took its case to the German council in Frankfurt and urged the Federation to mobilize against Prussia, but it had to fight on two fronts: Prussia and Italy.

On July 3, 1866, Austria was defeated. The old German Confederation was ended. Austria established a dual monarchy with Hungary, and by the Treaty of Prague, agreed to recognize "a new form of Germany without participation of the Austrian Empire." Bismarck decided to be lenient on Austria, as he might need an ally in the future.

The emergence of Prussia as the leading German power and the increasing unification of the German states were viewed with apprehension by Napoleon III after 1866. Meanwhile, Bismarck deliberately encouraged the growing rift between Prussia and France in order to bring the small States of South Germany into a national union. He made sure of Russian and Italian neutrality and counted correctly on British neutrality.

The immediate pretext for war occurred when the throne of Spain was offered to a prince of the House of Hohenzollern-Sigmaringen, a branch of the ruling house of Prussia. The offer, at first accepted on Bismarck's advice, was rejected on July 12, 1870 after strong French protest. But the aggressive French Foreign Minister, Antoine Alfred Agenor, the Duc de Gramont (Duke of Gramont), insisted on further Prussian assurances, which King Wilhelm I of Prussia refused.

The report on the informal conversations between King Wilhelm I and Count Vincent Benedetti, the French ambassador in Prussia on July 13 was sent to Bismarck by the King's permission. Bismarck cut out Wilhelm's concillatory phrases and emphasized the issue. It was designed to give the French the impression that Wilhelm I had insulted Court Benedetti; likewise the Germans interpreted the modified report as the Court insulting the King. Bismarck released the edited telegram to the media, known as the famous Ems Dispatch (or Elms Telegram), to inflame French feeling. On July 19, 1870 France under Napoleon III declared war on Prussia.

The Germans defeated the French in several battles, the French Emperor and 100,000 of his men were captured in Sedan. Paris held out until Jan. 28, 1871. In the Treaty of Frankfurt ratified on May 21, 1891, France agreed to pay an indemnity and to cede territories to Germany. Prussian militarism had triumphed and laid the foundation for German imperialistic ventures in the future

11.4.2.4 Comments.

This stratagem worked at the strategic level. It can involve various tasks at the tactical level where other stratagems, such as "Befriend a distant state while attacking a neighbour", "Find the way in the dark by throwing a stone", "Besiege Wei to rescue Zhao", and others. Though in many instances, it is publicized in political and diplomatic situations, yet it is very commonly found in human relationships.

(III) Play double-faced and attack somebody from behind.

9.4.3.1 Theme.

> Run with the hound and hold with the hare. One can get control of the scenario by manipulation. Sun Tze said, "When the enemies are united, one should try to cause internal dissension." (*The Art of War,* Chapter I). The adept in warfare always seeks victory from an opportune situation. This stratagem is very often used in diplomatic situations.
>
> However, to use this stratagem, there is a price to pay. It could trigger back fire from those being manipulated.

9.4.3.2 Source.

Zheng Xiu was very wicked. During the Warring States Period in China, the King of Wei presented a beautiful girl to Huaiwang, (reigned 328-299 BC), King of Chu who took great delight in her. His queen consort, Zheng Xiu, knowing how fond Huaiwang was of the girl, treated the newcomer as a sister supplying her with gifts and treasures. Learning about this, Huaiwang summoned Zheng and said, "A woman serves a man with her beauty and thus jealousy is a part of her nature. Yet you, knowing how much the new girl pleases me, have treated her more kindly than I have myself. You are in fact marvelous."

Zheng knew that Huaiwang did not suspect her of jealousy. After some time, when she met the girl, she said, "His majesty is much taken with your beauty but he dislikes the shape of your nose. When you serve him next time, be sure to cover your nose with your sleeve." The girl was grateful for this advice; she did accordingly when she served Huaiwang on the next occasion.

The next day Huaiwang asked Zheng, "The new girl covered her nose when she was with me. Do you know why?" Zheng said, "I know, she told me that she does not like the body smell of your Majesty." Huaiwang was furious about this, and ordered the naive girl's nose be cut off.

This story is from *Anecdotes of the Warring States* by Liu Xiang (77-6 BC).

9.4.3.3 Illustrations.

(1) **The manipulations of King Frederick II of Prussia.** In 1740, Charles VI, Holy Roman Emperor died without a male heir. Despite his efforts to secure his daughter Maria Theresa (German name: Maria Theresa Walburga Amalia Christina) (1717-1780) in her claim to the Austrian throne, her succession triggered the War of Austrian Succession (1740-1748).

Frederick II of Prussia promised to help Maria Theresa provided she ceded to him the Duchies of Silesia in which he pretended to have hereditary claims. Otherwise, he would ally himself with France, Bavaria and Saxony to fight against her. Declined by Austria of his claim, Frederick invaded Silesia, and led his forces to victory at Mollwitz in 1741 and at Chotusitz in 1742 in the so-called First Silesian War. As the Bavarians, French, and Saxon were advancing against Austria, Maria Theresa was compelled to arrange a truce with Frederick to avoid warfare from that side. Meanwhile, Frederick dispatched a cavalry to help his French ally.

In 1744, Frederick acquired East Friesland (now a region of Germany) on the death of the last ruler without heirs. In 1745, he again allied himself with France and Bavaria and broke the peace by invading Bohemia. But as France failed to send the promised army to help and Emperor Charles VII Albert (reigned 1742-1745) of the Holy Roman Empire died in January 1745, Frederick had to rely upon his own forces.

The Prussian victories at Hohenfriedberg, Soor-Trautenau, and Kesselsdorf overthrew the alliance and the Second Silesian War had to be settled by the Peace of

Dresden in which Prussia was confirmed its possession of Silesia.

By 1756, Maria Theresa was irresistibly impelled to punish Frederick and to recover Silesia. She allied with Russia, France, Sweden, and Saxony against Prussia and the U.K., but Frederick eventually managed to save Prussia. The Peace of Hubertusburg in 1763 awarded Prussia no new territory, as it merely confirmed the boundaries that had existed before the war. At the end of the war, however, Prussia was established as a rival to Austria for domination of the German states.

(2) ***Otto von Bismarck was a power manipulator.*** To expel Austria from the German Confederation was Prussian Premier Otto von Bismarck's chief objective. In 1866, Bismarck provoked Austria into declaring the Austro-Prussian War. A number of other German States, Bavaria, Nassau, Hessen-Kassel and Hannover joined the Austrian side. Bismarck intrigued Napoleon III of France for neutrality by vague assurance of the latter's claim for Luxembury. The Prussians won the Battle of Sadowa on July, 3, 1866.

By the Peace Treaty, Austria ceded Holstein to Prussia and withdrew from the German Confederation. It also ceded Venetia to Italy, which enabled Bismarck to earn Italy's goodwill. Elsewhere, Austria lost nothing. Bismarck decided to be lenient on Austria, as he might need an ally in the future.

In 1868, the throne of Spain became vacant. There were several candidates, among them a French Bourbon and a Hohenzollern. Napoleon III demanded that King Wihelm I of Prussia, as head of the Hohenzollern family, would denounce his nephew's claim to the throne. Wilhelm I compiled. Napoleon III demanded that Wilhelm I would once and for all declare that the Hohenzollern family, now and for the future would denounce its claims to the throne. Wilhelm I refused.

Bismarck published an abridged version of the telegram, the Ems Dispatch, containing the French demand. Napoleon III felt offended, and declared war on Prussia. In the Franco-German war, Southern German States fought on Prussian side. The Bavarian troops captured Napoleon III in Sedan. France had to cede Alsace-Lorraine and to pay reparations of 5 million gold francs.

9.4.3.4 Comments.

This stratagem aims at alienating enemies among their camps, playing double-faced to each of the enemies and seeking the opportunity to beat each of them. Lord Palmerston (1784-1865), a British politician and diplomat had his famous quotation: "We have no eternal allies and we have no perpetual enemies. Our interests are eternal and perpetual, and these interests it is our duty to follow."

King Frederick II of Prussia was an expert in maneouvering his competitors. However, this stratagem could fire back as France and Austria allied against Prussia in the Seven Years War (1756-1763). In 1762, Prussia was on the verge of disintegration. Frederick narrowly kept Prussia due to the sudden death of Empress Elizabeth of Russia, an event dubbed the miracle of the House of Brandenburg. Her successor, Peter III, an admirer of Frederick II pulled Russia out of the war. It relieved Frederick from the predicament. Then, Frederick was able to conclude the Peace of Hubertusburg which restored the prewar status quo.

Otto von Bismarck was a crafty power manipulator. His power plays were superb to undermine the politicians of Austria, France and Italy.

Exercises

1. The drugstore market is very competitive. They give flyer discounts, manufacturer's coupons, free delivery and 24 hours service. In the 1980's, one chain of stores installed certain machines (besides the weight scales) in their stores to be used for free. No hassle, no pressure to buy anything and no charges are required for the service. Each machine was deliberately placed in the store where the customers were required to walk a long way so as to be exposed to the various items stocked on the shelves of the drugstore.

(i) What was the machine?

(ii) What stratagem was used in this scheme?
   (a) Beat the grass to startle the snake.
   (b) Befriend a distant state while attacking a neighbour.
   (c) Cast a brick to attract a piece of jade.
   (d) Prod somebody into action

2. In the stock markets, once awhile some speculators would make use of scandals to drive the prices of the stocks (in the Dow Jones Index or in the NASDAQ index) down to scare the investors, or to over-exaggerate the positive expectations to boost the stock prices to attract investments. These people have the how how to make a fortune with their manoeuvres. In 1997, the financial storms swept the Asian Pacific Rim countries, and some of them have to take a long time to recover.

What stratagem do the speculators use in this case?
(a) Cast a brick to attract a piece of jade.
(b) Prod somebody into action.
(c) Beat the grass to startle the snake.
(d) Befriend a distant state while attacking a neighbour.

3. In June, 1942, Vononezh (a city about 400 miles to the northwest of Stalingrad) was used by the Germans as a base for the attack on Stalingrad and a key Don River crossing point. The assault was made by the German 4th Panzer Army whose commander was General Hermann Hoth. He captured Voronezh on July 6, and occupied the western river bank suburbs. However, it was followed by a Red Army counter-attack led by General Nikolai Fyodorovich Vatutin (In Service: 1920-1944).

Vatutin thought if he moved his army to reinforce Stalingrad, the Germans would follow him all the way to Stalingrad. If he stayed in Vononezh, he would be doing what his enemies expected him to do. He switched to be offensive, bombing the Germans lines, and sending troops to attack the Germans from their rear. The Germans had to ask for reinforcements. It took two more days for their infantry divisions to reach Vononezh to hold the line. Thus the German Panzer troops had to delay their move to Stalingrad.

Valutin was thus able to tie down the 4th Panzer Army, gaining the vital time for Stalingrad to make preparations for the epic Battle of Stalingrad that beat the German army to surrender.

Which of the following stratagems best describes General Nikolai Fyodorovich Vatutin's tactic in delaying the German 4th Panzer Army to move to Stalingrad?
(a) Cast a brick to attract a piece of jade.
(b) Prod somebody into action.
(c) Beat the grass to startle the snake.
(d) Befriend a distant state while attacking a neighbour.

4. Once upon a time there was a wise man that could bring disgruntled husbands and wives back together. He got famous by doing it. The King heard about this and wanted to play a practical joke on him. The King told the Queen to go to the summer resort, pretending to leave the King for grievances. He told the Queen no matter what the wise man said, she would refuse to come back to the Palace.

The King summoned the wise man to bring back the Queen as she had left due to grievances. The wise man saw through the King's ploy. He asked the King for some money. After this, nothing happened for a few days. Then, he led a band of musicians with carts of wedding gifts walking past the summer resort. The Queen was curious, and sent an attendant to ask the wise man, "What is happening?"

The wise man hesitated for a while before saying, "The Palace is going to hold a banquet..., a pretty bird arrives..." The Queen thought the King tricked her away from the Palace so as to arrange his wedding with a pretty girl. She hurried back to the Palace. Before she arrived at the Palace, the wise man told the King that his Queen was on the way back. When the Queen arrived, the King learned the whole story. He was amazed by the wisdom of the wise man, awarding him with many gold coins.

(i) Which of the following stratagems best describes the wise man's tactic to bring the Queen back to the Palace?
(a) Prod somebody into action.
(b) Entice snakes out of their lairs.
(c) Lengthwise and breadthwise, opening and closing.
(d) Beat the grass to startle the snake.

(ii) Do you think that the wise man could bring the Queen back to the Palace by his persuasions as he had done to others? Why or why not?

5.   Suppose you have two enemies to fight with. Naturally you will avoid fighting both at the same time. A father discovers that his daughter has developed two bad habits. She takes up an unhealthy program to reduce her weight, and she drives her car too fast. He has to focus on one problem at a time. He chooses to teach her responsible driving habits first, and refrain from talking to her about the weight control program for the moment.

What is the stratagem best describes this scenario?
(a) Cast a brick to attract a piece of jade.
(b) Prod somebody into action
(c) Befriend a distant state while attacking a neighbour.
(d) Play double-faced and attack somebody from behind.

6. Honda Soichiro had a dream to give people everywhere an economic form of transportation. In 1945, he came across a job lot of 500 war surplus two-stroke motors designed to power electric generations. He adapted them for attachment to push-bikes. By 1946, he produced motor-bikes running on turpentine. In 1948, he founded Honda Motor Company Ltd. Fujisawa Takeo was hired to manage the Company, while Honda himself focused on engineering.

At that moment, in Japan there were two hundred motor-bikes retailers who charged a lot in selling the merchandises. These people were more experienced to service motor-bikes. On the other hand, there were around 50,000 bike shops. Fujisawa proposed to contact them by letters soliciting for interested bike retailers to join the sales network for Honda. These retailers charged less make-up price and the sales network could be larger. Around 13,000 bike retailers showed their interests. Very soon, Honda motorcycles became popular in Japan.

Which of the following stratagems best describes Fujisawa Takeo's tactic in choosing retailers for Honda motor-bikes?

(a) Prod somebody into action.
(b) Entice snakes out of their lairs.

(c) Befriend a distant state while attacking a neighbour.
(d) Beat the grass to startle the snake.

7.   On October 14, 1809, the Treaty of Vienna signed between France and Austria imposed harsh peace terms on Austria because the latter was a loser. Klemens von Metternich was then appointed Foreign Minister of Austria in time to minimize Austria's loss.

Metternich initially supported an alliance with France, arranging the marriage between Napoleon Bonaparte and the Austrian Emperor Francis II's daughter, Marie-Louise. Though he allied with Bonaparte, yet he pledged to Russia in secret, not to assist Bonaparte in his invasion of Russia.

By 1812, realising the inevitability of Bonaparte's downfall, Metternich took Austria away from the alliance to neutrality and transferred himself into the role of an arbiter of Europe. As the Napoleonic Wars wound down, the victors gathered in Austria to make peace at the Congress of Vienna in 1815.

Metternich was anxious to ensure that the balance of power did not swing too far in any direction. In fact he counselled compromise and mutual concern to include France in the negotiations. He reached settlements regarding Germany, Poland, Italy and Austrian Netherlands that were precisely in accordance with his blueprint. His secret agenda was to ally with France and the U.K. to counter the growing strength of Russia and Prussia so as to achieve the political equilibrium he had desired.

Identify two stratagems used by Klemens von Metternich in perpetrating his balance of power postulate.
(a) Prod somebody into action.
(b) Entice snakes out of their lairs.
(c) Cast a brick to attract a piece of jade.
(d) Play double-faced and attack somebody from behind.
(e) Beat the grass to startle the snake.
(f) Lengthwise and breadthwise, opening and closing.

Chapter 10.

To strike and
to block the opponent's retreat path.

10.0   Introduction.

Actions 19-24 deal with the opponents faced directly and openly. Only Actions 23-24 are real confrontation with the opponents. We deal with Actions 23-24 in this chapter.

10.1 Action 23: To strike.

In order to bring the opponent under control, the last resort is confrontation. There are six situations in the consideration for making a strike.

Even at this stage, one must bear in mind Sun Tze's thesis: "The highest form of military leadership is to conquer the enemies by strategy, second to prevent the joining of their forces with their allies, third to attack them in the battlefield, and the worst policy is to besiege a walled city." (*The Art of War,* Chapter III). There are two categories of stratagems.

(I) Based on six combat scenarios.

(a) When in superior position. (When one is on the favored side of the combat).

10.1.1 The stratagem is: **Their name is Legion.**

10.1.1.1 Theme.

> When one's army has the superior strength, the best strategy is to win hands down, or to win without striking a blow. (Refer to 3.3.2.1). As a last resort, if he has to strike and his forces are ten to the enemy's one, he can surround them. (*The Art of War*, Chapter III). Sun Tze said, "When one's forces remain united while those of the enemy are scattered at ten different places, then he uses his entire force against one-tenth of the enemy's. As he can use many against few, the enemies will be weaker." (*The Art of War*, Chapter VI).

10.1.1.2 Source.

Sun Tze, *Art of War*, refer to 10.1.1.1.

10.1.1.3 Illustrations.

(1) ***The appeasement policy.*** The Treaty of Versailles limited the Germany National Defense to 100,000 men with few arms. Adolf Hitler became Chancellor of Germany in 1933. Almost immediately he began secretly building up Germany's army to 200,000 men and making heavy armaments such as tanks and offensive aviation forces. On October 14, 1933, he had Germany out of both the Disarmament Conference and the League of Nations. In 1935, he reintroduced conscription, and planned to expand the army to 300,000 men by April 1935 instead of 1938. The British and the French did nothing more than the official protests. They were more concerned about the rise of communism and believed that a stronger Germany might help to prevent the spread of communism to the West.

Immediately before September 1938, when Hitler wanted to occupy Sudetenland, the British Royal Army estimated that Hitler had 36 divisions, approximately 500,000 soldiers. In view of this, Britain and France had to resort to appeasement which was a policy of acceding to hostile demands in order to gain peace, so as to delay military confrontation with Hitler.

However, appeasement is supposed never to succeed for long. The aggressor always returns demanding further concessions. The implication is usually that refusal to 'appease' would have a happy ending as in any morality play.

(2) ***The Heroes in the North African Campaign 1942.*** In the literature on the North African Campaign in 1942, both German General Erwin Rommel and British General Bernard L. Montgomery were portrayed as strategic geniuses who turned certain defeat into victory. This is due to the fact that history prefers to focus on people and battles rather than on objects. Rommel's crowning glory is said to have been at Gazala and Montgomery's at El Alamein, but what is not mentioned is the startling similarity in their repective scenarios.

In May 1942, Rommel had a numerical superiority in armour after receiving supplies that the Allies had not detected. They were consisted of the vastly superior Tiger and Panther tanks, as well as the Panzer Specials equipped with larger guns and thicker face-hardened and spaced armour, and enough fuel to launch a prolonged offensive. Likewise in October 1942, Montgomery received 300 Sherman tanks more capable than the lower grade Panzer tanks and 100 self-propelled guns in time for the El Alamein offensive. For these statistics, it is clear that adequate supplies were the more decicive factors for victory than Second World War literature cares to highlight.

10.1.1.4 Comments.

Cowing the enemy into submission by making a big show of one's strength is the best move, while attacking with military force is an unwise move; even one has the superior force. Sun Tze advocated a preference for capturing the whole target intact rather than destroying it. This can be achieved when one's army has the superior strength.

Sun Tze said, "In the conduct of war when the enmey are out-numbered by ten to one, the best thing is to surround them; five to one, the best thing is to attack them, two to one, the best thing is to distract them before launching any assault. When the two forces are evenly matched, the best thing is to take the offensive. When the enemy's forces are larger and superior to a small extent only, the best thing is to prepare for defense. When the enemy's forces are larger and superior to a great extent, the best thing is dodge their attacks." (*The Art of War*, Chapter III).

Besides the numerical count and the level of training of the forces, supplies of food and equipment are equally important determinants.

(b) When in defensive position. (When one has to defend himself against his opponents).

10.1.2 The stratagem is: **Offend in order to defend.**

10.1.2.1 Theme.

> The ability to prevent defeat depends on oneself, while the opportunity for victory depends on the enemy. When one acts according to circumstance, he can flip between offensive and defensive tactics.
>
> "The adept in warfare is one who places himself in an invulnerable position and does not miss any opportunity to defeat the enemy." (*The Art of War*, Chapter IV). When one has an inferior force, it is best to adopt defensive tactics. When one has a superior force, it is best to adopt offensive tactics.

10.1.2.2 Source.

Sun Tze, *Art of War,* refer to 10.1.2.1.

10.1.2.3 Illustrations.

(1) *The wisdom of an ice cream and lollipops merchant.* It happened in a certain summer in the U.S. Manufacturers of ice creams and lollipops over-produced their goods. The inventory problems became accentuated.

While strolling on a sidewalk, Brandon (fictitious name), one of the manufacturers noticed the poster of a circus. He hit on an idea, and contacted the circus for an arrangement. He would provide everyone coming to the show a packet of fried beans free. During the intermissions, Brandon's cadets came in with ice creams and lollipops for sale. The response was tremendous because everyone would like to buy icy-cold stuff after eating the fried beans.

Brandon expanded his offensive sale strategy to ball-games stadiums. Very soon, he cleared his stock and made orders to other manufacturers to fill his markets. He was able to make a lot of profits in that year.

(2) *Surviving the consumer electronic retail competitions.* Consumer electrons include electronic equipment intended for everyday use in entertainment, communications and office productivity. The overriding characteristics of consumer electronic products are the trends of falling prices and the fast rate of obsolence.

Since 1970, there had been many electronic retailers going bankrupt or being taken over due to their throat-cutting price competitions. However, an electronic retailer BP (fictitious name) has been able to survive and prosper despite of the turmoils of the business. The management found out the faults of these retails: hard sale by the sale representatives, poor shop layouts, too many jargon and hidden costs in the items. Customers always felt disappointed after the purchases due to fast obsolence and falling prices.

BP Shops (fictitious) were renovated to allow customers browsing in a comfortable environment without unnecessary interferences. When being consulted, sale representatives explained functions of the equipment using easy to understand terms. Each item was clearly priced without strings. It did not emphasize on price knock down. While other retailers were struggling with their price cutting competitions, BP enjoyed rising sales and profits.

10.1.2.4 Comments.

The adepts in warfare can only prepare themselves secured against defeat, but they cannot be sure of opportunities for victory which must be provided by the enemy or the prevailing situation.

Brandon, the ice-cream and lollipops merchant turned to offensive tactics in order to save his company due to overproduction. BP Shops did not bother itself with the cut throats pricing competitions, but to take offensive measures in enhancing their shop layout and the sale strategies. In fact, price knocks may delay customers' buying decisions, and work negatively to discourage their enthusiasm to buy.

(c) When in attack. (When one is well prepared to launch the attack on his opponents).

10.1.3 The stratagems is: **Gain the initiative by striking first.**

10.1.3.1 Theme.

> When you are well prepared to seize favourable opportunity to initiate attack by striking first, you are sure to win.
>
> Sun Tze said, "If one is on the offensive, he finds his forces sufficient all the time." (*The Art of War,* Chapter VI). To

strike first is to offend. Being offensive, one has the advantage to make the enemy feel at loss as to where to put up defence. As he knows the place and time of the combats, he can make good preparations, even though his troops may currently be miles away. He should plan the attacks against the enemy's weakest points to make them irresistible.

10.1.3.2 Source.

Xiang Liang practiced what he preached. In around 207 BC, when the Qin Dynasty in China was disintegrating, Chen Sheng and Wu Guang rose in revolt against the imperial rule. Yin Tong, Prefect of Guiji who would like to fish in the troubled waters sought the advice of Xiang Liang, a general of the former State of Chu (in the Warring States Period).

Xiang said, "There have been some armed anti-Qin uprisings in many locations. This is the best chance to overthrow the Qin Dynasty. I've been told that he who strikes first will be the winner, while the late comers will be the loser."

Yin said, "You're descendant of the famous military clan in the Chu State. Only you can lead the insurgent troops."

Xiang was ambitious to seize some territories and to become king himself. He took an opportunity to kill Yin, so as to take over all the territories in the Guiji Prefecture. He declared to overthrow the Qin Dynasty.

This story is from *Records of the Historian* by Sima Qian (144-86 BC).

10.1.3.3 Illustrations.

(1) ***The Munich Beer Hall Putsch, 1923.*** In 1918, an Armistice was signed and brought an end to the WWI. Germany surrendered unconditionally to the Allies. In the following year the leaders of the Allies met at Versailles to decide how Germany was to be treated. When the terms of the Treaty of Versailles were published in June most Germans were angry. When the war ended, Adolf Hitler got a job working as an agent for the German Army. He was sent to a meeting of the German Workers Party in September 1919, which was led by Anton Drexler, who was very anti-Semitic. Hitler joined the party and became its leader in 1921.

Hitler wanted to attract as many people as possible to the party, so he changed the Party's name to the National Socialist German Workers Party. He hoped that the word "National" would attract nationalists who wanted to rebuild Germany after the WWI and the word "Socialist" would attract socialists who wanted to improve the lives of working people in Germany. In 1922-23, Germany had the hyperinflation problem, and many Germans found that their life-savings were lost. People who lived on pensions were in misery.

In 1922, Germany stopped paying reparations and the French and Belgian Armies invaded the Ruhr, the main industrial area of Germany. When the German workers went on strike they brought in their own workers and cut the area off from the rest of Germany. Hitler's party benefited by the reaction to this development, and exploited it by holding mass protest rallies despite a ban on such rallies by the local police.

The Bavarian government defied the Weimar Republic, accusing it of being too far left. Hitler endorsed the overthrow of the Weimar Republic, and declared at a public rally on October 30, 1923 that he was prepared to march on Berlin to rid the government of the Communists and the Jews. On November 8, 1923 Hitler led an attempt to take over the local Bavarian Government in Munich in an action that became known as the "Beer Hall Putsch."

It began with kidnapping the Bavarian officials in the Buergerbraukeller beer hall in Munich and proclaiming a new regime using their names. The following day, he led 2000-armed brown shirts in an attempt to take over the Bavarian government. This putsch was resisted and put down by the police, after more than a dozen were killed in the fighting. Hitler was arrested, sentenced to five years in prison. He was released after obtaining a pardon in December 1924.

(2) ***Israeli pre-emptive attack in the Six-Day War, 1967.*** Since 1949 when Israel was established in an area which Palestinian Arabs claimed as their homeland, the conflicts between Israel and its Arab neighbours never stopped.

In 1956, Israel overran Egypt in the Suez War; Egyptian President Gamal Abdel Nasser declared to avenge Arab losses and pressed the cause of Palestinian nationalism. He organized an alliance of Arab States surrounding Israel and mobilized for war. In April 1967, Israel and Syria engaged in serial clashes. Syria appealed to Nasser for help. In mid-May, the Egyptian army moved 100,000 troops and 1,000 tanks into the Sinai Peninsula on Israel's southern border. On May 17, Nasser called for the removal of U.N. observers in the region. On May 22, Nasser closed the Straits of Tiran. This move was regarded as an act of war by Israel.

Israel was aware that it had to fight on three fronts (Egyptians, Jordanians and Syrians). However, it preferred fighting to be done in Arab territories rather than Israeli. On June 5, Israel made a pre-emptive attack on the Egyptian military and air bases in Sinai. Within hours of the strike, they destroyed 309 of the 340 Egyptian aircraft in Sinai inflicting heavy casualties on the Egyptians. Israeli ground forces moved into Sinai and Gaza Strip. On the eastern front, the Jordanians air force was destroyed with minimum Israeli casualties. On the northern front, two-third of the Syrian air force was destroyed. Israel occupied West Bank, Golan Heights, and unified Jerusalem under its control.

The speed and scope of Israeli attacks were overwhelming to the Arabs. On November 22, the U.N. passed Resolution 242, calling for Israel to withdraw from the Occupied Territories, in return Arab countries would recognise Israel independence and guarantee secure borders for Israel. Unfortunately much of the peace negotiations involving the said parties for the past four decades have not resolved the disputes related to this Resolution.

10.1.3.4 Comments.

It requires much thorough planning and determination to strike first so as to gain the advantages. During the period 1921 to 1923, Adolf Hitler strived to build up the strength of the Nazi Party. He planned to overthrow the German Weimer Republic by force. Therefore he led the attempt to take over the local Bavarian officials, known as the "Beer Hall Putsch". Though he failed in this act, yet he gathered much support for his future endeavor.

In early 2003, U.S. President George W. Bush determined "to gain the initiative by striking first" by launching attack on Saddam Hussein's regime. His argument was instead of waiting for the terrorists to attack the U.S. homeland and U.S. interests round the world, he was going to hunt and fight them at their homeland. However, sceptics queried Bush's motive for doing this because it was Osama Bin Laden and Al Qaeda that were responsible for the September 11, 2001 attack, not Saddam Hussein of Iraq.

(d) When in confused situation. (The outcome of attack is unpredictable).

10.1.4 The stratagem is: **Work on the hearts and minds of others.**

10.1.4.1 Theme.

> Sun Tze was much concerned with the psychology and behaviour of the soldiers and the enemy. To prepare his soldiers for combat, discipline is rigidly enforced for all ranks. This includes forbidding superstitious practices, dispelling rumours and doubts, and living thriftily. Moreover, the troops are trained not to fear death. (*The Art of War*, Chapter XI).
>
> "When the general takes care of his men like infants, they will be willing to follow him even in the midst of dangers. When the general treats his men like his own children, they will be willing to support him even unto death." (*The Art of War*, Chapter X).
>
> "In order to kill the enemies, the troops must hate them." (*The Art of War*, Chapter II). "A whole army may become demoralized just as a general may be robbed of his presence of mind." (*The Art of War*, Chapter VII).

10.1.4.2 Source.

Zhao Kuangyin captured the heart of Qian Chu.

The Kingdom of Wu-Yue was established in 907 in the area of Hangzhou and the delta of the Yangtze River. Zhao Kuangyin (reigned 960-975) founded the Song Dynasty in 960. After the Song Dynasty had defeated the State of Southern Tang in 975, King Qian Chu (reigned 948-978) of the Kingdom of Wu-Yue was confused whether to submit to this new ruler of China or to fight against him.

Qian paid a visit to the Song Capital to see Emperor Zhao. Many Song officials wrote letters urging Zhao to kill or detain Qian. Zhao said, "If Qian does not want to submit to us, he would not come. After getting acquainted with us, I think he would make up his mind to submit."

After staying in the Song capital for a while, Qian decided to leave for home. On the question of submission, Zhao said to Qian, "When both of us are alive, we take this decision as pending." Zhao gave Qian many gifts including a wooden box which Zhao told Qian not to open until he arrived home. During Qian's trip, everyday, he burned incense in front of the box as a gesture of respect to Emperor Zhao.

When he arrived home, he opened the box. It contained the letters from the Song officials urging Emperor Zhao to kill or detain him. Qian was very moved by the trust and care of the Emperor. Then, Emperor Zhao passed away. In 978, Qian submitted to Zhao Kuangyin's successor, Zhao Guangyi (reigned 976-997). There was no bloodshed in this unification.

10.1.4.3 Illustrations.

(1) *Psychological warfare used in the Falklands War, 1982.* During the Falklands War 1982, (April 2 to June 14), the British and the Argentines conducted psychological warfare. Both sides used radio to a great extent.

On May 30, after bitter fighting Royal Marine Captain Roderick Bell who spoke perfect Spanish helped two Argentine senior non-commissioned officers to deliver a surrender message to the British Commander. They agreed to surrender and to the shock of the British, about 1,200 Argentines marched out of Goose Green and laid down their weapons.

On the other hand, the Argentine army broadcast to the approaching British fleet: "Would you like to be reminded of your hometown [sound of bells]. Yes it's good old Big Ben. It's been a long time since you listened to it."

To the Argentineans, the British Task Force was described as a pirate fleet, while Margaret Thatcher was portrayed as a Viking, a vampire and a Nazi Storm Trooper.

To undermine the Argentine garrison's morale, the British dropped down from air leaflets in Spanish: "The soldier who bears this pass has signaled his desire to cease fighting. He is to be treated strictly in accordance with the Geneva Convention and is to be evacuated from the area of operations as soon as possible. He is to be given food and medical treatment if he requires it and then be held in a place of shelter to await repatriations. By J. F. Woodward, Rear Admiral Commander, British Force."

On June 14, the Argentine Commander agreed to cease fire, and 9,800 Argentina soldiers threw down their weapons.

(2) ***US$10 million as the training expenses.*** In today's high-tech business, the payoff from high risk explorations can also be colossal. In the 1990's, there was a high-ranking business executive in charge of product development project in a Fortune 500 company in U.S. Due to "reasonable mistakes", the project had to be scrapped, resulting in a US$10 million to go down the drain.

Some people suggested to the CEO of the company to fire the executive responsible for the blame. After investigation, the CEO found that the failure was due to "reasonable mistakes". He was aware that "nothing ventured, nothing gained." In high-tech business, mediocre executives lacked the creativity and motivation in pioneering projects essential to the success of the company.

The CEO summoned the executive who was prepared to face the music. To the latter's surprise, he was assigned an equally important position in another division of the company. The executive asked, "Why don't you fire me?"

The CEO said, "We have spent $10 million on training you, are you ready to work?" Later, it proved that the CEO was right, because the executive was then able to apply his experiences and his wisdom in this new position to make the company profitable.

10.1.4.4 Comments.

Wu Tze (c. 435-381 BC) treated his soldiers like his own kith and kin. Thus, his soldiers were willing to fight to their death. Wu was victorious in 64 battles out of a total of 76.

Psychological warfare is the planned use of propaganda and other psychological actions to influence the opinions, emotions, attitudes and behaviors of hostile foreign groups or to incite positive attitudes among people in our camps to achieve our objectives. It is considered a type of unconventional warfare because it attempts to influence the mind of the enemy rather than destroy his military forces.

In the West, Alexander the Great (356-323 BC) was one of the first to care about psychological warfare because he was effective in swaying the mindsets of the populaces who were expropriated in his campaign. In order to keep the new Macedonian states from revolting against their new leaders, Alexander would leave a number of his men behind in each city to introduce Greek culture. Since this method of persuasion influenced loyalist and separatist opinions alike, it directly altered the psyches of the occupied people.

(e) When in gaining ground. (When one plots for gaining ground).

10.1.5 The stratagem is: **Outwit by novelty.**

10.1.5.1 Theme.

One can always beat his opponents with never thought of methods by surprises. Sun Tze said, "The adept in warfare can use indirect approaches, strategies and troops in such infinite ways like ever-changing forces of heaven and earth; and the ceaseless flowing water of rivers and streams." (*The Art of War,* Chapter V).

10.1.5.2   Source.

Tian Dan won by novelty. During the Warring States Period in China (475-221 BC), General Yue Yi was sent by the King Zhaowang (reigned 311-279 BC) of the Yan State to attack the Qi State. Nearly all the Qi cities fell except Jimo and Jucheng. Tian Dan was the Prime Minister of Qi, and he defended Jimo for three years. Then, Zhaowang passed away, and his son King Huiwang (reigned 278-272 BC) who did not like General Yue succeeded him.

Tian knew that this was an opportunity to fight back. He made use of the converted spies to inform King Huiwang that General Yue was afraid that Huiwang would kill him, therefore Yue would like to stay in the territories of Qi, waiting for the moment to enthrone himself as King. Since the Qi people had not completely submitted to Yue, the latter had to wait. That was the reason for Yue to besiege Jimo, but not to tear it down so as to win the hearts of the Qi people. Now, the Qi people did not have to worry about Yue. Their only worry was that King Huiwang would send another general to replace Yue, because any other Qi Commander would tear down Jimo, destroying everything.

King Huiwang learned about this. He replaced Yue by General Kei Je, and Yue fled to the State of Zhao. Tian tricked General Kei and his soldiers again with the converted spies to dig up the ancestral graves of the Qi people, and to cut off the noses and ears of the Qi captives, causing much public outrage against the Yan army.

Tian gathered about one thousand oxen. Sharp knives were tied to their horns, oil-soaked reeds to their tails, and scarlet streamers with dragon-patterns on their backs.

He organized a mission troop of five thousand soldiers. At night, the soldiers drove the oxen to the Yan camps. When they reached the camps, the reeds on the oxen's tails were set alight. The animals stampeded through the camps, and Tian's soldiers followed the animals to make the fatal blows to the Yan army. Tian was then able to recover much of the lost territories in the following months.

This story is from *Records of the Historian by* Sima Qian (145-86 BC). Tian's stratagem and war strategies were much praised by Sima Qian as a classic example of defeating the enemy by novel tactics.

10.1.5.3 Illustrations.

(1) ***Ingrid Bergman's choice of an aria for her audition.*** In 1932, at the age of seventeen, Ingrid Bergman (1915-1982) auditioned for the Royal Dramatic Theatre in Stockholm. The audition was extremely competitive. Many candidates chose famous arias from *Camilla* and *Macbeth* by famous composers, such as Giuseppe Verdi, to perform.

Instead of being conventional, Bergman chose an aria composed by a less known composer. It was about a farm girl, dancing on the farmyard and making a leap across a spring to stand in front of the boy she loved. She put her hands on her hips and giggled before she continued to sing. Bergman's performance was overwhelming successful. She sang with passion and made the most elegant leap. The adjudicators unanimously approved her admission.

Later on, Bergman became a three times Academy Award winning and two-times Emmy Awards winning actress.

(2) ***The fall of the Empire of mechanical watch-makers.*** Before 1970, Switzerland was famous for making watches and clocks. The first quartz watch movements were made in 1967 by a consortium of Swiss watches companies. It was called Beta 21.

Quartz is a crystalline mineral, silicon dioxide. The quartz used in today's watches is synthetic due to its more consistent properties. The quartz vibrates very quickly in response to an electric charge. It is these vibrations that enable the watch to keep time. A quartz watch is powered by electricity. The wide use of quartz in watches and clocks had to await the development of cheap semi-conductor digital logic in the 1960s.

The Swiss watch companies realized that in order to produce the quartz watches, they had to revamp their factories and to lay off many of their skilled mechanical watch-makers. They decided not to carry on the research any more.

However, in 1969, Seiko, the Japanese company valued this opportunity. It became the first company to offer quartz watches to the consumers. Between 1975 and 1980, 178 Swiss watch-making companies went bankrupt. Today, about 95% of the watches produced use quartz. The value of mechancal watches is derived from the craftsmanship and it takes up the status symbol.

10.1.5.4 Comments.

An innovative way of doing things always gives one an advantage. Ingrid Bergman's choice of the aria for audition was ingenious. Nowadays, new technologies emerge everyday to improve our quality of life. The quartz technologies were taken lightly by the Swiss watch-making companies. However, Seiko was enthused by these technologies.

Likewise for stratagems, we should not be confined to the classical 36 Stratagems. We should be receptive to other stratagems, and to take a new approach to study them.

(f)   When in desperate situation. (When one is on the unfavored side of the combat).

10.1.6 The stratagem is: **Break the cauldrons and sink the boats.**

10.1.6.1 Theme.

> One must fight with the courage of desperation to survive. If the enemy is strong and one's soldiers are uncertain and unwilling to fight with their efforts, defeat is at hand. One has to make the soldiers realize that there is no other alternative except to fight for survival. Burn the provisions; destroy the boats to dash the soldiers' hopes of escaping. In essence, it is to fight with one's back to the wall.
>
> To assemble all the divisions of the army and expose them to great danger is what a general is expected to do. Sun Tze said, "When the soldiers find themselves in desperate situation, they will struggle for survival. When they are threatened by death, they will fight hard for life." (*The Art of War,* Chapter XI).

10.1.6.2 Source.

Burning one's boats. Around 207 BC, the Qin Dynasty in China disintegrated, and people rose in revolt. After defeating the Chu army, the Qin General Zhang Han and his army marched north to attack the Zhao State. King Huaiwang of the Chu State appointed Song Yi as Commander-in-Chief and Xiang Yu as general to lead an army to rescue the Zhao State. Song Yi was afraid of the Qin army. He stayed by the Zhang River more than forty days without action.

Xiang killed Song and ordered the army to cross the river immediately. After crossing the river, Xiang ordered that all the boats be sunk, all the cauldrons smashed and the camp site burned. Each soldier was to carry only three days' food supply, showing the determination never to return alive without winning the battle. The Chu soldiers knew there was no way of retreat, so they fought with all their might, winning nine ferocious battles at the City of Julu against the powerful enemy. After this, Xiang rose greatly in prestige and became a leader of the armies fighting against the Qin Dynasty.

This story is from *Records of the Historian* by Sima Qian (145-86 BC).

10.1.6.3   Illustrations.

(1) ***Peter Rumantsiev knew "When death is certain, the soldiers will live."*** Conflicts between the Russian Empire and the Ottoman Empire broke out several times in the Eighteenth Century. In 1768, the Russian emissary to Istanbul was arrested and war was declared between the two countries. A Russian army under the command of Count Peter Rumantsiev drove the Turks across the Danube River.

In the naval Battle at Chesme, the entire Ottoman fleet was annihilated on June 26, 1770. Then, Rumantsiev's army amounting to thirty thousand was besieged by the Turks who had two hundred thirty thousand men. The worst thing was the Russian army's provisions had been depleted. The Grand Vizier (high executive official) Halil Hamid Pasa would avenge for their defeat at Chesme by killing every Russian soldier.

In view of the seriousness of the matter, Rumantsiev explained the situation to his men, and proposed one last move, to attack the Turkish camps at night by surprise. Every Russian soldier knew that there was no alternative but to fight for survival, and they did it well. Eventually, the Turks had to flee, losing twenty thousand men, while the Russians lost about one thousand. An armistice was signed in 1772. Peace negotiations dragged on. Only when an army under General Alexander Vaslyevich Suvorov crossed the Danube River, marching on to Istanbul, then the Sultan was willing to sign the peace treaty.

(2) *Hitachi Company instilled high employee morale during the recession 1974-75.* The Hitachi Limited includes many business divisions and companies, many technologies, products and solution technologies. The 1974 OPEC oil crisis devastated Japan which imported nearly 95 percent of its fuel for its industrial sector. In Hitachi, drastic cost cutting measures were taken to keep the company financially solvent, and the company executives voluntarily took 15 percent off their pay.

Two third of the employees, about six hundred seventy-five thousand, were not required to work, but they were given 97 percent of the pay. In April 1975, the Company postponed the commencement of work for the newly recruited personnel. Everybody felt the pressure.

In the second half of 1975, Hitachi sales began to increase. Every Hitachi employee made his best efforts. The recovery rates of sales and profits of Hitachi ranked first among similar manufacturers in Japan. Its management instilled high morale by having the employees to experience fighting with their backs to the wall.

10.1.6.4 Comments.

Morale and courage are the two indispensable factors for achieving victory. To instill in the soldiers or employees, a must-win attitude, the strategist must adopt some seemingly extreme measures. Sun Tze mentioned several times in *The Art of War* Chapter XI about fighting on "death ground". Death ground is an area in which one can only survive through fearless fighting and will definitely perish if one does not fight relentlessly. In that situation, the general and the army must fight as if they did not wish to live.

Court Peter Rumantsiev knew that when the soldiers felt that death was certain, they would win and live. Hitachi let their staff to experience such feeling during the 1974-1975 recession periods.

(II) Based on other considerations.

(a) When the opponent has a lot of supporters, it is best to capture their leader so as to facilitate the conquest.

10.1.7   The stratagem is: **Defeat the enemy by capturing their chief.** (One of the classical 36 Stratagems).

10.1.7.1 Theme.

> The most thorough way to dissolve the fighting capabilities of the enemy is to destroy the army's main force, and to capture its chief.
>
> Even though there are brave soldiers still fighting in the fields, sooner or later, they will be vanquished. This theme comes from *I Ching* which is the origin of Chinese thought.
>
> By winning battles but without capturing the chief of the enemy, complete success cannot be attained. When the chief is at large, possibly he is back to his hiding places. It is likely that he is coming back for revenge in the future. Thus, it is an advantage that the chief of the enemy is taken in captivity.

10.1.7.2   Source.

General Zhang Zin attempted to catch the rebel army's leader. It happened in the Tang Dynasty in China. General An Lushan rebelled against Xuanzong, the Emperor of Tang (reigned 712-755) in 755. General Zhang Zin confronted General Wan Ziki who belonged to An's camp. Zhang led his army to break into Wan's camps. Wan's troops panicked and fled in all directions. Banners and flags were thrown on the ground. Zhang did not know Wan, but he would like to capture the latter.

Zhang thought of a ploy. He ordered his archers to use straws as arrows. Wan's soldiers thought that Zhang's archers ran out of arrows, and they ran to report this to Wan.

Now, Zhang discovered where Wan was. Zhang's assistant shot an arrow and blinded Wan's left eye. But Wan managed to slip away. General Zhang won the battle only.

The story is from *Sin Tang Shu (New Standard History of the Tang Dynasty)* compiled by Ouyang Xiu (1007-1072) and Xong Qi (998-1061) of Song Dynasty during the period 1044-1060.

10.1.7.3 Illustrations.

(1) ***Nazi Germans rescued Benito Mussolini for setting up a new Italian Socialist Republic.*** The landing of Allied forces in Sicily in July 1943 prompted the downfall of the Fascist Italian leader and Adolf Hitler's ally, Benito Mussolini. On July 24, 1943, the Italian Fascist Grand Council, which had not met since the war began, summoned Mussolini to a meeting at which King Victor Emmanuel was appointed in his stead as Commander-in-Chief of the Italian armed forces.

The next day, the King dismissed Mussolini from all of his functions, had him arrested, and sent him to prison in an ambulance. Mussolini was imprisoned in the Grand Sasso Hotel on the Grand Sasso Plateau in the Abruzzi Mountains.

The Allied forces landed in Italy on September 2, 1943. Italy surrendered on September 8. From July 27 to September 12, the Italian Military Intelligence and German Intelligence agents played cat and mouse in the German attempt to locate Mussolini. On September 12, Otto Skorzeny piloted a glider to Grand Sasso and rescued Mussolini. The latter was flown to Hitler's Headquarters in Rasterbury.

On September 23, Mussolini was then flown back to Northern Italy. He proclaimed himself Head of State of the new Italian Socialist Republic, with the Capital at Salo. Mussolini would continue to promote his Fascist ideals and stated how he was let down by the Italian people. Mussolini ordered a revival of his military with a new uniformed military including the Republic National Guard, police and the 10th Squadron naval commandos. This government had no real power, and then the Nazi Germans invaded and occupied most of Italy. On April 27, 1944 the communist partisans captured Mussolini as he tried to flee to Switzerland, but just before the border, and shot him the next day.

(2) *The "Shock and Awe" air campaign in the War in Iraq 2003.* On March 19 2003, the coalition forces of the U.S. and U.K. launched the "Shock and Awe" air campaign in the first phase of the War in Iraq. They did this by bombing selected Iraqi military targets, followed by the (remarkably accurate) bombing of Saddam Hussein's presidential palace and several governmental ministries, all in downtown Baghdad.

It was a decapitation attack on the Iraqi leadership. U.S. Defense Secretary Donald H. Rumsfeld declined to use the traditional war tactics of massive invasion force, and thought he could accomplish the same objective with a smaller force and therefore fewer casualties.

General Tommy Franks, Commander of U.S. Central Command, said, "This will be a campaign unlike any other in history — a campaign characterized by shock, by surprise, by flexibility to make it so apparent and so overwhelming at the very outset of potential military operations that the adversary quickly realizes that there is no real alternative here other than to fight and die or to give up."

Theoretically, the "Shock and Awe" functions as the non-nuclear equivalent of the impact that the atomic bombs dropped on Hiroshima and Nagasaki during the World War II. The Japanese were prepared for suicidal resistance until both bombs were used, because the Japanese leadership changed their outlook and the average citizen changed their mindset after their "Shock and Awe" experience.

However, in the few days of "Shock and Awe", and despite of the coalition's air power, precision weapons and speedy data link, the Iraqi leadership did not fold. The Iraqis had their own ploys, e.g. guerrilla militias, intimate knowledge of the terrain, the willingness to use their own civilians as cover and the deception to surrender while seeking the chances to shoot the coalition troops.

10.1.7.4 Comments.

By winning battles but without capturing the chief (or commander), complete success cannot be attained. When the chief is at large, possibly he is back to his hiding places. It is likely that he is coming back for revenge in the future. Thus, it is important that the chief of the enemy is taken in captivity.

The Germans rescued Benito Mussolini for establishing a new Italian Socialist Republic to ally with Germany despite Mussolini being ousted by the Italian Fascist Grand Council. It was because Mussolini still had some influences of his own on the Italian people.

The decapitation attack in the first phase of the War in Iraq 2003 did not attain its maximum results because the "Shock and Awe" raids were not as overwhelming as those experienced by the Japanese in 1945.

To be able to grasp the essentials of the matter can facilitate solving problems. By the same token, to be able to identify the key figures of the group can help to communicate to the individuals of the group. If the enemy's army is strong but is allured to the chief only by money or threats, then aim at him. When the chief falls, the rest of the army will collapse.

But if the enemy's troops are affiliated to their chief through loyalty or religious fanaticism, this stratagem will not work, because the army would continue to fight after his death out of vengeance. This accounts for the fact that the Iraqi Republican Guards continued their resistance after the coalition forces seized Baghdad on April 9, 2003.

(b) The strategist will not like other people to take copy of his plot, and he would not give the late comer a chance.

10.1.8   The stratagem is: **Remove the ladder after the accent.** (One of the classical 36 Stratagems).

10.1.8.1   Theme.

> This stratagem is also known as "Cross the river and destroy the bridge." The saying was originally from Sun Tze, "The best time to mobilize our army is the moment that our enemy has ascended to the high place, and the ladder for ascent has just been kicked away." (*The Art of War*, Chapter XI). In this scenario, the enemy has no retreat path.
>
> With baits and deception entice your enemy into treacherous terrain, and ensnare him in this death trap by cutting off his rearguard support.
>
> There are other meanings associated with this saying. Removing the ladder after one's ascent will bundle up the people on the deck to share the same fate for whatever happening in the future.
>
> By removing the ladder, one can cut off all the troubles, which may occur, freeing one from all worries hereafter. It can also mean to put somebody in dilemma, having to choose "between the devil and the deep blue sea".

10.1.8.2   Source.

Liu Qi sought advice from Zhuge Liang after taking away the ladder. At the end of the Han Dynasty and around the year 206 in China, Liu Biao, the Governor of

Jingzhou favored his younger son Liu Zong to be his successor due to the influence of his concubine (mother of Liu Zong). His elder son, Liu Qi was disappointed. He would like to seek the advice from Zhuge Liang so as to save himself from any potential misfortune falling on him. However, Zhuge did not want to make any comments.

Once, Liu Qi and Zhuge toured the governor's private garden. They ascended a tower by a ladder to eat and drink. During the banquet, Liu Qi told his servants to take away the ladder. Liu Qi, "Now, we are half way between the sky and the earth. What you say can only be heard by me. Would you give me the advice?"

Knowing that he did not have to worry about the consequence of his words, Zhuge reminded Liu Qi about what happened in the reign of Duke Xiangong of Jin (reigned 676-651 BC). The Duke had a concubine called Li Ji. She would like to eliminate the Duke's two other sons, Sen Seng and Chong Er born by the Duke's other women, so that her son would be the sole successor to the Duke. Sen Seng preferred to stay in the court of Jin and he was eventually killed.

Starting from 669 BC Chong Er was on exile to seven states for a period of nineteen years so as to evade himself from his stepmother's plot. After the death of Duke Huigong (reigned 650-637 BC), with the help of Duke Mugong (reigned 659-621 BC) of the Qin State, he managed to return to his state as Duke Wengong of Jin (reigned 636-628 BC).

Liu Qi picked up the wisdom of this story. He made a petition to his father to be a governor of a district far away from Jingzhou. By doing this, he avoided the doomed fate of Sen Seng.

This story is from *History of the Three Kingdoms* by Chen Shou (233-297).

10.1.8.3 Illustrations.

(1) ***The Battle of Salamis, September 480 BC.*** The Battle of Thermopylae (August, 480 BC) was a pyrrhic victory for Xerxes I (reigned 485-465 BC), Great King of Persia and Pharaoh of Egypt against King Leonidas I of Sparta commanding an alliance of Greek city-states (cities having sovereignty themselves). But it offered Athens the invaluable time to prepare for the decisive naval Battle of Salamis, one month later.

The Persian fleet led by Xerxes I consisted of 650-1000 ships while the Greek fleet had only 220-366 ships commanded by Euryblades and Themistocles. Euryblades proposed to fight the Persians in the open sea. In case of defeat, they could retreat to the mainland. Themistocles argued in favor of luring the Persians into the bay area in front of the City Salamis. He thought that the bay was narrow and the currents were swift to nullify the effectiveness of the large Persian navy. Themistocles won his agruments.

Themistocles sent his agents to spread the news among the Persian fleet that the Greek sea-fighters would desert their ships at night to run for life. The bay entrance was not guarded. Xerxes I was elated by the news, and ordered his fleet to enter the bay. There was an island called Psythaleia situated at the entrance to the bay. The Persian fleet had to split into two streams. Its formation was disrupted. Once inside the bay, the Persian fleet had little space to maneuver because these ships had long oars. The Greek ships were agile due to their size, and they crushed the oars of the Persian fleet. The Persian ships crushed each other, and after eight hours of battle, more than 200 of them were sunk.

After the battle, Xerxes I retreated. He was compelled to send his soldiers home to prevent a revolt.

(2) **Hermann Goering plotted to remove Werner von Blomberg.** Werner von Blomber (1878-1946) was apppointed Minister of Defense in Adolf Hitler's government in 1933. In 1935, the Ministry of Defense was renamed to Ministry of War. Blomberg became Minister of War and Commander-in-Chief of the Armed Forces. In 1936, he was the first Field Marshal General appointed by Hitler. However, his subordinates, Hermann Goering and Heinrich Himmler conspired to oust him for power.

Unfortunately for Blomberg, he disagreed with Hitler in two policies, and made Hitler dissatified with him. First, in March 1936 Hitler gave order to reoccupy the demilitarized zone in the Rhineland. Second, in 1937, the quest for lebensraum (living space) and to stop a severe decline in living standards prompted Hitler to embark in the near future on a policy of agression to annex Austria and Czechoslovakia.

In January 1938, Blomberg then in his sixties whose first wife died in 1932 fell in love with a 26-year-old Erna Gruhn with a lowly working class background. He worried over how such a marriage would be received among his peers. He decided to ask Goering for his opinion, and was relieved when Goering said there would be no problem. Goering was the best man at the wedding that Hitler attended. Meanwhile, a police officer discovered that Gruhn had been a prostitute with a criminal record. The newlyweds departed for a honeymoon in Italy. In their absence, all kinds of nasty rumours began to surface about the bride's past. The police file was delivered to Hitler by Goering who hoped to benefit from Blomberg's downfall.

When Blomberg returned to Berlin, Hitler summoned him. He refused to annul the marriage, and consequently resigned all of his post on July 27, 1938 when Goering threatened to make his wife's past public knowledge. Hitler said he would restore Blomberg to duty when the controversy faded. Blomberg was never recalled to serve again.

A few days after Blomberg's resignation, Goering and Himmler accused another Commander-in-Chief Werner von Fritsch of being a homosexual. Goering did not want Fritsch to become Blomberg's successsor and thus his superior. It was called the Blomberg-Fritsch Affair.

10.1.8.4 Comments.

Themistocles' tactic was to lure King Xerxes I by disinformation into the bay where the Persian fleet lost its presumed strength. It was similar to the scenario when one had ascended to the roof of the house, but the ladder for ascent was then removed.

Hermann Goering seized an opportunity offered by Werner von Blomberg himself regarding his marriage to Erna Gruhn who had dubious past. Goering knew that Blomberg's downfall would benefit his own career. Adolf Hitler had been dissatified with the two highly ranking military officials, Blombery and Werner von Fritsch, blaming them as too hesitant towards his war plans. He made use of these chances to reorganize the Wehrmacht (the armed forces of Germany). In hindsight, some historians claimed that Hitler participated in the plot from the beginning.

Of all the stratagems, this stratagem is most frequently used to deal with people within one's camp. One's best friend could be one's most deadly enemy.

(c) Sometimes the strategist has to make use of a springboard to launch the strike. The strategist can also consider taking the springboard as an additional gain.

10.1.9 The stratagem is: **Borrow a safe passage to conquer Guo.** (One of the classical 36 Stratagems).

10.1.9.1 Theme.

> Use an ally's strategic location as a springboard to launch attack on a third party. The springboard can be borrowed and one may have to pay for it.
>
> After achieving the objective, one may turn against the ally that lent the springboard in the first place. It requires another schemer with equal or more calibers to decode the ploy.

10.1.9.2 Source.

Duke Xiangong used the Yu State as his springboard to invade the Gue State. In 658 BC, Duke Xiangong of the Jin State in China had the ambition to expand his territories. His Prime Minister, Xun Xi, proposed this stratagem "To kill two birds with one stone".

The Yu State stood in between the States of Guo and Jin. To reach Guo, the Jin army had to pass through Yu. The Duke presented gifts of beautiful jades, fast horses and pretty girls to the Duke of Yu, requesting the permission for his army to go through Yu's territories. Gong Ziqi, a minister of Duke of Yu, was sharp to see through the ploy, and he said to the Duke, "We mustn't give them the permission. The States of Yu and Guo are closely related as the lips and the teeth. When the lips are gone, the teeth cannot survive. If we allow the Jin army to come into our territories, the Guo State will be conquered, and we shall be the next victim." The Duke of Yu refused to listen.

The Jin army seized some territories of the Guo State. In 655 BC, the Duke made the same request again. Gong advised the Duke of Yu not to give the permission any more, but the advice was declined. Gong fled away from the Yu State with his family in a hurry. The Jin army overwhelmed the Guo State, and on its way back, it conquered the Yu State. Duke Xiangong recovered not only the gifts offered to the Duke of Yu, but also annexed the latter's territories.

This story is from *Zuo Qiuming's Chronicles* by Zuo Qiuming (c. 490 BC).

10.1.9.3 Illustrations.

(1) ***The Prague Spring, 1968.*** In the 1960s, an economic recession weakened the communist control of Czechoslovakia. In January 1968, Alexander Dubcek succeeded Stalinist tyrant Antonin Novotny as Secretary of the Czechoslovakia Communist Party. With full central-committee support, he began to institute political and economic reforms unprecedented in a Communist-bloc country: a free press, an independent legal system and religious tolerance.

In March, public rallies were held in Prague and in other cities in support of reform policies. Novotny resigned as President. The Prague Spring represented the fullest flowering of democracy behind the Iron Curtain.

On May 8, officials from Bulgaria, Poland, Hungary, East Germany and the Soviet Union at a secret meeting discussed the situation in Czechoslovakia. On May 30, high-ranking Soviet military officers arrived with 16,000 soldiers at Sumava, (situated in the Bavarian Forest on the south-western frontiers of the Czechoslovakia Republic with Germany and Austria) for military exercises. That was the springboard to Czechoslovakia. Inspired by the liberal atmosphere in Prague, a group of intellectuals issued the "Two Thousand Words manifesto" in June, calling for the full implementation of democracy.

With that, the vigilant Soviet Union decided it had to exterminate all counter-revolutionary activities. In late July, Leonid Brezhnev (in office: 1964-1982), the General Secretary of the Communist Party of the Soviet Union, called Dubcek to Moscow for an official rebuke. A hero's welcome greeted Dubcek's return to Prague. On August 21, the Warsaw Pact troops invaded Czechoslovakia through the Bavarian Forest where the springboard had been established. The Prague Spring was crashed absolutely.

This military action served also as a warning to similar movements that might happen in other States of the Warsaw Pact.

(2) **The North Atlantic Treaty Organization (NATO) agreements**. On April 4, 1949, the North Atlantic Treaty was signed in Washington D.C. U.S. by ten West European countries (i.e. Belgium, Denmark, France, Iceland, Italy, Luxembourg, the Netherlands, Norway, Portugal and the United Kingdom) the U.S. and Canada. This Treaty created N.A.T.O. It was an alliance that brought together free and sovereign countries in order to defend Europe against Soviet Communism. An attack against one or more of them in Europe or North America should be considered an attack against them all.

By the Treaty, U.S. can place troops in European countries that are within the N.A.T.O. organization. This strategy has brought in mutual benefits to both parties. It was a measure to check against the spread of communism, and to promote exchanging ideas on democracy as a form of government. It has also enabled U.S. products to break into the European markets.

By this stratagem the U.S. has acquired the springboards to dispatch their troops at times when it is necessary, and to ease the problems of supply lines because they are in the allies' territories. After all, it is not the U.S. own homeland that is the potential battlefield.

10.1.9.4 Comments.

A springboard is an efficient means to enable one to explore an area that he is not familiar. As a military stratagem, this is an efficient means. After achieving the goal, how to deal with the springboard is another tactical problem. The springboard concept is a step-by-step approach to reach the objective. It is a trial and error way of doing things. One can gather more experiences in the course of experimentation. Both the Eastern Bloc and the Western Bloc demonstrated their skills in putting this concept in practice.

In human relations, it is absolutely not advisable to turn against somebody who has helped you, and it is an ethical problem. People will be scared to help you in the future, and the consequence will ruin one's reputation. Certainly the outcome is more damaging.

10.2 Action 24: To block the opponent's retreat path.

This action is to block the opponent's retreat and then with him.

10.2.1 The stratagem is: **Shut the door to catch the thief.** (One of the classical 36 Stratagems).

10.2.1.1 Theme.

When dealing with a small and weak enemy surround and destroy him. If you let him go, you will be at a disadvantage in capturing him later. By capturing them, not only one can prevent the enemy to be at large, but also to avoid him to collaborate with his allies.

Sun Tze said, "In the conduct of war, if one's forces are ten to the enemy's one, the best thing is to surround them; if five to one, the best thing is to attack them; and twice as numerous, the best thing is to divide them." (*The Art of War*, Chapter III). The pursuit of the running fugitives may endanger the hunters to fall into the fugitives' traps. It is a weary game to catch these malicious doers. They distract us from the more important matters. If there are no preparations in blocking the retreat paths of these people, it is advisable to let them go to avoid desperate confrontations.

10.2.1.2   Source.

A fugitive could do anything to fight back when he did not care about his life. In the *Art of Warfare* by Wu Tze, it tells a story about a fugitive on the run. He ran into the wilderness.   The hunter gathered a thousand men to catch the fugitive. All pursuers had to be alert, keeping their eyes wide open. They had to be shrewd as the wolves. What were the reasons for doing this?

It was because they were afraid that the fugitive would act violently in his desperate situation. When the fugitive did not care about his life, he could do anything to fight back. Because of this, all the one thousand men in the pursuit had to be alert.

For the not so strong enemy, one can besiege him and subdue him. However, if one has to hunt for his enemy, one must be very careful, because it could be dangerous.

This story is from *The Art of Warfare* by Wu Tze (c. 435-381 BC).

10.2.1.3   Illustrations.

(1) *Henry Ford II recruited a skilled technician by buying a company.* In the 1960s, the Ford Motor Company installed a large generator. But it did not work well. After hiring several different teams of technicians to redress the problem, the generator still did not function well.

Somebody told Henry Ford II that there was a German technician working in a small company. He was an expert on generators. Ford contacted the company to send in the technician to examine the generator. After testing the generator many times, the technician used a piece of chalk to mark on the outside of the machine. He said, "Here is the problem, cut away 16 coils of wire." After cutting away the coils of wire, the generator functioned perfectly.

Henry Ford II gave the technician ten thousand dollars, and invited him to join his company with a salary ten times the going rate of a technician. But the technician politely declined the offer. He said that the employer of the company was very kind to give him a job when he needed it badly after immigration to the U.S from Germany. He would never leave the company. Henry Ford II was thrilled by this man's attitude. Later, he bought that Company so as to have the technician to work for him.

(2) ***Higuchi Drug Store strategically located its shops to bring in more customers.*** When Higuchi Toshio opened his drug store in the 1970s, the business was not good. One day, he happened to read a book. It read, "By joing 3 points not on a straight line, a triangle is formed. The surface is a plane." He was in deep thought about this.

He thought if he had three shops located at the vertex of a triangle, these shops could coordinate with each other to capture more customers and to minimize the out of stock situations.

Accordingly, he worked hard and saved money to operate two more shops in strategical locations so as to serve the customers in the area inside the triangle, and around the vertices of the triangle. It looked as if the customers were trapped inside the triangle as created by the three shops when they wanted to buy drugs. Suppliers were willing to give generous discounts in bulk sale to the Higuchi shops. Moreover, the advertising campaigns of the stores were more cost effective.

Higuchi's speculation worked out successfully. Soon, it was replicated in many Japanese cities. Consequently Higuchi drug stores became one of the successful drug chain stores in Japan.

10.2.1.4 Comments.

A wise fighter keeps track of his enemy's harmful deeds and maneuvers the situation so that the enemy's accumulated misdeeds come home to the enemy himself. When the enemies are trapped in their misdeeds, it needs only to shut the door behind them and kill them all. We can do this only if we are sure that the enemies have exhausted practically all their energies and means, or we are perfectly sure that we can overwhelm the enemy in the situation.

In many cases, one has to be careful not to interfere with the enemies when they were making their home journey. "When the enemy is surrounded, one should leave an outlet free. One must not press a defeated enemy so hard they become desperate." (*The Art of War,* Chapter VII). Before the Iraq War in 2003, on March 17 at 20.01 ET, U. S. President George W. Bush told President Saddam Hussein of Iraq to leave with his sons from Iraq within 48 hours to avert military conflict with the U.S. Apparently Bush made available an escape outlet to Hussein.

Henry Ford II valued highly the technical knowledge and the personality of the German technician. He would not let the latter go. By buying the Company in which the technician worked, Ford "shut the door" to get the man. Higuchi Toshio enclosed his potential customers within the triangle and around its vertices set up by his strategically located shops.

10.3 Action 25: To monitor.

To monitor is to control the current situation to make sure that it stays on track towards its goals. Sun Tze said, "... and the command and control structure so that everything can be deployed to the best advantage." (*The Art of War,* Chapter I).

10.3.1 The stratagem is: **Not to be bound by fixed rules, but vary the plan according to the situation of the enemy.**

10.3.1.1 Theme.

> Water has the unique characteristics of flexibility and adaptability. It was used as an analogy to illustrate the flexibility of deploying armies. It is fitting strategies to the circumstances of the enemy and the situation on the battlefield. (*The Art of War,* Chapter XI).
>
> "One should not be bound by fixed rules of conduct but vary his plans according to the requirements of the enemy until one can win a decisive battle." (*The Art of War,* Chapter XI)
>
> "The general who knows how to vary and adapt to changing situation so as to gain advantages is skilful in the art of war." (*The Art of War,* Chapter VIII).
>
> Norbert Wiener (1894-1964) defined cybernetics as "the science of control and communication, in the animal and the machine." Coordination, regulation and control are its themes (1948). Sun certainly had some rudiments of the cybernetics concepts in his book.

10.3.1.2 Source.

Sun Tze, *Art of War,* refer to 10.3.1.1.

10.3.1.3 Illustrations.

(1) *The Second Battle of El Alamein marked a turning point in WWII.* On August 18, 1942, Bernard L. Montgomery, known as "Monty", assumed control of the British 8th Army which had been driven back into Egypt by Field Marshal Erwin Rommel of the Axis with his Afrika Korps. He put a great deal of emphasis on organization and morale. He made a concerted effort to appear before troops as often as possible, frequently visiting various units and

making himself known to the men. He was determined to lead the army to fight the battles in a unified manner according to a detailed plan. All contingency plans for retreat were destroyed.

On August 30, 1942, Rommel attacked Alam el Halfa but was repulsed by the 8th Army (Battle of Alam el Halfa, August 30-September 6.) Monty implemented a number of unconvectional deceptions in the ensuing months to take by surprise on the Axis, not only as to the exact location of the forthcoming battles, but as to when the battles were likely to occur. The operation was codenamed "Operation Bertram". (Refer to 4.2.1.3 (2)).

After meticulous preparations, Monty launched an attack on the Axis forces entrenched at El Alamein in North Egypt on October 23. It came at the worst time for the Afrika Korps as Rommel was on sick leave in Austria. His replacement General George Stumme was killed during an Allied air raid on October 24. Rommel rushed back to the combat zones. Since he no longer had the resources to hold his line, he ordered his troops to withdraw. When the Axis lines broke, the British 8th Army pursued the enemy remnants into Libya and beyond.

Winston Churchill wrote in his memoirs about this war (October 23-November 3, 1942), "Before Alamein we never had a victory. After Alamein we never had a defeat."

(2) *Tommy Franks maintained that war should be fought based on adaptability and flexibility.* On March 19, 2003, the coalition forces of the U.S. and U.K. against Iraq was led by General Tommy Franks. He was well versed in Sun Tze's *Art of War*. The coalition forces encountered fierce resistance from the Iraqi forces and Franks had to face repeated questioning by the media why a larger U.S. force was not committed to the war in the first place. As at end March 2003, the U.S. had only 90,000 soldiers in Iraq, when many other military analysts would deploy at least 250,000.

Franks argued that the war would be a campaign characterised by shock, by surprise, by flexibility to make it so overwhelming that the adversary would quickly realize that there was no real alternative other than to fight and die or to give up. He maintained that war should be fought based on adaptability and flexibility. More troops would be committed when the scenario deserved that.

10.3.1.4 Comments.

General Bernard L. Montgomery managed to transform the morale of the 8th Army quickly. All contingency plans for retreat were destroyed, showing the determination never to retreat without winning victory. Monty made meticulous preparations in stocking supplies, and in implementing deception tactics preparing for the next confrontation. His offensive approach turned the scenario around to the Allies' favour by making the enemy feel at loss as to where to put up defense.

Monty was able to vary his plans according to the situation of the enemy. Therefore he displayed the brilliant leadership that firmly established his reputation as one of the greatest generals of WWII.

On January 10, 2007, President George W. Bush in his President Address to the Nation acknowledged the failing of his strategy for U. S. forces in Iraq. He announced a troop boosting plan of sending 20,000 to 22,000 men into Iraq. The sceptics doubted the wisdom of adding more troops, saying that the problem in Iraq was not troop strength. The war became primarily a sectarian struggle, and U. S. had no business being in the middle of a civil war.

Exercises

1.   In June 2002, President George W. Bush (in office: 2001-2009) in a commencement address at West Point talked about pre-emptive attack.   Surveying the post-September 11 scenarios, Bush said "If we wait for threats to fully materialize, we will have waited too long... We must take the battle to the enemy, disrupt his plans and confront the worst threats before they emerge."

Pre-emptive attack did happen at the start of the Six-Day War in 1967, when Israel fearing that Egypt was aiming to destroy the Jewish state, devastated Egypt's air force before its pilots had scrambled their jets. In 1981, Israel bombed the Osirak nuclear reactor in Iraq without warning, an incident that provoked worldwide disapproval.

Which of the following stratagems best describes Bush's move?
(a) Outwit by novelty.
(b) Gain the initiative by striking first.
(c) Offend in order to defend.
(d) Shut the door to catch the thief.

2. Skywriting is a form of advertising in which a pilot writes out a brief slogan, a catchphrase, or draws a simple diagram by smokes in the sky. The picture will only last as long as winds are relatively calm and the sky is clear.

On August 2, 1990, Iraq invaded and annexed Kuwait. It prompted the Gulf War (January 16-February 28, 1991) between Iraq and a coalition of 28 nations led by the U.S. Air offensive lasting six weeks during which "smart" weapons came of age, destroying one-third of Iraqi equipments and inflicted casualties.

One night, the coalition forces stopped the air raids. Two jets flew at high speed to draw a picture of the Iraqi flag over the sky of Baghdad. The aerial manoeuvres captured the attention of both the Iraqi and the coalition forces. The Iraqi soldiers were amazed, and shouted out with enthusiasm.

Then, the jets came back; each of them drew a diagonally white line, making an "X" over the Iraqi flag. The Iraqi soldiers were shocked and disenchanted, while the coalition forces started another wave of air raids. Iraq soon lost the war.

What was the stratagem used by the coalition forces in thwarting the morale of the Iraqi troops?

3.   In 1942, the Allies lost a considerable amount of merchant ships in the Atlantic Ocean due to German U-boat (submarine) attacks and lack of adequate air cover in the mid-Atlantic.

In U.K. Lord Louis Mountbatten was Chief of Combined Operations and part of the work of this department was to develop technology and equipment for offensive operations. One idea was that of an iceberg aircraft carrier. It was the idea of Geoffrey Pyke. As ice was unsinkable, the berg ship would be insulated and impervious to bomb and torpedo attacks. It would be easy to repair the holes by filling in water which would then be frozen.

One defect of ice was that it split too easily. Another scientist Max Ferdinand Perutz contributed by the discovery of pykrete that was a composite substance made of 14% sawdust or some other form of wood pulp and 86% ice by weight. Pykrete had small melting rate, and vastly improved strength and toughness over ordinary ice, actually close to concrete. The project was codenamed "Habbakuk", enthusiastically endorsed by both Mountbatten and Winston Churchill.

A prototype of the berg ship was built on Patricia Lake, Jaspar, Alberta in Canada. The berg ship was a complete success; it did not melt all through the summer. Eventually, the Habbakuk project never went beyond its experimental stage, because the U.S. had a secret weapon – the atomic bomb – in development to be used against Japan. It was an end to the war that would be brought about not by ice but by fire.

Which of the following stratagems best describes the objective of the Habbakuk project?
(a) Their name is Legion.
(b) Offend in order to defend.
(c) Outwit by novelty.
(d) Break the cauldron and sink the boats.

4.   Let us revisit the story of Count Peter Rumantsiev (refer to 10.1.6.3) leading his men to break through the siege.

If the Grand Vizier allowed an escape route to the Russian troops, or gave the Russian troops the choice of surrender without reprehension, what would likely be the outcome?

5.   The wind and the sun happened to challenge each other in ripping off the overcoats of the people walking in the fields. The wind blew hard, but the people in the fields embraced their overcoats tightly. No matter how hard it tried, its efforts were in vain.

Next, the sun had its turn. It radiated gently through the sky. Soon, everybody took off his or her overcoats. The sun said to the wind, "Kindness and warmth are more compelling than anger and violence. Always be good to others, and it will make a better world."

Which one of the following stratagems best describes the tactic used in the parable?
(a) Their name is Legion.
(b) Offend in order to defend.
(c) Outwit by novelty.
(d) Work on the hearts and minds of others.

6. In 1939, the German military established a rocket research site on the north German coast at Peenemunde. Scientists could conduct rocket test flights over water with monitoring along 200 miles of the coast.

In March 1943, British intelligence taped conversations between two German generals that confirmed they were building rockets in Peenemunde. The British Cabinet Defense Committee ordered Operation Crossbow to destroy the missile site. The primary objective of the raid was to kill as many personnel involved in the missile program as possible, so the housing area was the main target. Two lesser objectives were to destroy as many of the weapons production machines and documentation as possible, and to render Peenemunde unless as a reseach site.

In the evening of August 17, 1943, in order to divert German night fighters, a group of de Havillard Mosquitos (combat aircraft) conducted air raid on Berlin. Due to the proximity of Berlin and Peenemunde, German Luftwaffe (air force) was lured to Berlin. Meanwhile, nearly 600 aircraft of the Bomber Command changed their courses to raid at Peenemunde. They used low level attack tactics to achieve precision bombing. They dropped nearly 1800 tons of bombs on Peenemunde, 85 percent of this tonage was high explosive. The raid killed approximately 180 Germans, 500-600 foreigners mostly Poles in the workers camp and Dr. Walter Thiel, deputy director of the Army Research Center at Peenemunde.

Which one of the following best describes the stratagem used in Operation Crossbow to conduct the air raid at Peenemunde?

(a) Defeat the enemy by capturing their chief.
(b) Remove the ladder after the ascent.
(c) Shut the door to catch the thief.
(d) Borrow a safe passage to conquer Guo.

7.   Let us revisit the Prague Spring 1968 mentioned in 10.1.9.3. On August 3, 1968, representatives from Bulgaria, Poland, Hungary, East Germany, Czechoslovakia and the Soviet Union met in Bratislava and signed a declaration. It affirmed unshakable fidelity to Marxim-Leninism and proletarian internationalism. After the conference, Soviet troops left Czechoslovakia territory but remained along its border.

The Soviets were not satisfied with the talks and began to consider a military alternative. Leonid Brezhnev, the vigilant Soviet Party Secretary, decided he had to exterminate all counter-revolutionary activities as they would weaken the position of the Eastern Bloc during the Cold War.

In the night of August 20-21, 200,000 Warsaw Pact troops from the Eastern Bloc countries and 2,000 tanks invaded Czechoslovakia. Alexander Dubcek and a few Czechoslovak political leaders were arrested and taken to Moscow for negotiations. On August 25, they had to sign the Moscow Protocol that promised to protect socialism in Czechoslovakia, to restrain critical Czechoslovak media, and to reject any interference in the Eastern Bloc by the U. N. Security Council. Dubcek would remain in office for the moment.

What was the stratagem used by the Warsaw Pact to intervene Czechoslovakia political matters when its troops invaded Prague?

8.   During his term, U.S. President John Quincy Adams (in office: 1825-29) worked on a high tariff system to finance infrastructure development, such as road-building and a national bank to encourage productive enterprise and to launch a national currency.

Anne Newport Royall, a female reporter, had sought an interview with Adams but was repeatedly turned away at the White House. Then, she found out Adams' habit. Adams was an early riser. He often left the White House at the break of dawn, took a brisk walk to the nearby Potomac River, took off his clothes, swan in nude, dried himself off and returned to the White House before most people woke up.

One day, when Adams was in water, he noticed that a woman (i.e. Royall) sat atop his clothing on the river bank. Royall expressed her wish to make an interview with him. Adams asked if he could take a moment and get dressed, but she demanded he answered her questions while he was still in the water. Adams had to compel her wishes. It was an interview on Adams' views on matters relating to banks.

That was a remarkable incident in U.S. history in which a one-on-one interview between a female reporter and a nude President.

Which one of the followings best describes the stratagem used by Anne Newport Royall to get a one-on-one interview with John Quincy Adams?
(a) Defeat the enemy by capturing their chief.
(b) Remove the ladder after the ascent.
(c) Shut the door to catch the thief.
(d) Borrow a safe passage to conquer Guo.

9.   The Continental System of trade restrictions was designed by Napoleon Bonaparte to paralyse the U.K. through the destruction of the British economy. Economic warfare had been carried out before 1806, but the system itself was initiated by the Berlin Decree (1806) which claimed that the British blockade of purely commercial ports was contrary to international law. It was extended by the Milan Decree (1807) and the Fontainebleau Decree (1810) which forbade trade with Great Britain on the part of France, her allies and neutrals.

On July 7, 1807, after defeating both Prussia and Russia, Bonaparte compelled these two countries to join the Continental System to ally France and to boycott all trade with the U.K. by the Treaty of Tilsit. The U.K. retaliated by a counter-blockade which led indirectly to the War of 1812. Due to U.K.'s naval superiority, the counter-blockade was harmful to Bonaparte, because it alienated France from its allies.

What was the stratagem used by Napoleon Bonaparte in his economic warfare against the U.K.?

10. The Six-Day War in 1967 occurred between Israel and its Arab neighbours. Suez Canal was closed for some time and the sea route for oil tankers between Atlantic Ocean and Indian Ocean was intercepted. After the war, a Greek Oil Tanker Company was eager to look for more customers. Its director made a phone call to the British Petroleum Company (BP) which was the second largest chemical company in the U.K.

It offered a very competitive price to lease all its tankers to BP. But the reply must be received in 24 hours. Peter Walters, an executive vice president at that moment was to take the call. According to the Company's procedure, he did not have the power to make the decision. Meanwhile, Mr. Nelson, the Company's CEO was on a business trip to the U.S. Walters thought about the pening problem for a whole morning, considering all the risks incurred to the company. He made the decision to lease all the tankers of the Greek Oil Tanker Company.

Since Suez Canal was closed, all tankers had to take the route passed the Cape of Good Hope between Atlantic Ocean and Indian Ocean. Leasing all the tankers saved BP a lot of money. It proved that Walters made the right decision at the right time. Later, Walters took BP's helm in 1981.

What is the best stratagem to describe Peter Walters' action in this business deal? What are the pros and cons of taking this move?

Chapter 11.

To avoid and to reverse

11.0 Introduction.

Actions 26-28 are all negative actions, indicating the strategist is in an unfavourable position, so he would like to avoid something, to reverse the situation or to use some special stratagems to help. We cover Actions 26-27 (to avoid and to reverse) in this Chapter, and Action 28 in Chapter 12.

11.1 Action 26: To avoid.

In the course of combat, the strategist may find that the scenario has changed, and the opponent is on the favoured side. Now, he tries his best to avoid the adverse consequences. In the case of indictment for a crime, the accused keeps silent about major charges while admitting minor ones, or to dwell on other issues to distract attention.

11.1.1 The stratagems are:
    (I) **Avoid the important and dwell on the trivial.**
    (II) **Aim at swift victory and avoid prolonged campaign.**

259

(I) **Avoid the important and dwell on the trivial.**

11.1.1.1 Theme.

> To be able to avoid something happening is a very effective measure to reduce the risk to undergo the adverse consequences of confrontation with the enemy. This is especially true when the enemy is stronger. Sun Tze said, "One should avoid strength and attack weakness." (*The Art of War,* Chapter I).
>
> Many times, this stratagem is used as a temporary measure for relief. One has to wait for the best moment to deal with the more important matters or grapple with the more powerful enemy.
>
> Being in the adverse situation, you try to distract your enemy by focusing on minor issues. Deal with the major issues later when the situation is more favourable to you. Defendants of charges in courts keep silent about major charges and admit minor charges.

11.1.1.2 Source.

Zhuge Liang suggested no dealing with Cao Cao for the time being. In the late Second Century, the Han Dynasty lost control and authority. Warlords fought each other for power. Liu Bei had a virtuous reputation, and he would like to restore the rule of the Dynasty. However there were many strong competitors, such as Cao Cao, Yuan Shao and Sun Quan to name a few. In 207, Liu Bei was told by a learned man that in order to be successful, he must recruit the right advisor for help. It would be either the Hidden Dragon or the Phoenix Fledgling.

Liu found out that Zhuge Liang was the Hidden Dragon. Zhuge lived a cloistered life filled with introspection and studies of the classics. On the first and second visit, Zhuge's apprentice turned away Liu Bei. Finally, due to Liu's perseverance, on his third visit he was allowed to see the wise man. Liu outlined his desires to restore the Han Dynasty to its former state of glory. Zhuge was pleased with his goals and offered him advice based on Cao Cao's recent victory over Yuan Shao.

"Cao Cao did not have the power to overcome Yuan Shao, but he beat him with clever strategy. Now he has controlled the imperial court and uses it as a tool to control a vast military. Hence, you should avoid conflict with him at this time. Sun Quan is successful in the east of the Yangtze River; his family has held the area for three generations. He has the military strength therefore rather than attacking him you must befriend him. If you look to the west, Yizhou is a fertile land and holds auspicious meaning for your pursuit; it was the land of the founder of the Han Empire."

In other words, Zhuge pointed out that in order to achieve Liu's goal, the latter had to avoid confrontation with Cao Cao, the strongest competitor, at the moment. Meanwhile, Liu needed to ally with Sun Quan, and to acquire a base which might be Yizhou to work with. Thus, Zhuge had the vision of the Three Kingdoms design in his first meeting with Liu.

The story is from *Romance of Three Kingdoms* by Luo Guanzhong (c. 1330-1400).

11.1.1.3 Illustrations.

(1) ***Edward Kennedy's accident at Chappaquiddick in 1969.*** On July 19, 1969, when Edward Kennedy (1932-2009), aged 37 then, drove back from a party in Chappaquiddick, Massachusetts, his car went off the edge of a bridge. He was not severely injured. Edward's wife did not attend the party. However, Mary Jo Kopechne, a 29 years old blond secretary who was with him was killed. Kopechne had worked for Senator Robert F. Kennedy and Senator George Smanthers.

The accident was not reported until nine hours after the car sank into the river. Kennedy was charged for leaving the scene of the accident. In Massachusetts, a manslaughter charge was always given when someone left the scene of a deadly accident.

In fact, Kennedy's driver's license had expired on February 22, 1969 (nearly 5 months before the accident) and had not been renewed. But this problem was "fixed" by officials at the Registry of Motor Vehicles before the legal proceedings began. Moreover, Kennedy had a record of serious traffic violations in Virginia. But these traffic violations did not show up in the Inquest due to the fact that they were regarded as out-of-state convictions.

In Kennedy's written statement to the police, he wrote: "I was driving my car on Main Street on my way to get the ferry back to Edgartown. I was unfamiliar with the road and turned right onto Dike Road (leading to the accident site) instead of bearing hard left on Main Street..." But, at the Inquest, however, the judge concluded that Kennedy drove over Chappaquiddick Road (the Main Road) three times, and over Dike Road and Dike Bridge twice the day before. It was very suspicious that Kennedy was found in a car with a young woman who was not his wife in the late hours (11:15 p.m. July 18 to 12:45 a.m. July 19). Kennedy claimed that he delayed reporting the accident to the authorities because he was "confused and in shock". His statements about his rescue attempts suggested that in fact he was quite aware that Kopechne's life was at stake and that prompt actions were needed.

However, a police detective said Kennedy's actions did not reflect a state of shock, but instead suggested a deliberate and calculated effort to cover up his involvement in the accident, while at the same time concealing the fate of Kopechne from those who could have saved her if prompt actions were taken.

On July 25, 1969, Kennedy pled guilty to leaving the scene of an accident. He was sentenced to serve two months in the House of Correction at Barnstable. But, the sentence was suspended.

(2) *The Iran-Contra Affair in 1985.* In 1985, while Iran and Iraq were at war, Iran made a secret request to buy weapons from the U.S. The Iran-Contra Affair occurred. It was a secret arrangement to provide $30 million to the Nicaraguan right-wing Contra guerrillas from profits gained by selling arms to Iran. Congress had strictly prohibited sale of arms to a government, like Iran, deemed hostile to the U.S. as well as aid to the Contras.

Robert C. McFarlane, one of the national security advisers, sought President Ronald Reagan's (in office: 1981-1989) approval, in spite of the embargo against selling arms to Iran. He explained that the sale of arms would not only improve U.S. relations with Iran, but might in turn lead to improved relations with Lebanon, increasing U.S. influence in the Middle East. Meanwhile, Reagan had become frustrated because he was unable to secure the release of the seven American hostages being held by the Iranian terrorists in Lebanon. As President, Reagan felt that "he had the duty to bring those Americans home."

The arms-for-hostages proposal divided the administration. Long-time policy adversaries Defense Secretary Caspar Weinberger and State Secretary George Shultz opposed the deal, but Reagan, McFarlane and C.I.A. Director William Casey supported it. With the backing of the President, the plan proceeded.

By the time the sales were discovered, more than 1,500 missiles had been shipped to Iran. Three hostages had been released, only to be replaced with three more, in what the State Secretary Shultz called "a hostage bazaar."

Discovery of the arrangement in 1985-1986 shook President Reagan's administration. Most directly involved were Adm. John M. Poindexter and Marine Lt. Col. Oliver North, both of the National Security Council (N.S.C.). It was deemed "unclear" whether Reagan and then-Vice President George H. W. Bush were also involved, though North later claimed Reagan knew of the secret arrangement. But Reagan later testified in court that he did not "recall".

While probing the question of the arms-for-hostages deal, Attorney General Edwin Meese discovered that only $12 million of the $30 million the Iranians reportedly paid had reached government coffers. North explained the discrepancy: he had been diverting funds from the arms sales to the Contras, with the full knowledge of Poindexter and with the unspoken blessing, he assumed, of President Reagan.

Speculation about the involvement of Reagan, George H. W. Bush and the administration at large grew rankly. Poindexter resigned, and North was fired, but the Iran-Contra was far from over. Independent Counsel Lawrence Walsh investigated the matter for the next eight years. Fourteen people were charged with either operational or "cover-up" crimes. In the end, North's conviction was overturned on a technicality, and President George H. W. Bush (in office: 1989-1993) issued six pardons during his term, including one to McFarlane who had already been convicted and one to Weinberger before the latter stood trial.

11.1.1.4 Comments.

There were a lot of cover-ups in both the Chappaquiddick accident and the Iran-Contra Affairs. Edward Kennedy pled guilty to leaving the scene of an accident despite of the fact that similar cases could be charged as manslaughter. This one incident gave him and his family a bad name and caused him to decide not to run for the U.S. Presidency any more.

In the Inquest on the Iran-Contra Affair, Oliver North was in the limelight. Obviously, the stratagem "The plum tree dies for the peach tree" was used. (Refer to 13.1.1). His conviction was overturned on a technicality. Again, the focus was on the trivial. However, in spite of the Iran-Contra Affair, Ronald Reagan has always been regarded as one of the most honest Presidents in the U.S. history.

(II) **Aim at swift victory and avoid prolonged campaign.**

11.1.2.1 Theme.

> Speed and aggressiveness usually defeat a static defense. But one should avoid a protracted war. Sun Tze said, "In the conduct of war speed is most important." (*The Art of War,* Chapter XI).
>
> He emphasized that the purpose of raising a large army was to secure swift and decisive victories in war. Once a war becomes protracted, it is hard to predict its outcome, and it will incur high costs.
>
> "The stupid may sometimes score quick success but even the cleverest fails in a protracted warfare. There has never been a case where a prolonged warfare proved beneficial to any state." (*The Art of War,* Chapter II).

11.1.2.2 Source.

Sun Tze, *The Art of War,* refer to 11.1.2.1.

11.1.2.3 Illustrations.

(1) ***Nazi Germany's Blitzkrieg (Lightning War).*** Blitzkrieg was an offensive military doctrine which involved an initial bombardment followed by the use of motorized mobile forces attacking with speed and surprise to prevent an enemy from taking a coherent defense. It was instituated by the Wehrmacht (armed forces of Germany) in the invasion of Western Europe and initial operation against the Soviet Union. Its success was based on astounded movements, general enemy unpreparedness and an inability to react quickly according to the situation.

On September 1, 1939, Nazi Germany invaded Poland by the tactic of blitzkrieg. In mid September, the Soviet Union occupied the Eastern Part of Poland according to the secret terms of the Molotov-Ribbentrop Pact (Tready of Non-aggression between Germany and the Soviet Union) signed on August 23, a few weeks earlier. In April, 1940, Germany invaded Demark and Norway. Demark immediately capitulated, and Norway was subjugated in two months despite of support from the Allies.

On May 10, Germany attacked France and the Low Countries. The Netherlands and Belgium were overwhelmed by the blitzkrieg tactic in a few weeks. The British Expeditionary Force sent to help the French and the Belgian armies against the Germans had to evacuate from the continent at Dunkirk on May 26.

The Battle of France (May 10- June 21) was a decisive German victory. Paris fell on June 14. France had to sign the Second Armistice at Compiegne on June 22, establishing a German occupation zone in Northern France.

(2) *The Vietnam War 1969-1975.* It is also known as the American War in Vietnam. It took place from 1969 to April 10, 1975, with the North Vietnamese victory at the end. At various stages the war involved clashes between small units patrolling the mountains and jungles, amphibian operations, guerrilla attacks on the villages and urban areas, and large-scale conventional battles.

It offers a classical example of the negative impact of a protracted military campaign. The U.S. troops had to be rotated regularly to prevent them from being worn out. As the war dragged on, additional and compulsory military conscription was introduced, causing greater protests and declined support among the U.S. citizens. Eventually the U.S. had to concede defeat and withdraw from Vietnam on April 10, 1975. The Vietnam War caused U.S. military casualties of 58,209 deaths, 2,000 missing and 305,000 wounded.

11.1.2.4 Comments.

Alexander Vasilyevich Suvorov (1729-1800), the greatest Russian commander of all time, rarely if ever lost a battle, usually won without losing many troops. He achieved seemingly impossible victories. Suvorov's innovative offensive operations, employing long, rapid marches and surprise attacks supported by his detailed training of his men, gained him the enduring admiration of the Russian people. One of his aphorisms on war was "Speed is essential, but haste harmful" sharing similar thesis with that of Sun Tze.

On March 20, 2003, the U.S.-led War for Iraqi Freedom began. It was originally planned to be a short war that would end within a couple of weeks. The U.S. used a "shock and awe" strategy supported by precision and heavy bombing to bring down Saddam Hussein and his regime. Unfortunately the U.S. met with severe resistance even after the fall of Hussein. The war evolved to be civil war within Iraq, and U.S. had to increase its troops to deal with the increased threats.

On October 12, 2007, Lieutenant-General Ricardo Sanchez, U.S. former Commander in Baghdad for a year after the 2003 invasion, issued a damning indictment of the War. He denounced President George W. Bush's government as "incompetent" and "negligent" for presiding over "a nightmare with no end in sight." Apparently, the U.S. has not learned the lessons from the Vietnam War.

11.2 Action 27: To reverse.

The best defence is to offend. The strategist tries to reverse the prevailing condition. When it is not possible to offend by the conventional means, one can do it by other means.

11.2.1 The stratagem is: **Turn the guest into the host.** (One of the classical 36 Stratagems).

11.2.1.1 Theme.

> Defeat the enemy from within by infiltrating his camp under the guise of co-operation, surrender or peace treaties. Extend your influence skilfully stepwise so as to swallow up the enemy.
>
> In ancient China, a noble usually provided food and lodgings to his "hangers-on". There were two classes of these "hangers-on" or guests: temporary and permanent. The temporary guests could not participate in the noble's business. The permanent guests were in the inner circle of the noble by his favour. The latter participated actively in running the noble's business. Gradually these guests achieved the status of being regarded as the hosts.
>
> Literally, the term "host" stands also for the offense role, on the positive side, and being active while the "guest" stands for the defense role, on the negative side, and being passive.

11.2.1.2 Source.

Chunshen was tricked by an opportunist.   In China, King Kaoliewang (reigned 262-238 BC) of the Chu State was barren. His Prime Minister Lord Chunshen (314-238 BC) worried about this. All the high officials in those days kept a group of hangers-on in their houses. These hangers-on were proficient on a particular skill, and they helped their master to carry out various jobs.

Li Yuen, an opportunist, hatched a scheme. As a first step, Li submitted himself as a hanger-on of Lord Chunshen. Then, he offered his younger sister as one of Chunshen's concubines. Soon, the girl was pregnant. Next, Li instructed the girl to talk to Chunshen, "King Kaoliewang has got no heirs. When he passed away, his brother would be the successor. He has his own favoured confidants. As you are not his confidant, you will be cast away to obscurity."

Chunshen agreed to her analysis and asked for suggestions. The girl said, "I am now pregnant. Since King Kaoliewang trusted your lordship, it would be wise to offer me to the King as a concubine. If I can give birth to a boy, the boy will be the successor to the throne, and you will continue to hold your official post without any worry."

Chunshen did accordingly. Then, the King's new concubine gave birth to a boy who became the heir of the Kingdom. Gradually, Li as an uncle of the prince grew powerful and schemed to eliminate Chunshen. In spite of the warnings by some of his hangers-on, Chunshen found it difficult to believe that Li would do anything harmful to him, because he had been kind to Li and they collaborated in the succession plot.

In 238 BC, King Kaoliewang passed away. Li took the initiative to hide some of his troops in the palace. When Chunshen showed up in the funeral, he was murdered on the spot. Chunshen learned his lesson of "to return evil for good" in a tragic way. Li took over Chunshen's official post.

11.2.1.3 Illustrations.

(1) ***Toyota surpassed General Motors in global auto sales in April 2007.*** Toyota Motor Corporation was founded by Toyoda Kiichiro (1894-1952) as a spin of his father's company Toyota Industries to make automobiles in 1937. Early vehicles had their designs based on the Dodge Power Wagon and Chevrolet.

In 1957, Toyota entered the American market. At that time, General Motors (GM) accounted for half of the American auto market, and four out of every five cars in the world were being produced in the U.S. Toyota was a small company that only produced 25,000 cars, compared to 4 million manufactured by GM. With the exception of individual years in the 1970s and 1980s when production was cut due to labor strikes, GM has held the number-one spot for every year since 1931 including the depths of the Great Depression years.

Based on many market research conducted in U.S., Toyota adopted the strategy to produce small fuel-efficient cars to a high level of quality. Gradually, GM, Ford Motors and Chrysler had to struggle for survival as Toyota and other Japanese cars continued to cut into their market shares with the rise of gasoline prices. In 2003, Toyota surpassed Ford Motors in terms of vehicles sales. During the first three months of 2007, Toyota sold more cars and trucks worldwide than General Motors for the first time ever, as the Japanese company moved closer to becoming the world's largest automaker in terms of annual global sales.

(2) **Mark Twain: The magician muttered, and knew not what he muttered.** Samuel Langhorne Clemens (1835-1910) better known by his pen name Mark Twain, was an American humorist, satirist and writer. He enjoyed immense public popularity and his keen wit and incisive satire were remarkable.

In his book *Eruption,* he wrote, "A banquet is probably the most fatiguing thing in the world except ditchdigging. It is the insanest of all recreations."

Once, he attended a banquet in which people talked and laughed loudly. He preferred a quieter environement. He talked to a woman sitting next to him about this, and the woman agreed with him. He hatched a plot that required the help of the woman who was willing to do so. He told her to lean her head to him pretending to listen carefully to something interesting while he muttered. Soon, some people caught sight of this, and stopped talking because they would like to hear what Twain was saying. Gradually, silence prevailed in the banquet hall, and Twain was still muttering.

Now Twain stood up and say, "Ladies and gentlemen, we had an experiment. The objective was to reduce the rumbling sound a moment ago in this hall. I think many of us here prefer a civilized and calm environment for dining." All the people agreed to Twain's point of view, and they enjoyed the banquet in a serene atmosphere.

11.2.1.4 Comments.

The steps in reversing the positions of the host and the guest are gradual moves:
(a) to be permitted to come as a "guest",
(b) to make use of any opportunity to sell one's skills,
(c) to get into the inner circle of the host,
(d) to grab the power and to lead, and
(e) to establish oneself as the leader of the main stream.

This stratagem enables one to swallow up an ally instead of an enemy, and the turning over process is gradual. It aims at role reversal with the other side. Some critics took the long-awaited eclipsing of GM symbolic not only for what it reflected the demise as the once-mighty automobile giant, but also for what it revealed the decline of American capitalism in the present scenario.

Mark Twain was a guest at the party. He and some of the guests preferred to enjoy the banquet in a serene atmosphere. Twain was able to make it, while the actual host might find it difficult to do himself.

Exercises

1. In 1975, Mr. Black (fictitious name) of a Food Processing Company in U.S. happened to read from the newspaper about the outbreak of foot and mouth disease in livestock in a small Mexican town. He believed that such disease might spread to Texas and California which were major meat supply states.

Black hired a veterinarian to make a trip to ground zero to investigate the matter. Later, the veterinarian confirmed the news. Immediately, Black raised all the funds to purchase as much frozen meat (beef and pork) as possible, and transported all these meat to the storage depots in the East Coast. Sometime later, the outbreak of the foot and mouth disease spread to the West Coast of the U.S. The Food and Drug Administration (FDA) banned all meat products from on the West Coast from the market. The price of meat soared, and Black made a fortune of nine million dollars in this venture.

Which of the following strategies best describes the moral of the story?
(a) Avoid the important and dwell on the trivial.
(b) Fish in murky waters.
(c) Speed is essential.
(d) Aim at swift victory and avoid prolonged campaign.

2. Once there was a man who quarreled with somebody on a loan outstanding. Then, they fought against each other, and the man picked up an axe. He wounded the other person's leg, and he was taken to court, charged for assault with an axe. His lawyer defended him, claiming that during the struggle, the axe fell out from his hand, dropping onto the other person's leg.

What was the stratagem used by his lawyer?
(a) Turn the guest into the host.
(b) Avoid the important and dwell on the trivial.

(c) Aim at swift victory and avoid prolonged campaign.

(d) Outwit by novelty.

3.   In 1940, Operation Sealion was Germany's plan to invade the United Kingdom. But the operation was postponed indefinitely on September 17, 1940 by Adolf Hitler because he was aware that Germany could not get control of the skies. The operation lapsed, never to be resumed.

Meanwhile, Hitler was convinced that U. K. would sue for peace when Germany triumphed over Soviet Union. Operation Barbarossa was the codename for Germany's invasion of Soviet Union. Due to the military strength of Soviet Union, Hitler deployed many deceptive tactics to cover the operation. Cargoes of "military supplies" were loaded on trains to the shores of the British Channel. A lot of commotions were created by the battleships, landing exercises and mobile troops. Bombers frequently made their attacks to the British skies. In fact, by June 1941, three million German soldiers were assembled in the East Front.

Diplomatic ties between Germany and Soviet Union were cordial. Senior Nazi officials praised the relationship between the two countries established by the Molotov-Ribbentrop (or Nazi-Soviet) Pact signed on August 23, 1939. Hitler spoke publicly on the favourable relations with the Soviets.

On June 22 1941, Operation Barbarossa was launched. Hitler was over-confident due to his success on the Western Front. He expected victory in a few months and he did not prepare for a war lasting into the winter. By the Blitzkrieg tactic, the German armies penetrated 100 km into the Soviet territories in a week. At the end of July, the German armies reached 600-700 km beyond the Soviet borders.

(i)   The Blitzkrieg tactic required some of the following strategems to make it effective. Identify these stratagems.

(a) Avoid the important and dwell on the trivial.

(b) Besiege Wei to rescue Zhao.

(c) Gain the initiative by striking first.
(d) Hide a dagger in a smile.
(e) Make a feint to the east and attack the west.
(f) To win hands down.
(g) Turn the guest into the host.

(ii) Napolean Bonaparte invaded Russia with about 600,000 men and over 50,000 horses in the 1800s. Use web searching to find out the date to begin his campaign, compare it to that of Adolf Hitler's, and one will be thrilled by the finding.

4. In the Seventeenth Century, the Qing Dynasty in China adopted a close-door policy, not to trade with foreigners. The British came to China, looking for trade opportunities, and they were disappointed. Finally the British thought of a snare to hook the Chinese people on opium. By doing so it created the need not only to trade with Britain, but making them dependent on the British in the opium trade.

Which of the following stratagems was used by the British merchants?
(a) Avoid the important and dwell on the trivial.
(b) Aim at swift victory and avoid prolonged campaign.
(c) Work on the hearts and minds of others.
(d) Turn the guest into the host.

5. Since 1950s, the Soviet Union had always tried to extend its broad gauge railway lines into Eastern European countries for strategic reasons. But the latter declined such action, saying that they had no interest.

In early 1970s, the giant Huta Katowice steel mill was built in Southern Poland. The new steel mill had to install large amount of machinery. The Polish authority sought the aid of the Soviet Union which expressed its consent to help. A contract was signed.

Then the Soviet authority revealed that in order to transport the machinery to Poland, the existing Polish standard gauge railway tracks were inadequate. An entirely new broad gauge line had to be built to transport the machinery and later on the iron ore from Ukraine to the steel mill. The line ran as a single track line for almost 400 km from the Polish-Ukrainian border to Slawkow (near Katowice). Without the new machinery, the steel mill project had to be scrapped.

The Polish authority had no choice, but gave its consent to the building of the broad gauge rail. The construction began on November 15, 1976 and completed on November 30, 1979.

It was the westernmost broad gauge railway line in Europe that was connected to the broad gauge rail system of the countries which before 1991 constituted the Soviet Union.

What was the stratagem used by the Soviet Union in dealing with the Polish authority to extend its broad gauge railway to Eastern Europe?

Chapter 12.

To use some special stratagems.

12.0 Introduction.

Actions 26-28 are all negative actions, indicating the strategist is in an unfavourable position, so he would like to avoid something, to reverse the situation or to use some special stratagems to help. We have covered actions 26-27 in Chapter 11, and we shall discuss Action 28 in this chapter.

12.1 Action 28: To use stratagems.

The stratagems available to reverse the unfavourable scenario are to use beauty traps, to sow distrust among the opponents, to inflict injuries on oneself to win the confidence of the opponent, and to plot a set of interlocking stratagems to change the prevailing conditions.

Sun Tze began his book with a treatise on detailed planning and ended with the discussion of intelligence and espionage. In fact, detailed planning cannot be carried out without reliable intelligence. To obtain the necessary information, agents (or spies) and moles are planted in the enemy's camps. Their targets could be bribed, blackmailed or extorted.

12.1.1 The stratagems are:

(I) **The beauty trap.** (One of the classical 36 Stratagems).

(II) **Let the enemy's own spy sow discord in the enemy's camp.** (One of the classical 36 Stratagems).

(III) **Inflict injury on one's self to win the enemy's trust.** (One of the classical 36 Stratagems).

(IV) **The Stratagem with a set of interlocking stratagems.** (One of the classical 36 Stratagems).

(I) **The beauty trap.**

12.1.1.1 Theme.

When the enemy is too strong, the adept in warfare will not confront him directly. One will pay tributes to the enemy denoting submission. It will be a bad move if one has to cede land or cities, because it will enable the enemy to get more provisions. In the Warring States Period (475-221 BC) of China, the Qin State was able to annex the other six States eventually because these states always appeased Qin by ceding land and cities.

Likewise, it is also a bad move to pay indemnity in terms of gold and silver, because it will enrich the financial strength of the enemy. These were the mistakes made by the Song Dynasty (960-1279). The Song Dynasty paid a lot of indemnities to the Liao State (907-1125) and the Jin State (1115-1234) which were founded by the nomads in the north.

When dealing with an able leader, exploit his indulgence of sensual pleasures in order to weaken his fighting spirit. This strategy works on three levels. First, the leader would be indulged in pleasures that he neglected his duties and allowed his vigilance to wane. Second, he would also alienate from his courtiers, disrupting co-operation and destroying morale. Third, the females at court, motivated by jealousy, began to plot intrigues, aggravating the disparity.

Lu Shang (actual name was Jiang Ziya) who helped Wenwang to found the West Zhou Dynasty (1122-256 BC) wrote *Liutao* (means the six stratagems). He mentioned about this stratagem. "If one cannot subdue his enemy by military means, his can bribe their corrupt officers with riches and pretty girls. These girls can bewitch the enemies with charm, making them neglect their duties."

12.1.1.2 Source.

The beauty trap classic - Story of Xishi. Around 500 BC, Xishi lived in the Yue State. At that time, China was divided into many states fighting for power. The Wu State had just annexed the Yue State, and King Goujian of Yue was forced to serve King Fuchai of Wu for three years. After being humiliated during these years and after Goujian was released to return to the Yue State, he plotted to revenge himself. He commissioned men to seek for girls whom he could present as tributes to Fuchai.

One day when Fan Li, the Prime Minister of Yue, was walking along the countryside, he met Xishi, the most beautiful maiden he had ever seen in his life. He recruited her, together with another pretty girl Zheng Dan. He taught them the art of poetry, song and dance, and transformed them into the most irresistible of all women. During the three years of her coaching, Xishi and Fan Li fell in love with each other, but did not confess their true feelings until making the journey to the Wu State. There, Xishi together with Zheng Dan were presented as tribute gifts to Fuchai, who fell so madly in love with these girls that he revealed all the state secrets to them.

Xishi never lost sight of her mission. Her aim was to bewitch Fuchai so that his subjects would grow restless and his friends would desert him. She managed to relay all state secrets to Fan Li. The political chaos that ensued enabled Goujian to invade the Wu State, recompensing him for his former humiliation.

After the victory, Fan Li and Xishi quietly disappeared from public life. She lived in relative obscurity with Fan Li who became a successful merchant. This story is exceptional in the history of feudal China, as no one has ever blamed Xishi, even though she had caused the collapse of the Wu State.

This story is from *Records of the Historian* by Sima Qian (145-86 BC).

12.1.1.3 Illustrations.

(1) ***Mordechai Vanunu fell into the beauty trap.*** In 1985, Mordechai Vanunu, an Israel former nuclear technician who had worked in the Dimona Nuclear Power Plant in the Negu Desert was laid off because he was influenced by one of Israel's left wing groups.

He travelled to Nepal, Burma, Thailand and eventually arrived at Sydney, Australia. His movements were monitored by ASIO (Australian Security Intelligence Organization.) In fall 1986, he met Peter Hounam, a journalist of *The Sunday Times*. He wanted to provide evidence to *The Sunday Times* that Israel was developing nuclear weapons. ASIO kept close surveillance on Vanunu and informed the British MI6 about his activities. Vanunu flew with Hounam to London. In violation of his non- disclosure agreement, Vanunu revealed to *The Sunday Times* his know- ledge of the Israeli nuclear program.

The Sunday Times was prudent, and gave order to Hounam to verify Vanunu's story with the nuclear weapon experts. So, the publication of Vanunu's story was delayed. Vanunu contacted a rival newspaper the tabloid *Sunday Mirror* whose owner was Ian Robert Maxwell. It was speculated that Maxwell might tip off the Mossad (the national intelligence agency of Israel) possibly through the

British secret agents. It was also possible that the Mossad was alerted by enquiries made to the Israeli Embrassy in London by *Sunday Mirror* journalists. The Israeli governement ordered Mossad to arrest Vanunu. In consideration not to harm the good relationship with the British government, Vanunu should be lured away from U. K. before arresting him.

Mossad agent Cheryl Bentov masqueraded as an American tourist called Cindy got acquainted with Vanunu in Leicester Square near the hotel in which the latter resided. Vanunu was deeply attracted by her charm, and started to date her. On September 29, Cindy said she would like to visit her sister in Rome, and persuaded Vanunu to go with her. Once in Rome, Mossad agents captured Vanunu and smuggled him to Israel in a freighter. On October 5, *The Sunday Times* published Vanunu's disclosed information, and established that Israel had produced more than 100 nuclear warheads. In 1988, Vanunu was put on trial in Israel on charge of treason and espionage, and was sentenced to 18 years' imprisonment from the date of his arrest.

(2) ***The KGB's ploy on Christina Onassis.*** In 1974, Christina Onassis took the helm of the Onassis Shipping after the death of her father Aristotle Onassis. During this time, the cold war between the East and the West prevailed. The Onassis family owned Skorpios, a large island in Greece, with tremendous strategic value to the agents of both the Eastern and the Western Blocs.

The Soviet KGB had a "Beauty trap" for Christina. Sergei Kausov was a loyal member of the Communist Party. A traffic accident was staged during which Kausov risked his life to save Christina's car from being crashed by another car driven by a drunken driver. Gradually, Kausov managed to charm Christian during their meetings, and the two eventually began to fall into love, first clandestinely, then openly. Sex with him was a revelation for Christina, and he was the first man who could make her feel beautiful despite that she had two marriages before. Christina and Kausov married on August 1, 1978.

Shortly after their return from Carnival in Rio, Kausov was captured by the KGB and forced to work in a small village in Siberia. Christina spent nearly a million dollars to free him so that she could live with him in Moscow. Her decision to live in Moscow caused an explosion in both sides of the Iron Curtain. Governments of the Western Bloc and her shipping company were concerned about her "defection" to the Eastern Bloc, while the Soviets made the immense propaganda value of her decision.

Slowly, Christina found out the KGB's ploy and that Kausov might have been married before and he was working for the KGB. Meanwhile, Christina felt that she could not adjust to life behind the Iron Curtain. She began to look for an excuse to evade from the scenario.

A crisis in her company provided an opportunity to travel to the West as the Saudi government was concerned about her marriage, fearing that the KGB would be allowed to infiltrate her company. They threatened to destroy the company if she did not dissolve the marriage. Christina decided to leave the Soviet Union so as to competently manage her business. She promised Kausov not to mention about a divorce until he and his mother had been safely brought out of the Soviet Union. Then, she departed for Switzerland. Eventually she divorced Kausov in May 1980.

12.1.1.4 Comments.

Needless to say, stories of beauty traps happen not only in the James Bond movies, but also in the real world. With the rise of female administrators or executives in government and in commerce, the baits used in the beauty traps are not confined to beautiful women but also handsome men as illustrated by the Christina Onassis case. Very frequently rivals in political campaigns tapped in the private lives of their opponents, and to blow them off by scandals of homosexuality or outside marriage affairs based on real facts or rumors.

The beauty trap is ubiquitous in the marketing place today. Merchants apply the concept of beauty trap to all advertisements, sales promotion and packaging. Merchandises are beautifully wrapped to take on an appealing look to the potential consumers. By doing these, the customers' attentions are attracted and their buying decisions are prompted.

(II) Let the enemy's own spy sow discord in the enemy's camp.

12.1.2.1 Theme.

Use the enemy's agents to work for you and you will win without any loss inflicted on your side. Sun Tze said, "Efforts must be made to ferret out the enemy' agents" (*The Art of War,* Chapter XIII). You have caught the enemy's agents, but you spare them from punishment, and win them over by immense bribes or benefits. Or, in other cases, when you discover the enemy's agents, you play dumb. Meanwhile feed them with some false information so that they will bring it back to their masters.

Another objective of this stratagem is to split the enemy internally by misinformation causing mistrust among the people in the enemy's camp. While the enemy is preoccupied settling internal disputes, his ability to attack or defend is alleviated.

Sun Tze classified agents into five categories. (*The Art of War,* Chapter XIII).
(a) The Local Agents are recruited from the inhabitants of the country.
(b) The Inside Agents are recruited from the discontented officials of the enemy.
(c) The Double Agents are recruited from the agents whom the enemy has sent to do espionage work.

(d) The Doomed Agents are those who having purposely imparted false information are denounced to the enemy by their colleagues.

(e) The Missionary Agents are those who are ostensibly sent on some mission to bring back useful information.

12.1.2.2 Source.

Zhan Ping framed Fan Zeng. At the fall of the Qin Dynasty (207 BC) in China, Generals Xiang Yu and Liu Bang emerged as the chief contestants for the throne. Xiang had a lot of courage, but not as much wisdom, therefore two of his followers, Zhan Ping who was a master of stratagems and Hann Xin who was a military expert defected to Liu Bang.

Xiang had several counsellors with him, notably Fan Zeng, Zhung Limei and a few others. After defection, Zhan Ping plotted to get rid of these two persons. Zhan paid many inside spies to spread the message in Xiang's camps that Zhung and other generals were not happy with the unfair reward system of Xiang, and these people would defect to Liu's camp. Being suspicious, Xiang stopped discussing military matters with Zhung and the other generals.

Later, Xiang sent his delegate Yue Tzeki to discuss with Liu Bang about armistice; meanwhile Yue had the secret mission to espy the current status of Liu's camps. Zhan held a formal banquet to welcome the guests.

When Zhan met Yue, Zhan bade Fan Zeng greetings, and whispered to Yue, "What are the messages from Mr. Fan?"

Yue said, "King Xiang sent me here, not Mr. Fan."

Zhan pretended to be scared and said, "I thought Mr. Fan send you here." Zhan hurried away, and Yue and his companions were led to a catering room where simple meals were served to the guests.

A few days later, Yue was able to discuss the agenda for armistice with Liu Bang. Liu agreed to some of the terms, and told Yue to report the matter to King Xiang. When Yue returned to Xiang's camps, he reported about his meeting with Liu, what he had seen inside Liu's camps, and about his humiliated experiences by Zhan. Xiang became very suspicious of Fan despite of Fan's claim for innocence. Finally Fan was sacked, and he died on his way back to his hometown.

This story is from *Records of the Historian by* Sima Qian (145-86 BC).

12.1.2.3 Illustrations.

(1) ***The scenario observed by a Spanish Falangist during his U.K. tour in October 1940.*** In October 1933, the Spanish Falange was established. It condemned socialism, Marxism, republicanism and capitalism, and proposed that Spain should become a Fascist state similar to the one established by Benito Mussolini in Italy. After the Spanish Civil War (1936-1939), General Francisco Franco (in office: 1939-1975) united the Falange with other right-wing parties to form a single party under his control.

Starting July 10, 1940, the German Air Force (Luftwaffe) launched a bombing campaign to destroy British air defense or to compel the U.K. out of the war by forcing an armistice or surrender. It was known as the Battle of Britain (July 10, 1940-October 31, 1940) Meanwhile, Winston Churchill was convinced that Spain would enter the war on the side of Adolf Hitler after receiving reports that Franco and Adolf Hitler were planning to invade Gibraltar.

In October, the British Foreign Office received the application of visa from a representative of "Spain Youth Movement" to visit U.K. on the pretext of studying the Boy Scouts organization. In fact, the mission of the Falangist was to collect information on the British anti-aircraft activities. The British secret service and the MI5 convinced the Foreign Office to issue the visa because they hatched a plot. On arriving at London, the guest was warmly greeted, and escorted to the Athena Hotel located around seven minutes walk from Hyde Park. The guest room was equipped with eavesdropping devices.

In London, there were only three anti-aircraft weapon units. One of the units was deliberately moved to the Hyde Park. Whenever the German Air Force launched raids on London, this unit would strike whether or not the intruding planes were in the vicinity. The guest was escorted to visit the Windsor Castle. A fully equipped tank battalion stayed close to the Castle, and the guest was told that it was the King's Guard. In fact, it was the only fully equipped tank battalion left in the British Isles.

The guest was flown to Scotland. On his way, several squadrons of British fighting aircraft such as the Dehaviland Mosquito, the Unsung Hero, the Spitfire Magic and etc. flew past-by. Actually, it was a show, and the squadron was ordered to repeat its flight to impress the guest, despite of the fact that the U.K. was running short of fighting aircraft. Next, the guest was escorted to a seaport which was packed with various battleships to show that the U.K. was armed to the teeth.

Years later, the British secret service found out that in the Falangist's report to Berlin, he gave the advice not to invade the British Isles due to its preparedness to fend off attacks. Hitler dropped Operation Sealion (invasion of the U.K.) on October 31, 1940.

(2) *A deadly hoax committed by the British Intelligence.* After Nazi occupation of the Netherlands on May 17, 1940, the Dutch resistance went underground. There were many small decentralized groups engaged in independent activities. They produced forged ration cards and counterfeir money, collect intelligence, published underground newspaper, sabotaged phone lines and railways, and hid away the Jews who would otherwise be captured and put to concentration camps.

In Hague, January 1942, a Duch informer told Lt. Colonel H. J. Giskes, one time chief of German military counterespionage in the Netherlands, about the radio-communication activities of H. M. G. Lauwers, a Dutch agent working for the British Intelligence. The latter was caught red handed. Giskes wanted to make the links theirs and to compel Lauwers to collaborate with him, codenaming the operation "North Pole".

Suspecting that Lauwers might doublecross them, the Germans were ready to jam the signal at the first misplaced dot or dash. In fact, according to the British instruction, he had to garble every 16th letter. By omitting the prearranged errors, he would be informing the British Intelligence that he had been caught. He kept this secret to himself and typed the text for his German captor as he was told.

But the British Intelligence had forgotten its own verification checks. Lauwers sent, and London replied. Now, German Intelligence could access the information supplied by the British Intelligence.

The British told Lauwers that five gigantic cargoes would be parachuted down on March 28: four containers of materials and an agent. The Germans received all of them. For 20 tragic months, this deadly hoax continued as German Intelligence handled the Dutch operations of British Intelligence, receiving about 200 drops of men and materials. The Nazis executed 47 out of the 54 British agents through this source.

In order to win London's confidence, Giskes printed articles in the Dutch press about spurious exploits and explosion of a junk-laden barge in the Maas River at Rotterdom as damages caused by British sabotages. Eventually two agents escaped and told the British about their mistakes. It estimated that 1,200 Dutch resistance people lost their lives due to their identities being exposed in the Operation North Pole.

12.1.2.4 Comments.

Sun Tze advocated that the enemy's agents must be actively sought out. (*The Art of War*, Chapter XIII). They must be bribed and counselled so that they would provide information on the situation of the enemy. They can help in the recruitment of local and inside agents. They can be used to bring back fabricated information to their masters as doomed agents. But these converted agents are difficult to manage. Just as they are "bought over" by heavy bribes, there is no guarantee they will not cross over again to the enemy or even to a third party.

Sun Tze stressed that it is very important for the sovereigns and the generals to know how to use and work with the different types of agents. The British secret service and MI5 made use of this stratagem to create an impression on their Falangist visitor about the British military preparedness of Germany's invasion. In the Operation North Pole case, Lt. Colonel H. J. Giskes outwitted the British Intelligence in the sabotage of materials, men and information due to latter's neglience in verification check of the messages.

(III) **Inflict injury on one's self to win the enemy's trust.**

12.1.3.1 Theme.

To inflict injury on one's self is to relax the vigilance of the enemy and to gain his condidence. Then the stratagem to sow discord in the enemy's camp will pay off. It is human nature not to get himself/herself hurt. After one has inflicted injury on one's self, many times people tend to believe his/her story. Mencius (331-289 BC) supported the notion that "every man is good by nature". He delineated "the four good beginnings" as "the sense of mercy is the beginning of *jen* (benevolence); the sense of shame should lead man to a sense of righteousness; the sense of courtesy, if allowed to develop, would give man decorum; and the sense of right and wrong is the foundation of wisdom." Thus, sympathy is a virtue, but it could be the Achilles' heel of the honourable person.

This stratagem has two aims. First, the enemy is lured into relaxing his vigilance since he no longer considers his competitor an immediate threat. Second, it is a way to win the enemy's trust by pretending a mutual enemy has caused the injury.

12.1.3.2 Source.

The tragedy in Chunshen's home. It happened in the Spring and Autumn Period in China. King Qingxiangwang (reigned 298-263 BC) of the Chu State appointed Huang Xie as his Prime Minister and bestowed him the title of Lord Chunshen. One of the Lord's beloved concubines, Yue, would like to plot against the Lady. Yue inflicted her with scratches, and she told the Lord that the Lady had ill-treated her in this manner.

Later, in another occasion, Yue tore her clothing and exposed herself. She accused the Lord's son, a designated successor; for this sexual assault, and it was a ploy schemed by the Lady. The Lord was mad about this, and ordered the execution of the Lady and his son. Yue was then able to take up the title of Lady Chunshen.

12.1.3.3 Illustrations.

(1) ***Rudolph Hess, number 3 man in Hitler's Germany, flew to Scotland, 1941.*** Rudolph Hess (1894-1987) joined the Nazi Party in 1920. He served for several years as Adolf Hitler's personal secretary. In 1932, Hitler appointed him Chairman of the Central Political Commission of the Nazi party and a SS General as a reward for his loyal service. On April 21, 1933, he was made Deputy Führer, a figurehead position with mostly ceremonial duties.

Hess was a shy, insecure man who was totally and deliberately subservient to his Führer. In 1939 Hess was even designated to be the number 3 man in Hitler's Germany after Hermann Goering. As time passed, his limited power was further weakened by the political intrigue of the top Nazis around Hitler as they were constantly craving for personal power. Hess had only one desire, to serve the Führer, and thus lacked the will to engage in self-serving struggles for power and he lost out to other people. As a result, Hitler gradually distanced himself from Hess.

Hoping to regain importance and redeem himself in the eyes of his Führer, Hess put on a Luftwaffe uniform and flew a German fighter plane alone toward Scotland on a "peace" mission on May 10, 1941, just before the Nazi invasion of the Soviet Union (June 22, 1941).

Hess intended to see the Duke of Hamilton, whom he wrongly believed to be a leader of a peace party. With extra fuel tanks installed on the Messerschmitt ME-110, Hess, an skilled pilot, made the five hours, 900 miles flight across the North Sea and managed to navigate within 30 miles of the Duke's residence near Glasgow, Scotland. At 6,000 feet Hess parachuted safely to the ground.

Hess would like to negotiate peace with the British, assuring that there was no wish to destroy a fellow "Nordic" nation. Certainly he knew Hitler's plans to attack the Soviet Union and would try his best to avoid Germany getting involved in a two-front war. But Hess also displayed signs of mental instability to his British captors and they concluded he was half-mad and he represented only himself. Hess was imprisoned. In 1945, he was returned to Germany to stand trial before the International Military Tribunal at Nuremberg that sentenced him to life imprisonment.

(2) *Double agents misled the Nazis.* In 1941, two Norwegians Helge Moe, nicknamed Matt, and Tor Glad, nicknamed Jeff, working for Gestapo (secret police of Nazi Army) landed by rubber dinghy on a Scottish beach. They brought with them sabotage equipment. Their missions were to conduct terrorist attacks and to collect military

information in U.K. Soon they defected to the U.K. MI5 converted them to double agents working for it.

So as to gain credibility from the Nazi Intelligence, MI5 organized bogus sabotages. The first stunt was bombing of a London flour warehouse. It was followed by four successful German parachute drops of sabotage equipment over the turnip fields in Scotland. In 1943, these agents were ordered to conduct mischief in the countryside. MI5 chose the electricity generating station at Bury St. Edmunds, Suffolk. Matt and Jeff detonated a small explosion among unimportant equipment and left a large unexploded bomb as evidence. The local constables failed to find the evidence. Then came the MI5 agents and they were able to find the bomb. A Nazi radio broadcast boasted it as "The big East Anglican" sabotage.

Matt and Jeff gained the trust of the Nazi seniors. By doing this, MI5 obtained the information on most of the German agents in the U.K. These double agents convinced Nazi planners that a British invasion of German-occupied Norway was imminent, and misled them into thinking the 1944 D-day landing would be in Calais rather than Normandy.

12.1.3.4 Comments.

The motive of inflicting injury on oneself is to relax the vigilance of the enemy towards him. However, when the stratagem works, the strategist has suffered body infliction himself. If the stratagem does not work, the strategist loses the game in addition his body injuries.

Though Sun Tze did not mention this stratagem in his book, yet he praised highly "Those who are able to vary military strategies to win victories according to the requirements of the enemy may be compared to gods." (*The Art of War*, Chapter VI).

The British Intelligence unit should be credited for its scrupulous work in the case of Hess. The British disregarded the "peace talk" with Hitler's Germany, and continued to thwart the Germans in Western Europe, so that Hitler could not deploy most of his troops to invade the Soviet Union, and have to fight on two fronts. In the case of the Norwagian double agents, their fake sabotages gave them the credibility to mislead their Nazi seniors on the Allies' military strategies in the war.

(IV) The Stratagem with a set of interlocking stratagems.

12.1.4.1 Theme.

So far, we have described each stratagem and how it works. In reality, in order to achieve an objective, one may use several stratagems simultaneously or in sequence. There is a master plan for these stratagems. Keep different strategems operating in the overall plan. Each stratagem aims at a particular facet of the operation, on a particular person or for a specific time. The launch of each stratagem may be dependent on the outcome of the preceding stratagem, or on the conditions of the prevalent scenario to be used with other stratagems.

Again this stratagem is used when the enemy is distinctly stronger, and it is not advisable to deal with them at the moment. It usually involves the use of stratagems to create confusion to weaken the enemy's perception and judgment, and to bring disorders inside the enemy's camps to alleviate their spirits.

Let the enemy entangles himself in the network of stratagems set up for him. Next, strike the enemy with another stratagem to destroy him. In case one of the stratagems failed, there are other stratagems to rectify the situation.

12.1.4.2   Source.

The Battle of Chibi, 208.   In 208, Cao Cao led an army 200,000 strong on war vessels for a southern expedition to destroy Liu Bei of the Kingdom of Shu and Sun Quan of the Kingdom of Wu. Liu then had only an army of 20,000. His advisor Zhuge Liang suggested him to ally with Sun and planned to use fire in the battle to put Cao Cao to rout.

Pong Tong pretended to be very unhappy with Zhou Yu, the Commander-in-Chief of Wu, for not giving him any opportunity to try his talents. He defected to Cao Cao. He noticed that Cao Cao's troops were not accustomed to ships and the waves made them vomiting and ill. He advocated joining the war vessels together by iron chains, so that there would be no fear of the wind, the waves and the rising and falling tides. Cao Cao liked this idea, because it would overcome the ailment of the soldiers. In fact, after the vessels had been chained together, the use of fire to destroy the ships would be most efficient and effective.

Meanwhile Divisional Commander Huang Gai of the Kingdom of Wu was cruelly beaten before all the officers in Zhou Yu's camps, using the "person injury ruse". Huang claimed that he was grievously angry with this and wished to defect to Cao Cao that he might avenge. Cao Cao believed in his story.

In fact, Huang feigned to defect to Cao Cao so as to lead boats carrying incendiary materials under the pretence of grains to get close to Cao's fleet. When they were near, they threw burning materials to set fire to the vessels. Finally, Cao Cao suffered a disastrous defeat in the Battle of Chibi (Red Cliffs) in November 208.

This story is from *Romance of Three Kingdoms* by Luo Guanzhong (c1330-1400).

12.1.4.3 Illustrations.

(1) **_The Battle of Khalkhin Gol, 1939._** In the 1930s, after the occupation of Manchuria and Korea, Japan became interested in the Soviet territories in the Far East. Clashes between Japan and the Soviet Union frequently occured on the border of Manchuria as they claimed different border lines in their own favour. The first major Soviet-Japanese border was was the Battle of Lake Khasan in 1938, in which the Soviet Union defeated Japan.

Manchuria was a puppet state of Japan known as Manchukuo. The principal occupying army was the Kwangtung Army of Japan, consisting of some of the best Japanese units at that time. The western region of Manchukuo was garrisoned by the newly formed 23rd Division under General Komatsubara Michitaro. In May, 1939, skirmishes occurred again in the disputed territories. Concerned with a possible threat to the Trans-Siberian Railway, Josef Stalin dispatched to the region his ablest commander Lt. General Georgi K. Zhukov, later a marshal of the U.S.S.R.

Zhukov arrived at Nomonhan, a village near the river Khalkhin Gol to find that the Japanese had secured some vital high ground and realized that he needed reinforcement. Before August, he had acquired 550 front line aircraft, 500 state-of-the-art T34 tanks, 20 cavalry squadrons and 35 infantry battalions. All these were done in secret using the stratagem "Cross the sea by deceiving the heaven."

Zhukov was one of the first commanders to use radio signals intelligence to gain advantage. He sowed disinformation to the Japanese by broadcasting fictitious command orders, ciphered in codes he knew the Japanese could break. He misled the Japanese to believe that he was defensive only, using the stratagem "Make a feint to the east and attack the west." Richard Sorge, a Soviet agent of German-Russian parentage, the press attaché to the German embassy in Tokyo, also helped by providing Zhukov with the Japanese military information.

The Soviets were proficient in intelligence analysis, command, control and communication. They received the information that the Japanese planned a major offensive operation on August 24.

Zhukov's preparation for the critical battle was remarkable. His battalions and squadrons were not made aware that an offensive action was planned until three hours before the units moved out. Zhukov decided to "gain the initiative by striking first" on August 20. The Japanese army had been misled, and many Japanese officers were away from their units at the time of the attack.

Zhukov's blitzkreig combination of armour, artillery, air support and infantry wiped out the Japanese 23rd Division, killing 18,000 Japanese troops out of 60,000 men. As Zhukov annihilated the Japanese army on August 31, the very next day on September 1, Adolf Hitler launched his invasion of Poland. Stalin was in favour to sign a cease-fire agreement with Japan so that he was free to go ahead with his invasion of Eastern Poland on September 17. Thus, the Soviets advanced no further than the border line they had claimed before this Battle.

(2) ***Adolf Hitler's stratagems in the devious conquest of 1933-1938.*** When Adolf Hitler became Chancellor of Germany in 1933, together with his aides, he determined to rearm Germany and to dismantle almost the entire remaining legacy of the Treaty of Versailles. Hitler knew that there were discrepancies between France and the U.K., the two major powers.

By aggravating these discrepancies, and winning the U.K. as an ally, he would be able to weaken the alliance against Germany. Hitler thought that the British, given their growing concern about the increasing strength of Japan and the United States in the Far East, would let him expand in Eastern Europe, as long as he would not threaten the U.K. directly.

In 1933, Hitler withdrew Germany from the League of Nations because he did not want to violate openly the League's disarmament clauses. His Tirpitz's fleet-building plan had passed a danger zone. It might trigger an attack by France and its eastern allies, Poland and Czechoslovakia, before Germany was ready. So as to impress the French and British diplomats, he made peaceful declarations. Though these people remained suspicious of German rearmament they did not consider the situation serious enough to restrain Germany. Moreover, Hitler made foreign countries believed that his foreign policy was no more than the traditional revisionism of the Weimar governments by keeping the Foreign Minister Ernst von Neurath in office until early 1938.

In 1934, Hitler secured a non-aggression pact with Poland. So far, Germany had always cooperated with the Soviet Union in order to ward off a Polish attack and, eventually, to win back the territories lost to Poland after 1918. It was a pragmatic and cynical move, because Poland was the key power in French plans to contain Germany. This pact marked a blow to the French security system against Germany.

In January 1935, the Saar district, ceded to France by the Treaty of Versailles, voted overwhelmingly for return to Germany. The people in the Saar district had never consented to French rule. In March, Hitler reintroduced general conscription and this act prompted France, the U.K. and Italy to form an alliance to condemn Germany in a conference held in Stresa. But Hitler undermined this Stresa alliance by signing a bilateral treaty with the U.K., in which the Germans agreed to limit their future naval build-up to 35% of the Royal Navy's strength. Hitler also promised not to build more than 45% of the submarines the British owned.

Meanwhile the Soviet Union signed a treaty with France. It signalled that the Soviets had continuing interests in containing Hitler's Germany together with the western powers. France and the U.K. adopted the controversial policy of appeasement. Appeasement means "giving a bully what he wants". When they finally became alarmed about German rearmament, it was too late for them to stop it.

In 1936, Hitler adopted a more clamorous anti-Communist foreign policy. He war-tested his armed forces to support General Francisco Franco, the fascist militia, in the Spanish Civil War against the left-wing liberals. He moved his troops into the Rhineland. The appeasement here was that France did nothing to stop this breach of the Versailles Treaty. The alliance of Germany, Italy and Japan worked out, and it was called the Axis, which suggested an axis of anti-communist resistance.

Japan invaded China in July 1937. This alarmed the U.K. and the U.S. which both had important trade interests and power political concerns in the Far East. It signalled to Hitler that it would make concessions regarding Danzig, the city under League of Nations control, Austria and the Sudetenland. In return, the British demanded that Hitler respected the international commitments he signed.

The British Prime Minister Neville Chamberlain was not sure whether Sudetenland was a "great issue" which needed war. Instead, he thought it was "a quarrel in a far-away country between people of whom we know nothing" and, at Munich on September 29, 1938, the U.K. and France gave Sudetenland to Germany. Hitler, in fact, simply wanted a British alliance giving him a free hand in Eastern Europe. He secretly ordered the German Army to get ready for war by October 1, 1938. In public, he declared his peaceful intentions and promised that annexation of the Sudetenland was Germany's last territorial claim in Europe.

12.1.4.4 Comments.

In the real world, it is seldom enough to use only one stratagem to accomplish an undertaking. It is always advantageous to outwit the enemy by deploying a set of interlocking stratagems. In the Battle of Khalkhin Gol, Lt. General Georgi K. Zhukov deployed several stratagems in his preparations to fight against the Japanese best army, the Kwantung Army, at that time.

Though a brief account of what Hitler did during the period of 1933-1938 is presented in the above, one can identify the stratagems used by Hitler:

(a) Find the way in the dark by throwing a stone,
(b) Cross the sea by deceiving the heaven,
(c) Pretend to advance along one path while secretly going along another,
(d) Conceal a dagger in a smile,
(e) Cast a brick to attract a piece of jade
(f) Befriend a distant state while attacking a neighbor,
(g) Lengthwise and breadthwise, opening and closing, and
(h) Take away a goat in passing.

Exercises

1.   Many famous generals make it a point of honor to eat exactly what their troops eat while in the fields. They do not enjoy luxuries until they go home, and when the war is over.

(i) What is the purpose for doing this besides winning over the hearts of their troops?

(ii) Besides sex, name some other "beauty traps".

2. The King of the Autocrat State suspected that some people were plotting an overthrown or coup. He worked out a ploy with his trusted assistant. This man openly criticized the King for being extravagant. The King ripped off his authority and privileges, and put him in jail. The King's enemies, already nursing grievances, soon got in contact with the man. Finally, an assassination attempt on the King was foiled due to information gathered by this man.

      What stratagem did the King use in his ploy?
(a) The beauty trap.
(b) Inflict injury on one's self.
(c) Let the enemy own spy sow discord in the enemy's camp.
(d) Turn the guest into the host.

3.   There was a shopkeeper who carried the sale proceeds home at night. In a dark corner, a mugger with a gun robbed his money. As he was turning over the money, he pulled down his hat and said, "Man, would you mind to shoot at this hat, so that I can tell my boss that I was robbed."

      The mugger did accordingly, and shot twice at the hat. Next, the man took off his jacket, and begged the mugger to shoot at it. The mugger very impatiently shot at it, but there were no more bullets. The man knocked the mugger down quickly and snapped back the money.

What stratagem did the shopkeeper use in his encounter with the mugger?

(a) The beauty trap.

(b) Let the enemy own spy sow discord in the enemy's camp.

(c) The stratagem with a set of interlocking stratagem.

(d) Inflict injury on one's self to win the enemy's trust.

4.   Suleyman Demirel became Prime Minister of Turkey in 1965. He was the leader of the Justice Party, and followed a moderate pro-Western policy to govern the country. In 1966, the Tukish government seized a file of letters showing that the CIA of U.S. was lobbying some Turkish military officers to help the Justice Party in suppressing the activities of the other demoncratic parties.

One letter was written by an agent within the Justice Party to a person with the initial of "E.M." and another letter from "E.M." to U.S. military officer Colonel Dickson stationed in Ankara. The Turkish newspapers reported on this matter, and speculations were made as who was "E.M."

There was an official with the name Edwin Martin working in U.S. Embassy in Ankara, and Colonel E. Morgan headed the Turkish-American Joint Organization. Some people believed that Colonel Dickson was in charge of the CIA matters in Turkey.

Anti-US atmosphere flared in Turkey, stressing "No Turkish government allows the foreign influence to turn into a form of colonialism." The U. S. government examined the matter thoroughly, and found that CIA or U.S. agents had nothing to do with it. Years later, it was discovered that the ploy was mastered by KGB to alienate the Turkish-American relationship.

What was the stratagem used by KGB in alienating the Turkish-American relationship?

5.   The parents of Johanna Marie Magdalena Ritschel, or "Magda" (1901-1945) divorced in 1904. Her stepfather was a Jew, Max Friedlander. Her association with Judaism was

increased by her schoolgirl intimacy with Lisa Arlosoroff and her charismatic brother Victor Chaim Arlosoroff.

In 1921, she married Gunther Quandt, a wealthy industrialist over twenty years her age. As Quandt spent little time with her, Magda divorced Quandt in 1929. She was two-timing with Arlosoroff and Dr. Joseph Paul Goebbels. Magda was attracted to Adolf Hitler. In 1931, her marriage to Goebbels was somewhat arranged. Since Hitler intended to remain unmarried, it was suggested that as the wife of a leading and highly visible Nazi official, Magda might eventually act as "First lady of the Third Reich." Goebbels had many affairs with other women. Magda intended to provoke him by saying that to certain degree, she was Jewish.

Goebbels found the situation threatening to his careers. Meanwhile, Victor Arlosoroff became the Zionist representation in the negotiation with the new Nazi government to let German Jews immigrate to Palestine with their property. Goebbels ordered the Gastapo to murder Arlosoroff, not in Germany but in Tel Aviv, Palestine, in June 1937. He would like to kill two birds with one stone, i.e. to eliminate Arlosoroff for his personal affairs with Magda, and to interrupt with what Arlosoroff was doing.

People thought that the murder was done by the Jabotinsky factor of the Zionist movement or by the Arabs.

(i) What is the master stratagem used by Joseph Goebbels in his elimination of Victor Chaim Arlosoroff?

(ii) Can you identify at least two stratagems covered in previous chapters and used in the ploy to eliminate Arlosoroff?

6. Tokugawa Ieyasu (1543-1616) was the founder and first shogun of the Tokugawa Shogunat of Japan. The Shogunat ruled from 1600 to 1868. He was the son of a daimyo (feudal lord) in Mikawa Province. In 1558, he defeated the military forces of the Mikawa Monto within the Province. The Monto

was a warlike group of monks ruling Kaga Province, and they had many temples elsewhere in Japan.

In one battle, Tokugawa moved his troops to the back of the Monto in one big circle. During the day, the Monto sent in two farm girls to gather information on the disposition of Tokugawa's soldiers. Tokugawa's assistant caught these girls and brought them in, informing his master of his suspicion. Tokugawa hatched a plot. He pretended to talk to another samurai that he wished his reinforcement would arrive soon to bring in more men and supplies. The girls were kept in custody, but the keepers pretended to be busy so that the girls could slip away easily.

When the girls returned to their masters, they reported what they heard. The Monto thought it made sense to attack Tokugawa before his reinforcement arrived. Thus, they prepared themselves to launch the attack that evening by a short cut going through a ravine. Meanwhile, Tokugawa hid his troops in ambush round the ravine, because he speculated that the monks would come by the short cut to make a surprise attack. Both Tokugawa's army and the Monto forces used the new gunpowder weapons which the Portuguese had introduced to Japan in the 1550s. The monks were overwhelmed, and later all their temples were demolished.

What stratagem did Tokugawa Ieyasu use in his plot against the Monto monks?
(a) The Beauty Trap.
(b) Let the enemy own spy sow discord in the enemy's camp.
(c) The stratagem with a set of interlocking stratagem.
(d) Inflict injury on one's self to win the enemy's trust.

Chapter 13.

To abandon and to run away.

13.0   Introduction.

Actions 29-30 include to abandon and to extricate oneself from the scenario.

13.1   Action 29: To abandon.

(a) A good strategist must be able to trim his sail according to the direction of the wind. In an unsuccessful engagement, he is prepared to give up the less important in order to protect the more important.

13.1.1 The stratagem is: **The plum tree dies for the peach tree.** (One of the classical 36 Stratagems).

13.1.1.1 Theme.

According to the Chinese fable, the plum and the peach have devoted friendship between them. When one party is in danger, the other one will try its best to save its friend, even sacrificing itself so as to let the other to live.

> This stratagem aims at substituting one thing for another when sacrifice has to be made. On deliberation of the prevailing conditions, when loss is inevitable, sacrifice something that is less valuable in lieu of something more precious.
>
> In playing chess, the stratagem known as "Save the king by abandoning the knights" has the same theme. Even though something has to be foregone, yet the overall result merits the move.

13.1.1.2 Source.

Tien Ji's horses beat the King's horses by 2:1. It happened in the Warring States Period (475-221 BC) in China, General Tien Ji of the Qi State loved to have horse racing with the nobles. In general, Tien's horses were not as good as those of the King, Weiwang of Qi (reigned 378-343 BC). Sun Bin (descendant of Sun Tze) was the Chief-of-staff of Tien. He knew that among the horses of Tien and those of the King, there were grades of supreme, mediocre and plain. Sun thought of a ploy to help Tien.

In routine horse racing, Tien's horses of each grade lost to the King's horses of the same grade. Sun proposed the following scheme to Tien. They arranged Tien's plain horses in the match against the King's supreme horses. For the match with the King's mediocre horses, they used Tien's supreme horses. Likewise, for the match with the King's plain horses, they used Tien's mediocre horses. Of course, they did these without letting the King or other people know. Eventually, Tien won two races, and lost only one race to the King.

This story is from *Records of the Historian* by Sima Qian (145-86 BC).

13.1.1.3 Illustrations.

(1) ***"Hold to the last man" to keep control of the*** ***bridgehead.*** After an unsuccessful siege of Stalingrad (August 1942 to February 1943) Germany lost momentum in Russia. German forces withdrew partially because of an expected Allied invasion in Western Europe. The Soviets quickly became offensive and it was Germany's turn to retreat.

On August 4, 1943, the Soviets took Orel. Byelgorod fell that same day. Kharkov was also recaptured three weeks later. Almost all key German occupied cities in the Soviet Union were liberated with ease. The Soviets kept on liberating Bryansk, Smolensk, Dnepropetrovsk (an important dam), Kiev, Dnieper, and Zhitomir. The Soviets were only 67 miles from the conquered Poland. By October, all the Ukraine east of the Dnieper River together with deep bridgeheads across much of its length was now in the Soviet hands.

In crossing the Dnieper River, the vanguards of the regiments were ordered to hold and die to keep the bridgehead, diverting the attention of the Germans. The main force crossed the river from other locations. The vanguards all sacrificed themselves. However, the number of casualties in the main force was kept to the minimum. Soon, the German forces were finished in the Soviet Union.

(2) ***Sidney Carton died for Charles Darnay due to*** ***his love for Lucie Manette.*** In Charles Dickens' classic, *A Tale of Two Cities,* Sidney Carton loved Lucie Manette so much that he promised "I would embrace any sacrifice for you and for those dear to you." He made the ultimate sacrifice for Charles Darnay, Lucie's husband who looked exactly like him.

Dr. Alexandre Manette was released from the Bastille after seventeen years of unjust imprisonment. His young daughter Lucie took him from Paris to live with her in London. On the voyage home, Lucie and her father befriended a young Frenchman Charles Darnay. Five years later, Charles was arrested on mysterious treason charges upon his arrival in England. At Darnay's trial, he was discharged, because the lawyer's clerk, Sidney Carton looked exactly like him. The witness could have been mistaken for identifying Darnay as a spy.

Having saved Darnay's life, Carton found that Darnay was his main rival for Lucie's affections. However, Carton had no faith in himself and knew that he could not win her love, but he vowed that he would do anything possible to keep a "life she loves" beside her. Although Manette had misgivings about Darnay because of his aristocratic background, he gave his blessing for his daughter to marry Darnay. They had a little girl and lived peacefully for a time with Carton a frequent visitor.

When the French Revolution broke out, Madame Therese Defarge, a fanatic constantly plotted on the destruction of Darnay's aristocratic family, lured Darnay back to France. With Darnay sentenced to be executed, Carton again found himself all that stood between Darnay and disaster.

Carton managed to get into Darnay's cell. He forced Darnay to exchange clothes with him, and caused Darnay to faint with the odour of the poisons. Darnay was carried out and brought to join his family by an old acquaintance that Carton was blackmailing. Satisfied that he would live in Lucie's memory, Carton willingly went to the guillotine as if he were Darnay.

13.1.1.4 Comments.

This is one of the most popular stratagems used in politics. The leaders have never committed, or can commit, or will commit any wrongdoings. When things went wrong, somebody down in the hierarchy must be responsible for the processes and the consequences.

In terms of economics, peaches were sold at a higher price than plums (in China when the fable was first used), so the plum tree must die for the peach tree. Even today, in some countries, the political leaders always have aides around them. These people are the scapegoats whenever and wherever to be called upon.

In the military, it may not be possible to win all battles, because that is very difficult. Minimising the loss is one useful objective if it is inevitable. Certainly this stratagem can put us in the opportune situation. By defeating the Germans, the Soviets certainly gained much in establishing the Communist regime in Eastern Europe after WWII.

(b) Sometimes, it is easier to win by leaving the opponent for the moment. Things will be better when they are at their worst. The action is to allow the opponent more latitude first to keep a tighter rein on him afterwards.

13.1.2 The stratagem is: **In order to capture, one must let loose.** (One of the classical 36 Stratagems).

13.1.2.1 Theme.

Cornered prey will often mount a final desperate attack. Careful delays in attack will demoralise the enemy and bring him down.

Sun Tze said, "One must not try to interfere with the enemies when they are bent on returning home. When the enemy is surrounded, one should leave an outlet free. One must not press a defeated enemy so hard that he becomes desperate." (*The Art of War*, Chapter VII).

13.1.2.2 Source.

Zhuge Liang captured and released Meng Huo seven times. During the period of the Three Kingdoms (220-280) in China, Zhuge Liang, the Prime Minister of the

Kingdom of Shu planned to expand Shu's territory to the southwest areas. At that time, aborigines considered as barbarians by the mainland Chinese occupied this region. In view of the potential threats from the Kingdoms of Wei and Wu, Zhuge wanted to avoid being engaged in prolonged guerilla warfare with the aborigines, he thought of a scheme.

Meng Huo was the Chief of one of the aboriginal tribes. He was the fiercest fighter. Zhuge managed to capture him, but also release him later. These were repeated seven times. At first, Meng was unwilling to submit. By the seventh release by Zhuge, Meng was so moved that he vowed to live peacefully with the people from the mainland. Finally, Zhuge's patience was rewarded; both the mainlanders and the aborigines enjoyed prosperity.

This story is from *Romance of Three Kingdoms* by Luo Guanzhong (c. 1330-1400).

13.1.2.3 Illustrations.

(1) *Vernon Kell cracked the German spy ring in 1914.* German intelligence placed agents in the U.K. before the WWI to spy on the Royal Navy's ships. It uncovered some useful intelligence to the Kaiser's naval staff.

In 1909, Military Operation 5 (MO5) responsible for investigating espionage, sabotage and subversion within and outside the U.K. was under the leadership of Major Vernon Kell. Later in 1916, the organization became known as MI5.

It happened in 1911, Stanley Clarke, one of Kell's officers overheard a conversation on a train. Two Germans talked about a strange letter that one of them had received from Potsdam asking questions about British preparations for war. The letter was sent to the proprietor of the Peacock Hotel in Leith. When approached by Clarke, the proprietor provided full details of the mysterious correspondence. The letter was from a "Mrs. Tony Reimers", who was a senior member of the German Intelligence Service with the name Gustav Steinhauer. Kell obtained the permission to intercept this and other correspondence, from which a ring of agents and intelligence "post boxes" were uncovered.

Karl Gustav Ernst was an Islington hairdresser of German descent, and he was a British citizen. He had been under investigation since October 1911. Interception of his mail had revealed that he had been in regular contact with "Mrs. Tony Reimers." The Germans were particularly interested in the activities of the Intelligence Department of the War Office. Though some people in MO5 would like to arrest the German spy ring, yet Kell preferred to delay action so as to gather some more information from the correspondences. As the German messages were written in invisible ink, techniques to read these messages without detection were developed.

On August 4, 1914, the day of the outbreak of the WWI, Kell ordered an arrest of twenty-two German agents all at once throughout England, so as to prevent anyone from escaping due to being tipped off.

(2) *The Hitachi conspiracy, 1980.* In November 1980, Raymond Cadel , an ex-IBM staff took 10 of IBM's 27 secret workbooks describing the 308X series before he left to work for National Advanced Systems (NAS) a Silicon Valley subsidiary of National Semiconductor. Cadet's boss at NAS, an Iranian named Barry Saffaie, learned about the ten IBM workbooks and made several photocopies of them.

In the summer of 1981, Saffaie went to Japan and delivered one set of the workbooks to Hitachi whose computers were marketed by NAS in the U.S. Hitachi realized their value and would like to get the other workbooks.

Hayashi Kenji, one of Hitachi's senior engineers, was acquainted with Maxwell Paley, a computer consultant previously worked for IBM. Paley offered Hayashi a legitimate study of the 308X project, a report that his consulting firm had developed from other sources. Hayashi told Paley that he did not want the study, but he would like to have the rest of the workbooks, admitting that he had ten of the total volume. Paley knew that something was wrong.

IBM spent more than $50 million a year on security. Richard Callahan, ex-FBI agent was in charge of the IBM's security. It was important to IBM to verify that Hitachi actually had the workbooks before going further. Callahan called his friend Alan Garretson, a FBI agent to collaborate in the inquiry of the Hitachi's conspiracy. Paley agreed to act as a double agent for IBM.

Paley telexed Hayashi that he might be able to get the other workbooks, and set up a meeting with the latter in Tokyo in October, 1981. On October 2, Paley met Hayashi and gave the latter a handwritten index to the whole set of IBM workbooks. Paley brought an associate and IBM's Callahan with him. He told Hayashi he could arrange somebody not in his company to do the job. Paley asked Hayashi to give him some copies of the workbooks so he would know if his contact brought in the right ones. On October 6, Hayashi gave Paley three of the ten workbooks and a long "shopping list" on the IBM items that Hitachi needed to get their copycat computer system to work. Later, when Callahan looked at the workbooks, he immediately identified them as the stolen IBM materials.

IBM decided to take the case to the Justice Department with the evidence. The FBI ran a company under the cover of Glenmar Associates in San Jose, California, to investigate the theft of high-tech items to alien countries with Alan Garretson as its head. Callahan, Garretson, and Paley hatched a plot. They would take more time to draw the maximum number of Hitachi employees into the FBI net.

In November 1981, Hayashi came to Los Angeles to see Paley, Callahan as "Richard Kerigan" and Alan Garretson as "Al Harrison" whom Paley referred to as a source from which the other IBM workbooks could be obtained. Though "Harrison" had impressed Hayashi, and each of the Hitachi employees involved in the scheme that what they were doing was illegal, yet these people were ardent to their mission. Through bargaining, they agreed to pay one hundred thousand U.S. for the workbooks. The Hitachi team requested to physically inspect the "3380" computing system themselves by paying ten thousand dollars.

On November 15, "Al Harrison" bribed his way into a secret-filled room at Pratt & Whitney's Hartford, Connecticut plant to allow Hitachi's Naruse Jun to photograph a new IBM disk drive memory device installed there for testing. In fact, the FBI agents kept surveillance of the scenario by taping.

Between November 1981 and June 1982, Hitachi paid six hundred thousand to fill its "shopping list" to "Al Harrison" Meanwhile, Mitsubishi learned about Hitachi's conspiracy and sent Kimura to contact "Al Harrison" to work for them also.

The FBI team liked to look into the people in the highest echelons of Hitachi involved in this conspiracy. They told Hitachi contacts that two very senior IBM executives about to retire would like to make more money. They could deliver highly confidential hardware, software and manuals. The IBM men would not deal unless they could meet a Hitachi official of comparable rank.

At last, Dr. Kisaburo Nakazawa, Head of Hitachi's computer factory at Odawara came up to talk to Callahan and Garretson. "Al Harrison" asked for $5,250,000 to deliver all the materials and information of IBM 3081K computing system. On June 22, 1982, the Hitachi team consisting of Hayashi Kenji and Ohnishi Isao, Hitachi's software expert, was told to pick up the goods at the FBI cover office in San Jose. They were caught red-handed. Investigation revealed that 11 Hitachi executives were involved.

Ultimately, however, Hitachi paid little for its transgressions. In San Francisco, on February 8, 1983, Judge Spencer Williams fined Hayashi $10,000-the maximum fine-and Ohnishi $4,000. He also levied a fine of

$10,000 against Hitachi, which paid its employees' fines. Kimura and others from Mitsubishi were also arrested.

13.1.2.4 Comments.

By letting the enemies to flee, it would reduce their pride and spirit. Their will to fight is thus dampened by the desire to flee. However, the enemies are still being monitored at arm's length. To abandon pressing the enemies is not to forget about them, or to do nothing. The essence is patience, waiting for the attrition of the enemies' morale so as to strike for a total victory.

In the Hitachi conspiracy case, the FBI agents took more time than usual to draw the maximum number of Hitachi employees into the FBI net. The theft of IBM secrets apparently did not tarnish Hitachi's image as an innovative company. In fact, the Japanese newspaper insisted on calling it the "IBM industrial espionage" case as if IBM had been the offending party. Hitachi's sales actually rose in the months following the revelation that Hitachi had stolen IBM's secrets.

13.2 Action 30: To run away.

When the scenario is deteriorating for the strategist, he has to find a way out to save himself by running away. He may find it difficult to extricate from the scenario, unless he does this in a delicate and tactful way.

13.2.1 The stratagems are:
- (I) **The cicada sheds its shells.** (One of the classical 36 Stratagems).
- (II) **Retreat is the best option.** (One of the classical 36 Stratagems).

(I) **The cicada sheds its shells.**

13.2.1.1 Theme.

> The shell of the cicada serves as a decoy to make its enemy think it is still holding its position, so that the latter will not dare to attack. Meanwhile, the cicada is on its way elsewhere secretly.
>
> "It is the duty of the general... to keep the army in ignorance of his plans by presenting false appearances. He must frequently alter his arrangements and his plans so that no one can be sure of his true intentions. He must frequently shift his camps and his routes so that no one can anticipate his movements." (*The Art of War,* Chapter XI).
>
> When one is in danger of defeat, and he does not want to surrender, the option left is to retreat. However, by retreating one may leave his army extremely vulnerable to a rout and slaughter. He should create an illusion that attracts the enemy's attention, while secretly he withdraws his troops leaving behind only the facade of his presence.

13.2.1.2   Source.

Butt Joiyeo hung goats to beat drums in retreat. In 1206, during one of his combats with the much more powerful invading Jurchens, General Butt Joiyeo of the Song Dynasty decided to retreat overnight.

In order to avoid rout and slaughter, Butt ordered his men to leave all banners and camps behind, and to tie tens of goats by their hind legs and hang them up. They put the drums below the fore limbs of the goats, so that when the goats struggled, their fore limbs would beat the drums. It created an illustion that the Song soldiers were still in the camps, but in fact they had left stealthily.

13.2.1.3 Illustrations.

(1) **Nikolai Vatutin moved his 3rd Guards Tank Army north without being noticed.** In the autumn of 1943, the successful offensive of the Soviets against the Nazi German invaders enabled the Soviets to secure several bridgeheads over the Dnieper River. General Vatutin commanded the First Ukrainian Front held the southeast bridgehead in the rugged terrain of the Bukrin bend about 140 km from Kiev. Nazi General Walther Nehring and his 24th Panzer Corps occupied an effective defensive position.

STAVKA was the General Headquarters of armed forces in the Soviet Union, with Georgi K. Zhukov as Head of General Staff. After thorough consideration of the scenario, STAVKA ordered the First Ukrainian Front to cross the Dnieper River back to the east bank by brute force, and moved northwards to the Lyutesh, bridgehead to the north of Kiev. Over there, the German forces were relatively weak.

Vatutin had the problem to move his powerful 3rd Guards Tank Army north to the Lyutesh bridgehead without being noticed by the Germans. He came up with an idea. In the dark of the night, a Soviet major and two soldiers slipped into the combat zone. They found a corpse, and dressed it with the uniform of a Soviet captain. They put an order with the words "Suspend offense, switch to defense, Vatutin," into his pocket. Quickly they slipped back.

At dawn, the Germans opened fire, and the Soviets withdrew from the front-most trenches to the second trenches so that the Germans could find the corpse of the Soviet captain. Meanwhile, the Soviet radio broadcast the message of strengthening defense for a new attack at Bukrin bend.

The Bukrin bend command feigned to be busy with anti-aerial attacks drills. The communication center worked without stopping day and night to direct construction of defense infrastructures. In fact, the powerful 3rd Guards Tank Army moved northwards to the Lyutesh bridgehead under cover of darkness and diversionary attacks out of the Bukrin bend.

On November 3, while Adolf Hitler was planning to destroy the Soviet forces at Bukrin bend, the Nazi forces camped at the Lyutesh bridgehead awoke to a mass Soviet bombardment. The Germans were smashed. Kiev was very soon liberated.

(2) *How Amadeo Pietro Giannini got around the Federal Reserve Board's order.* In 1904, Amadeo Pietro Giannini opened the Bank of Italy in San Francisco to serve the "little fellows" ignored by the larger banks. He was the first to attempt at branch banking to bring bank services close to the clients. By doing so, he repeatedly offended influential members of the financial community, and state and federal regulators. The Bank of Italy bought its first branch, the San Jose Bank in 1909, and grew rapidly.

Giannini shrewdly sidestepped the regulation by establishing separate state banks and put them under the control of a new holding company, Bancitaly. At that time, John Pierpont Morgan and his few peers (The Global Elite) had overwhelming influence on the American economy and banking practices. Through the intervention of the Federal Reserve, Bancitaly was alleged to infringe anti-trust. It had to sell a large part of its stocks.

Giannini resigned from the Bank of Italy, and began his lobby work among the President, the officials in the Under Secretary for Domestic Finance for the support of branch banking. In 1928, Giannini purchased the Bank of America of Los Angeles, with its 21 branches. In this way Giannini sidestepped the order of the Federal Reserve Board prohibiting member banks from opening new branches. After the U.S. Congress relaxed the restrictions on branch banking in 1927, Giannini established Bank of America branches in several Western States.

In 1928 Giannini formed the TransAmerica holding company. In 1930, under the TransAmerica umbrella, he consolidated Bank of Italy and Bank of America as the Bank of America National Trust and Savings Association.

13.2.1.4 Comments.

Throughout history, there have been numerous people who for various reasons had to flee away from their enemies. In order to do things right, the best stratagem is to create an illusion to the hunters that one is still under his scope of surveillance. The cicada leaves its shell, and the lizard sheds its tail to deceive their predators. After escaping, one may have to change his name or hide himself up for some time till the hunters are no longer interested in him.

As to the reason for taking the flight, usually it is because the enemies are too strong to deal with at that time. By escaping and hibernating, one manages to gather his strength and resources preparing for the next combat. It is said that the final victory is determined in the last five minutes of all the battles.

General Nikolai Vatutin used deceptions to mislead the Germans to think that the Soviet armies were holding the Bukrin bend. In fact, the Soviets moved north to the Lyutesh bridgehead. Amadeo Pietro Giannini was under pressure to give up Bancitaly, but he had in mind an even bigger vision.

(II) **Retreat is the best option.**

13.2.2.1 Theme.

> When overwhelmed, you cannot fight to win; you surrender, compromise or flee. Surrender is complete defeat, compromise is half defeat, and flight is not defeat. Return when the time is right to fight again.

"If you are greatly outnumbered then retreat. While it is possible for a small force to put up a great fight, in the end it will lose to superior numbers." (*The Art of War*, Chapter III). For the strategist, after he has failed in all his ploys, the best option left for him is to flee. There is a well-known saying, "Of the 36 stratagems of Master Tan Daoji, running away is the best." (Refer to 1.4.1).

For the retreat, one can make use of the stratagems such as "Cross the sea by deceivng the heaven" (Refer to 4.3.1.1) or "The cicada sheds its shells". (Refer to 13.2.1.1).

However, sometimes one has to fight his bloody path to escape. It is wrong to think that to retreat is cowardly. Many times before the empire builders or the heroes were successful in their exploits, they had to flee from their deadly enemies. How, when and where to make the retreat are very important decisions.

Another important thing is the will power of the person in making the retreat decision. One must be very decisive. If one lingers around, and does not retreat when it is still possible to do so, he will lose that opportunity forever. When one cannot make up his mind to go, he will bear the consequences of not taking the flight.

13.2.2.2 Source.

Chong Er was on exile to evade his stepmother's plot. It happened during the Spring and Autumn Period in China, in the reign of Duke Xiangong of Jin (676-651 BC). The Duke had a concubine called Li Ji. She would like to eliminate the Duke's two other sons, Sen Seng and Chong Er born by the Duke's other women, so that her son would be the only successor to the Duke.

Sen Seng preferred to stay in the court of Jin and he was eventually killed. Since 669 BC, Chong Er was on exile to seven states for a period of nineteen years. By doing this, he evaded from his stepmother's plot. After the death of Duke Huigong of Jin (reigned 650-637), and with the help of

Duke Mugong of Qin (reigned 659-621 BC), Chong managed to return to his state as Duke Wengong of Jin (reigned 636-628 BC).

This story is from *Records of the Historian* by Sima Qian (145-86 BC).

13.2.2.3 Illustrations.

(1) ***Evacuation at Dunkirk.*** When the WWII broke out against Nazi Germany on September 3, 1939, British soldiers, known as the British Expeditionary Force (B.E.F.), were sent across the Channel to help the French and later the Belgian Armies against invasion by Nazi Germany. But the Allied forces underestimated the strength of the German Army, which used tanks and bombers to smash the Allied defenses and pen them back into a tiny area around the French port of Dunkirk. In May 1940, as the B.E.F. trickled into Dunkirk, they found themselves stranded without shelter or supplies. The German tanks were just ten miles away and the capture or death of the 400,000 soldiers seemed imminent.

The British new Prime Minister Winston Churchill (took office on May 10, 1940) decided to launch Operation Dynamo - the evacuation of the B.E.F. by sea on May 26. This enormous rescue mission was led by Vice Admiral Bertram Ramsay, who rounded-up a huge fleet of vessels - from tiny tugs and barges, to lifeboats and navy destroyers - to send to Dunkirk. As the Allied rescue ships approached Dunkirk they became the easy targets for the German Stuka bombers. The harbour became partially blocked by ships sunk under constant bombardment. The smaller ships picked up soldiers from the shallow beaches to transport them to the destroyers. Of the 850 vessels which took part in Operation Dynamo, 235 were sunk.

The soldiers were packed crowdedly onto the ships for the hazardous journey back to the U.K. When they arrived, being exhausted, at the ports of Dover, Ramsgate and Margate they were greeted as heroes. The B.E.F. lost more than 68,000 soldiers at Dunkirk, but 338,226 soldiers were evacuated, making it the greatest mass rescue of all time. By June 4, Dunkirk was occupied by the Germans. Churchill said it was "a miracle of deliverance". He reminded the British people that it was a defeat which would need strong determination to overcome. Despite heavy losses, the B.E.F. soon regrouped and became the nucleus of the new alliance which, five years later, won the WWII.

(2) ***Charles de Gaulle carried with him "the honour of France" in his escape to London.*** Charles de Gaulle proposed the theories of mechanized warfare in contrast to the static defense doctrines which were in vogue among many of his colleagues, including his mentor Marshal Philippe Pétain. He wrote a book published in English with the title *The Army of the Future*. On May 10 1940, Nazi Germany invaded France, Belgium, Luxembourg and the Netherlands. German First Panzer army used Gaullist tactics in their attacks.

On June 6, French Prime Minister Paul Reynaud appointed de Gaulle as Undersecretary of State for national defense and war, and put him in charge of coordination with the U.K. As a junior member of the French government, he unsuccessfully opposed surrendering; advocating instead that the government be removed to North Africa to carry on the war as best it could from the French colonies. He served as a liaison with the British government and, in collaboration with Winston Churchill proposed a political union between France and the U.K. on the morning of June 16 in London.

This was a desperate last-minute effort to strengthen the resolution of those members of the French government who were in favor of resistance. De Gaulle took the plane back to Bordeaux (provisional seat of the French government) that same afternoon. But he was disappointed to learn that Pétain had become the French Premier with the intention of seeking an armistice with Germany.

De Gaulle made the most important decision in the modern history of France. He refused to accept French surrender and instead rejected Pétain, calling for the continuation of the war against Germany. On June 17, when de Gaulle escorted a British envoy to board the plane to London, he slipped into the plane at the last minute and fled, narrowly escaping from the pursuit of German aircraft. On June 18, when he arrived at London, Winston Churchill said, "De Gaulle carried with him, in that small airplane the honor of France." In the U.K., de Gaulle commanded the Free French Movement which earned him the death penalty in Occupied France. The Free French rejected the armistice and fought with the Allies to liberate France.

13.2.2.4 Comments.

There are two primary motives for people running away from the places they live. The first is to make a living, and the second to evade from the harsh rule.

No doubt, there are other personal reasons to make one running away from his present situation. Chong Er wanted to evade his stepmother's plot, only returned to his state as Duke of Jin (reigned 676-651 BC) after nineteen years in exile. Winston Churchill wanted to save the British Expeditionary Force by the Evacuation at Dunkirk to fight on another day against Nazi Germany.

General Charles de Gaulle refused to accept French surrender and fought with the Allies to liberate his country by leaving France and commanding the Free French Movement in the United Kingdom. No doubt, "Retreat is the best option" is the most well known stratagem among all the stratagems.

Exercises

1. Nazi Germany conducted devastating boming raids in Coventry, England, on the evening of November 12, 1940. Since 1900, Coventry had been a centre of U.K.'s munitions factories. The attack codenamed Operation Moonlight Sonata was to undermine Coventry's ability to supply the Royal Air Force and the British Army by destroying factories and industrial infrastructure in Coventry.

The raid was made by 515 German bombers. It destroyed or damaged about 60,000 buidlings over hundreds of hectares in the centre of Coventry, killing about 1,000 people.

The raid could have been avoided. In fact, the British cryptanalysts had some success in breaking the German's Enigma cipher machine codes (information from which was termed Ultra). Winston Churchill had to evaluate whether to play dumb or take measures to avoid the disaster. The latter alternative exposed the Allies' capability to break the German codes. The Germans would use another set of machine codes which the British cryptanalysts could take a long time to crack. Churchill made the decision to sacrifice Coventry in order to enhance Germany's confidence in its unbreakable Enigma.

Which of the following stratagems best describes Winston Chruchill's choice of action in this case?
(a) The plum tree dies for the peach tree.
(b) In order to capture, one must let loose.
(c) Play dumb.
(d) The cicada sheds its shells.

2. The Chinese generals who wrote extensive commentaries on Sun Tze have observed that feeding and clothing prisoners of war means you are really feeding and clothing recruits. The opportunity to be magnanimous reveals to the enemies that you are not the devil he assumed you to be.

After being defeated, a proud fighter may be much more approachable and agreeable when treated with dignity and respect.

(j)   What is the stratagem used in this scenario?

(ii)   It is said that relying on the loyalty of a former leader of the enemy can be dangerous to the point of disastrous. What will you do to obtain the best results from this stratagem?

3.   Spartacus (c. 109-71 BC) was born in Thrace. He became a soldier, and was captured by the Romans. He might have served as an auxiliary in the Roman Army in Macedonia. He deserted the army, and was outlawed, captured and sold into slavery. He was eventually purchased by Lentulus Batiatus and trained at his gladiatorial school in Capua. In ancient Rome, a gladiator was a man trained or hired to fight for the amusement of the audience.

Once when Spartacus was in the arena taking part in the team fights, his team-mates had been killed. He was the only survivor. But in the other team, there were three merciless gladiators remaining. He was in no march against three of them together. So he ran as fast as he could in the arena. The spectactors thought he was such a coward. But to retreat was his stratagem. The other gladiators could not run as fast as he could. As soon as one of the pursuers got close, he turned back suddenly and knocked him down. By the same token, he finished the other two gladiators.

Later on with 70-80 comrades, Spartacus escaped. He hid in Mount Vesuvius and raised a large army of slaves. With this army, he defeated two Roman legions. Spartacus intended to lead the slaves over the Alps and out of Italy, but the slaves forced him to march on Rome. A new Roman army under Crassus finally vanquished Spartacus and his men. After his defeat, six thousand slaves were crucified along the Via Appia as a warning to other slaves.

Which of the following stratagems best describes Spartacus' tactic to find the best moment to strike back at the gladiator getting close to him?
(a) The plum tree dies for the peach tree.
(b) In order to capture, one must let loose.
(c) The cicada sheds its shell.
(d) Retreat is the best option.

4. In late 1970s, the Matsushita Communication Industrial Group announced to abandon the manufacturing of mainframe computers. The Company was a subsidiary of Matsushita Electrical Works owned by Matsushita Konosuke. He had spent five years and over one billion yens in the research and development of mainframes.

In view of the keen competitions in the Japanese market among the mainframe manufactures, such as Fujitsu, Hitachi, NEC and Toshiba, Matsushita thought it would be better to shift resources freed up by the pullout from mainframe computer development to other electronic consumer goods. It was a brave decision, but it was wise. International companies such as Siemens Corporation and RCA had abandoned their mainframe computer production.

In Japan, Matsushita had always been respected as "the god of management". One of the most lasting of his business sayings was, "If we cannot make a profit; that means we are committing a sort of crime against society. We take society's capital, we take their people, we take their materials, yet without a good profit, we are using precious resources that could be better used elsewhere."

(i) What was Matsushita Konosuke's stratagem in dealing with the company's mainframe computer production?

(ii) Discuss the validity of the quoted Matsushita's saying in the North American scenario.

5.   After the lost of the Naval Battle of Guadalcanal (Nov. 12-15, 1942), the Japanese Navy Command was in favor of abandoning Guadalcanal. On January 4, 1943 order came from Tokyo that Guadalcanal was to be evacuated within a month, and the mission was codenamed Operation Ke.

The Operation began on January 14, with the delivery of a battalion of infantry troops to Guadalcanal to act as rear guard for the evacuation. Meanwhile, Japanese army and navy air forces began an air superiority campaign around the Solomon Islands and New Guinea. In the Battle of Rennell Island, a U.S. cruiser was sunk. Two days later, Japanese aircraft sunk a U.S. destroyer near Guadalcanal. The actual withdrawal was carried out on the nights of February 1, 4, and 7 by Japanese destroyers. Allied forces did not actively attempt to impede the evaculation because their commanders believed the operation was actually a reinforcement operation, not an evacuation.

In total, the Japanese evacuated 10,652 men from Guadalcanal at a cost of one destroyer sunk and three damanged. The retreat was so stealthily that it was not until February 9 that the Americans knew for certain the Japanese had gone.

Which of the following stratagems best describes the tactic used by the Japanese in Operation Ke?
(a) The plum tree dies for the peach tree.
(b) In order to capture, one must let loose.
(c) The cicada sheds its shell.
(d) Retreat is the best option.

Chapter 14.

Sun Tze's teachings and the stratagems.

14.0 Introduction.

Sun Tze believed that to conquer the enemy without raising war is most desirable. He said, "One who has a thorough knowledge of oneself and the enemy is what leads to victory. If one knows himself but not the enemy, one has an even chance of winning and losing a battle. If one knows nothing the enemy or himself, he is sure to lose in every battle." (*The Art of War,* Chapter III).

When we examine the 30 basic behaviours in our systematic classification of stratagems, actions 19-22 (i.e. to attract, to warn, to prod, and to chart the best course for action) deal with the opponents faced directly and openly. Only actions 23-24 (i.e. to strike and to block the opponent's retreat path) are real confrontations with the adversaries. The other actions are basically acts of exploration, deception and extrication.

Sun makes it clear that "one must not fight unless the situation becomes so critical that there is no other alternative." (*The Art of War,* Chapter XII). "A sovereign must not embark on a military campaign simply out of anger. A general must not go into battle out of pique." (*The Art of War,* Chapter XII). One of Sun's key mottoes is "War is based on deception and started by the desire for gain." (*The Art of War,* Chapter VII). However he emphasised on how to reduce the loss of lives and resources in the eventuality of waging war. Even in war, "one should aim at swift victory and avoid prolonged campaign". (*The Art of War,* Chapter II).

14.1 The Stratagems from Sun Tze's *The Art of War.*

Sun's teachings provide a way of thinking on military strategies, and stratagems. The stratagems offer a means for comprehending other people's behavior, including both inadvertent and deliberate actions, and for analyzing all kinds of scenarios, those arising naturally as well as those emerging by design. We shall quote the teachings from Sun's book, starting from the first chapter, and relate them to forty-five stratagems (out of a total of sixty stratagems covered in this book) that have the same tenet. The section in which the stratagem is discussed in detail is put inside the parentheses.

14.1.1 *Chapter I.*

"Those who carry out planning in the temple beforehand will win if the plans are thorough and detailed."

The stratagem is: **Take counsel in one's temple.** (3.3.1.1)

"When one is active, he must feign inactive."

The stratagem is: **Play dumb.** (4.1.1.1)

"When one is near, he must feign that he is far away. When one is far away, he must feign that he is near... One should attack the enemies where they are least prepared and when he is least expected."

The stratagem is: **Pretend to advance along one path while secretly going along another.** (4.2.2.1)

"When the enemies are thrown into disorder, one can crush them with ease."

The stratagem is: **Fish in murky waters.** (7.1.2.1)

"When the enemies like small gains, one should entice them by baits."

The stratagem is: **Cast a brick to attract a piece of jade.** (9.1.1.1)

"If the opponent is of choleric temper, one should seek to irritate him."

The stratagem is: **Prod somebody into action.** (9.3.1.1)

"The adept in warfare can use indirect approaches, strategies and troops in such infinite ways like ever-changing forces of heaven and earth; and the ceaseless flowing water of rivers and streams."

The stratagem is: **Outwit by novelty.** (10.1.5.1)

> "One should avoid strength and attack weakness."
>
> The stratagem is: **Avoid the important and dwell on the trivial.** (11.1.1.1)

14.1.2 *Chapter II.*

> "When the army's ardor and morale are dampened, when the fighting strength is exhausted, and when the state treasury is spent, it will be an opportunity for the other state sovereigns to spring up and take advantage."
>
> The stratagem is: **Loot a burning house.** (3.5.1.1)

> "The stupid may sometimes score quick success but even the cleverest fails in a protracted warfare. There has never been a case where a prolonged warfare proved beneficial to any state."
>
> The stratagem is: **Aim at swift victory and avoid prolonged campaign.** (11.1.2.1)

14.1.3 *Chapter III.*

> "To win every battle by actual fighting before a war is won; it is not the most desirable. To conquer the enemy without resorting to war is the most desirable."
>
> The stratagem is: **To win hands down.** (3.3.2.1)

> "When the army is beset with disorder and lack of faith, the other state sovereigns are sure to take advantage and cause troubles."
>
> The stratagem is: **Take away a goat in passing.** (3.5.2.1)

"In the conduct of war, if one's forces are ten to the enemy's one, the best thing is to surround them; if five to one, the best thing is to attack them; and twice as numerous, the best thing is to divide them."

The stratagem is: **Shut the door to catch the thief.** (10.2.1.1)

"If you are greatly outnumbered then retreat. While it is possible for a small force to put up a great fight, in the end it will lose to superior numbers."

The stratagem is: **Retreat is the best option.** (13.2.2.1)

14.1.4 *Chapter IV.*

"The adept in warfare is one who places himself in an invulnerable position and does not miss any opportunity to defeat the enemy."

The stratagem is: **Offend in order to defend.** (12.1.2)

14.1.5 *Chapter V.*

"One who is skilful to weary the enemy on the move maintains deceitful appearance."

The stratagem is: **Make a feint to the east and attack the west.** (4.2.1.1)

"The adept in warfare is able to push his army in a manner comparable to the onrush of stones falling from the great heights of mountain - due to momentum."

The stratagem is: **Push the boat along with the current.** (6.2.2.1)

"He would make the enemies leave their positions by holding out baits so that his men could ambush them."

The stratagem is: **Lure the tiger out of the mountain.** (8.1.1.1)

14.1.6 *Chapter VI.*

"Scheme to discover their plans and plots... use tactics to ascertain their strength and weakness, and by contact one will know the areas of their strengths and weaknesses."

The stratagem is: **Find the way in the dark by throwing a stone.** (3.2.1.1)

"The clever combatant always forces the enemies to traverse distances and dangers in order to meet him, while he waits for them at ease."

The stratagem is: **Wait at one's ease for an exhausted enemy.** (3.4.1.1)

"If we do not wish to fight ... all we need do is to throw something odd and unaccountable in his way."

The stratagem is: **Empty Castle ploy.** (5.1.1.1)

"One may advance and may be absolutely irresistible, if he makes for the enemy's weak points."

The stratagem is: **Steal the beams and pillars and replace them with rotten timber.** (5.2.2.1)

"If one wants to engage the enemies in battle and if the enemies seek refuge behind inaccessible shelter, he can draw them out by attacking some places, which they will be obliged to rescue."

The stratagem is: **Besiege Wei to rescue Zhao.** (6.1.1.1)

"By holding out baits one can make the enemies go to places where he wants them to go." But for the expert strategist, he would devise a ploy to take the bait as offered by the enemy and beat the latter with some other ruses afterwards.

The stratagem is: **Beat somebody at his own game.** (6.2.1.1)

""By provocation one can ascertain their mood and movement; by tactics one can ascertain the vulnerability of his enemy."

The stratagem is: **Entice snakes out of their lairs.** (9.1.2.1)

"When one's forces remain united while those of the enemy are scattered at ten different places, then he uses his entire force against one-tenth of the enemy's. As he can use many against few, the enemy will be weaker."

The stratagem is: **There name is Legion.** (10.1.1.1)

"If one is on the offensive, he finds his forces sufficient all the time."

The stratagem is: **Gain the initiative by striking first.** (10.1.3.1)

14.1.7 *Chapter VII.*

"When there are apparent disorders within the enemies, it is best to wait and watch."

The stratagem is: **Watch the fire across the river.** (3.1.1.1)

"A whole army may become demoralized just as a general may be robbed of his presence of mind."

The stratagem is: **Remove the firewood under the cooking pot.** (8.2.1.1)

"One has to drive a wedge between the enemy's front and rear, to prevent the enemy from co-operation with his allies, reinforcement and rally among their fighting forces."

The stratagem is: **Befriend a distant state while attacking a neighbor.** (9.4.1.1)

"One must not try to interfere with the enemies when they are bent on returning home. When the enemy is surrounded, one should leave an outlet free. One must not press a defeated enemy so hard that he becomes desperate."

The stratagem is: **In order to capture, one must let loose.** (13.1.2.1)

14.3.8 *Chapter IX.*

Sun Tze proposed thirty-two methods to observe signs of the environment and enemy's behaviors.

The stratagem is: **A straw will show which way the wind blows.** (3.1.2.1)

"When the envoy of the enemy speaks humbly while preparations are being intensified, it indicates that they are about to advance."

The stratagem is: **Retreat in order to go forward.** (4.3.2.1)

"When without warning of distress the enemy suddenly sues for peace, it indicates a plot."

The stratagem is: **Hide a dagger in a smile.** (5.3.1.1)

14.1.9 *Chapter X.*

"When the general takes care of his men like infants, they will be willing to follow him even in the midst of dangers. When the general treats his men like his own children, they will be willing to support him even unto death."

The stratagem is: **Work on the hearts and minds of others.** (10.1.4.1)

14.1.10 *Chapter XI.*

"At the beginning one may appear as shy as a young maiden when he tries to entice the enemy to war. Afterwards he must act as fast as a fleeing hare when he wants to catch the enemy unprepared."

The stratagem is: **Hide one's light under a bushel.** (4.1.2.1)

"One should not be bound by fixed rules of conduct but vary his plans according to the requirements of the enemy until one can win a decisive battle."

The stratagem is: **Not to be bound by fixed rules but vary the plan according to the situation of the enemy.** (10.3.1.1)

"Order the officers and soldiers to carry out tasks, but do not inform them of the reason or intention. Order them to go after advantages and gains, but do not divulge the dangers involved."

The stratagem is: **Cross the sea by deceiving the heaven.** (4.3.1.1)

"When the enemies are united, one should try to cause internal dissension."

The stratagem is: **Play double-faced and attack somebody from behind.** (9.4.3.1)

"When the soldiers find themselves in desperate situation, they will struggle for survival. When they are threatened by death, they will fight hard for life."

The stratagem is: **Break the cauldrons and sink the boats.** (10.1.6.1)

"The best time to mobilize our army is the moment that our enemy has ascended to the high place, and the ladder for ascent has just been kicked away."

The stratagem is: **Remove the ladder after the accent.** (10.1.8.1)

> "The general should act like a shepherd who forces his flock of sheep to run hither and thither without their knowing the final destination."
>
> The stratagem is: **Make a cat's paw of someone.** (6.3.3.1)

> "It is the duty of the general... to keep the army in ignorance of his plans by presenting false appearances. He must frequently alter his arrangements and his plans so that no one can be sure of his true intentions. He must frequently shift his camps and his routes so that no one can anticipate his movements."
>
> The stratagem is: **The cicada sheds its shells.** (13.2.1.1)

14.1.11 *Chapter XIII.*

> "Though the enemies possess a large army, they may be rendered powerless."
>
> The stratagem is: **Turn around one thousand catties with the strength of four liangs.** (6.3.2.1)

> "Efforts must be made to ferret out the enemy's agents."
>
> The stratagem is: **Let the enemy's own spy sow discord in the enemy's camp.** (12.1.2.1)

14.2   The guiding principle in stratagems.

According to Sun Tze, the guiding principle in military strategy may be compared to that of water. "Just as water has no fixed form, warfare has no fixed rules". (*The Art of War,* Chapter VI). The stratagems are heuristics or ad hoc rules of thumb for the strategists to develop solutions to many kinds of problems and to be challenged by many kinds of contingencies. However, heuristics cannot guarantee absolute success; likewise the stratagems may not achieve their full functions due to various random factors.

Broadly speaking, the objectives of the stratagems are:
(a) to hide one's real goals;
(b) to make the competitor or enemy weaker; and
(c) to prevent his own weakening.

The stratagems by which victories are obtained must be varied indefinitely according to the variety of circumstances. One should not repeat the stratagem by which a victory is obtained, but let the methods be regulated by the infinite variety of the scenario. Being unpredictable makes it difficult for the enemy to know one's plan of action. It is an additional advantage contributing to one's ultimate success.

Sun Tze said, "One should not be bound by fixed rules of conduct but vary his plans according to the requirements of the enemy with the sole object of winning a decisive victory." (*The Art of War,* Chapter XI). As a rule, deception plays an important part in these stratagems, causing confusion and disorder among the adversaries. Therefore, being unpredictable, flexible and deceptive is the guiding principle of stratagems.

The fundamental words of caution repeatedly emerged: no single stratagem can ever dominate nor be applicable in every situation. At times, two scenerios are similar except for one or two factors, in one case the strategist should evade from the situation, yet in the second case he should launch attack despite of all the odds against him.

14.3 Rules for the strategist.

A successful strategist must process two sets of knowledge. The first set of knowledge concerns how to formulate effective stratagems. The second set concerns how to skillfully apply these stratagems. Fundamental to these is the strategist must be familiar with the background philosophy of the stratagems and the recorded experiences in using each of the stratagems. Every stratagem was designed under specific situation for a special purpose. Successful use of the stratagems depends on one's intelligence and it is always helpful if he knows a lot of past events.

There are ten rules for such application (Chien Chiao, 1995):

* plan carefully,
* put oneself in an advantageous position,
* be forbearing,
* take precautions against everyone on all occasions,
* be kind in words and gesture,
* be flexible; vary the plan according to situation,
* always be prepared,
* be unpredictable,
* save face for others,
* be ruthless.

Ross Ashby, a British cyberneticist (1903-1972) formulated his famous Law of Requisite Variety. The law states that as a system becomes more complex, the controller of that system must also become more complex, because there are more functions to regulate. In other words, the more complex the system that is being regulated, the more complex the regulator of the system must be. In line with this theme, the thesis is when your competitors have a repertoire of 36 stratagems; you should be equipped with these classical stratagems, more stratagems from Sun Tze, and a new approach to monitor the scenerio. It is not the quantity of strategems that matters much, but the way in which they are deployed.

However, we prefer the antithesis derived from the Chinese philosophical teachings: "He who knows not the stratagems is respectable, but he who plays no stratagems in spite of knowing them deserves more respect." The choice is entirely yours.

Appendix A

A Chronology of Chinese Dynasties

Xia Dynasty		21st Century – 16th Century BC (approx.)
Shang Dynasty		16th Century – 11th Century BC (approx.)
Zhou Dynasty	Western Zhou	11th Century-770 BC
	Eastern Zhou:	770-221 BC
	Spring and Autumn Period	770-476 BC
	Warring States	475-221 BC
Qin Dynasty		221-207 BC
Han Dynasty	Western Han	206 BC - 24
	Eastern (Later) Han	25-220
Three Kingdoms	Wei	220-265
	Shu	221-263
	Wu	222-280
Western Jin Dynasty		265-316
Eastern Jin Dynasty		317-420
Southern Dynasties	Song	420-479
	Qi	479-502
	Liang	502-557
	Chen	557-589
Northern Dynasties	Northern Wei	386-534
	Eastern Wei	534-550
	Northern Qi	550-577
	Western Wei	535-556
	Northern Zhou	557-581
Sui Dynasty		581-618

Tang Dynasty		618-907
Five Dynasties	Later Liang	907-923
	Later Tang	923-936
	Later Jin	936-946
	Later Han	947-950
	Later Zhou	951-960
Song Dynasties	Northern Song	960-1127
	Southern Song	1127-1279
Liao Dynasty		916-1125
Jin Dynasty		1115-1234
Yuan Dynasty		1171-1368
Ming Dynasty		1368-1644
Qing Dynasty		1644-1911

Appendix B

Map of China
Warring States Period (475-221BC)

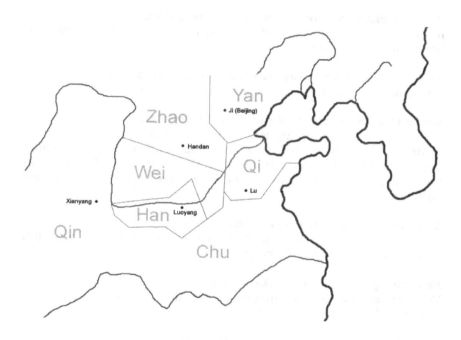

Appendix C

A synopsis of the stratagems.

A straw will show which way the wind blows.
It is important to interpret the various signs, symptoms and behaviour of the enemy.

Aim at swift victory and avoid prolonged campaign.
Speed and aggressiveness usually defeat a static defence.

Avoid the important and dwell on the trivial.
Being in the adverse situation, you try to distract your enemy by focusing on minor issues. Deal with the major issues later when the situation is more favourable to you. Defendants of charges in the court keep silent about major charges and admit minor charges.

Beat somebody at his own game.
Devise a ploy to take the bait as offered by the enemy and beat him with some other ruses afterwards.

Beat the grass to startle the snake.
Frighten or startle the enemy to see how he reacts so as to ascertain his situation.

Befriend a distant state while attacking a neighbour.
It is more advantageous to attack the nearby enemies due to logistic reasons, than those far away. Ally yourself with your distant enemies to prevent them joining forces with your present enemies.

Besiege Wei to rescue Zhao.
Let the enemy fully commit himself against his prey, and then instead of rushing to the rescue, attack something he holds dear.

Borrow a safe passage to conquer Guo.
Use an ally's strategic location as a springboard to launch attack on a third party. Once the enemy has been defeated, one may turn against the ally who lent the springboard.

Break the cauldrons and sink the boats.
One must fight with the courage of desperation to survive.

Cast a brick to attract a piece of jade.
Use baits to entice the other person and takes him in.

Create something out from nothing.
Get what you need by creating a false idea in the enemy's mind and fix it in his mind as a reality.

Cross the sea by deceiving the heaven.
To create a front that eventually becomes imbued with the impression of familiarity, within which you may manoeuvre unseen while all eyes are trained to see obvious familiarities.

Decorate the tree with bogus blossoms.
Use deceptive appearances to make one looks much more powerful than he really is.

Defeat the enemy by capturing their chief.
If the enemy's army is strong but is allured to the chief only by money or threats, then aim at him. If the chief falls, the rest of the army will collapse. If, however, they are allured to the chief through loyalty, the army can continue to fight after his death out of vengeance.

Empty castle ploy.
When the enemy is superior and your situation is such that you expect to be overrun at any moment, then deliberately make your defensive line defenceless to confuse the enemy.

Entice snakes out of their lairs.
Use allurement to entice the conspirators or hidden objects to come forward or to reveal themselves.

Find the way in the dark by throwing a stone.
You can gather information about the enemy's situation and intention by this handy and inexpensive method. Politicians call it "releasing the balloons" to attract comments before the launch of new laws or regulations.

Fish in murky waters.
Throw your enemy into chaos; exploit his weakened position to seize every advantage for you.

Gain the initiative by striking first.
When you are well prepared to seize favourable opportunity to initiate attack by striking first, you are sure to win.

Hide a dagger in a smile.
Charm and ingratiate yourself to your enemy. When you have his confidence, you move against him in secret.

Hide one's light under a bushel.
When one is capable, he must feign incapable.

In order to capture, one must let loose.
Cornered prey will often mount a final desperate attack. Careful delay in attack will demoralise the enemy and brings him down.

Inflict injury on one's self to win the enemy's trust.
To inflict injury on one's self is to relax the vigilance of the enemy and to gain his confidence; then the stratagem to sow discord among the enemies will pay off.

Kill with a borrowed knife.
Induce others to fight your battles for you, so as to conserve your strength.

Lengthwise and breadthwise, opening and closing.
Be tactful in political and diplomatic situations so as to gain advantages.

Let the enemy's own spy sow discord in the enemy's camp.
Use the enemy's spies to work for you and you will win without any loss inflicted on your side.

Loot a burning house.
Use the misery and distress of your enemy to gain something for yourself.

Lure the tiger out of the mountain.
Lure the enemy to come out from a situation that favours him to a situation that favours you.

Make a feint to the east and attack the west.
Spread misleading information about your intention in order to induce your enemy to concentrate his defence on one front and thereby leave another front vulnerable to attack.

Make a cat's paw of someone.
To put a job into the hands of another without letting him know.

Not to be bound by fixed rules, but vary the plan according to the situation of the enemy.
It is fitting strategies to the circumstances of the enemy and the situation on the battlefield.

Offend in order to defend.
The ability to prevent defeat depends on oneself, while the opportunity for victory depends on the enemy. When one acts according to circumstances, he can flip between offensive and defensive tactics.

Outwit by novelity.
One can always beat his opponents with never thought of methods by surprises.

Play double-faced and attack somebody from behind.
Run with the hound and hold with the hare. One can get control of the scenario by manipulations.

Play dumb.
At times, it is better to pretend to be foolish and do nothing than to be reckoned intelligent and act recklessly.

Point at the mulberry only to curse the locust.
To discipline, control or warn others whose status excludes them from direct confrontation by analogy and innuendo.

Pretend to advance along one path while secretly going along another.
Set up a false front deliberately, and then penetrate your enemy's territory on other fronts to make a surprise attack.

Prod somebody into action.
Irritate the enemy to get him excited and emotional, while you keep cool and cautious. Prodding is usually done by the use of linguistics, such as ridicules, sarcasms, scorns and insults.

Push the boat along with the current.
By making use of the momentum of the scenario, one can accomplish tasks more efficiently and effectively.

Raise a corpse from the dead.
Exploit and manipulate by reviving something from the past and give it a new purpose.

Remove the firewood under the cooking pot.
When confronted by a powerful enemy, do not fight him head-on but weaken him by undermining his foundation and destroying the source from which he obtains his support.

Remove the ladder after the accent.
With baits and deception entice your enemy into treacherous terrain, and ensnare him in this death trap by cutting off his rearguard support.

Retreat in order to go forward.
If the enemy are far superior in numbers and training, it is best to avoid them at the moment.

Retreat is the best option.
When overwhelmed, you do not fight; you surrender, compromise or flee. Surrender is complete defeat, compromise is half defeat, and flight is not defeat. Return when the time is right to fight again.

Shift the misfortune to somebody else by moving the corpse to his place.
The strategist manoeuvres the victim by framing a third party for the crime. The strategist can conceal his/her identity.

Shut the door to catch the thief.
When dealing with a small and weak enemy surround and destroy him. If you let him go, you will be at a disadvantage in capturing him later.

Steal the beams and pillars and replace them with rotten timber.
Replace the enemy's strength with weakness.

Take away a goat in passing.
Any negligence of the enemy must be turned into a benefit for you.

Take counsels in one's temple.
It is similar to an English idiom "Take counsel of one's pillow", meaning one has to weigh and consider the matter, preferably with others people.

The beauty trap.
When dealing with an able leader, exploit his indulgence of sensual pleasures in order to weaken his fighting spirit.

The cicada sheds its shells.
The shell of the cicada serves as a decoy to make its enemy think it is still holding its position, so that the latter will not dare to attack. Meanwhile the cicada is on its way elsewhere secretly.

The plum tree dies for the peach tree.
When loss is inevitable, sacrifice the lesser for the benefit of the greater.

The Stratagem with a set of interlocking stratagems.
You should use several stratagems simultaneously. Keep different plans operating in an overall scheme. Should any one stratagem fail, you would still have others to fall back on.

Their name is Legion.
When one' army has the superior strength, the best strategy is to win hands down, or to win without striking a blow.

To win hands down.
To win hands down is to win without striking a blow.

Turn around four kilograms with the mass of one gram.
In the traditional Chinese martial arts, a basic tactic is to borrow strength according to the principle of leverage.

Turn the guest into the host.
Defeat the enemy from within by infiltrating his camp under the guise of cooperation, surrender or peace treaties. Extend your influence skilfully stepwise so as to swallow up the enemy.

Wait at one's ease for an exhausted enemy.
Tire your enemy by carrying out an active defense, in doing so, his strength will be reduced. Keep evading him and force him to come to you from far away, while you stand your ground.

Watch the fire across the river.
Delay entering the battlefield until all other players has become exhausted fighting among them. As for you, observe closely and be prepared for any advantages that may come from it.

Work on the hearts and minds of others.
The general must be concerned with the psychology and behaviour of the soldiers and the enemy.

Appendix D

Answers to odd-numbered exercises

The followings are the suggested solutions to the exercises. In line with Sun Tze's teachings "it is always advantageous to outwit the layman's thinking by clever manoeuvres." (Chapter VII). If you think yours a better solution than the one suggested, please take our hearty congratulations.

Chapter 3.

1. (a)
3. (i) (c)
(ii) Stressed on business negotiations and nothing else. If the business negotiations were not done by the first week, Mr. Smith should consider flying back to New York at once.
5. (i) (d)
(ii) Probing into the information that the enemy might carelessly leave behind, especially computer files and internet websites. Look at how an enemy treats others. Note where he makes trouble for himself or where he has blinded himself. Analyze what irritates him and what scares him most. All this information can help in a thorough understanding or how the enemy is doing.
7. (b)
9. (i) (d)

(ii) The scheme to steal a sample of the chemical was foiled. However, Jean would like to save the faces of the delegation members by presenting them souvenirs. (Refer to 14.3).

Chapter 4.

1. (i) (a)
(ii) "Sir, I have sold a dozen cats by the display of this feeding bowl. Each buyer asked for that bowl."
3. (i) (d)
(ii) Greed and entertainment; making the victim feel carried away by his shrewdness.
5. (b)
7. (i) Mr. Lawrence packed the left handed gloves as pairs of ordinary gloves with one right hand and one left hand.
(ii) Cross the sea by deceiving the heaven.

Chapter 5.

1. Empty castle ploy.
3. (d)
5. (i) Hide a dagger in a smile.
(ii) Japan took the initiative to launch the Pearl Harbor attack on December 7, 1941, to annihilate U.S. fleet in the Pacific.

Chapter 6.

1. (a)
3. (c)
5. Push the boat along with the current.
7. Make a cat's paw of someone. "Someone" is not limited to a third party; it can be the opponent himeself.

Chapter 7.

1. Create something out from nothing.

3. (i) Create something out from nothing.
(ii) People tend to have confidence in what they find out themselves especially through their ingenuity.
5. Fish in murky waters.
7. (c)

Chapter 8.

1. Lure the tiger out of the mountain.
3. (i) The British fleet provided supplies to the resistance force inside Toulon. Another objective was to draw away the British soldiers from the city to the ships which could carry them away in case of emergency.
(ii) "If one wants to engage the enemies in battle and if the enemies seek refuge behind inaccessible shelter, he can draw them out by attacking some place which they will be obliged to relieve." (*The Art of War*, Chapter VI).
5. Remove the firewood under the cooking pot.

Chapter 9.

1. (i) The automatic blood pressure measuring machine.
   (ii) (c)
3. (c)
5. (c)
7. (d)

Chapter 10.

1. (b)
3. (c)
5. (d)
7. Borrow a safe passage to conquer Guo.
9. Shut the door to catch the thief.

Chapter 11.

1. (c)
3. (i) (c), (d)

(ii) Napoleon Bonaparte's invasion of Russia commenced on June 22, 1812. Adolf Hitler's invasion of Soviet Union commenced on June 22, 1941.

Chapter 12.

1. (i) The general must be a man of integrity and moral uprightness so that he will not be trapped by luxury.
(ii) Besides six, the beauty traps include drugs, gambling, cash, riches, even sympathy and flattery, that will break the will of a general.
3. (d)
5. (i) The Stratagem with a set of interlocing stratagems.
(ii) (a) Kill with a borrowed knife.
    (b) Shift the misfortune to somebody else by moving the corpse to his place.

Chapter 13.

1. (a)
3. (d)
5. The cicada sheds its shells.

Bibliography

Books

Ban, Gu (32-92), *History of the Han Dynasty.*
Chen, Shou (233-297), *History of the Three Kingdoms.*
Chien, Chiao (1984), *Playing by Rules, Chinese-style,* in Course by Newspaper, Thought & Action II, Hong Kong.
Chien, Chiao (1995), *Strategic Behavior of Chinese Political Elites,* in Working Paper, Department of Anthropology, CUHK.
Fan, Ye (389-445), *Hou Hanshu (History of the Later Han Dynasty).*
Liu, Powen (c. 1300), One Hundred Strategies of War.
Liu, Xiang (77-6 BC), *Anecdotes of the Warring States.*
Luo, Guanzhong (c. 1330-1400), *Romance of Three Kingdoms.*
Ouyang, Xiu (1107-1072) and Xong Qi (998-1061), compiled *Sin Tang Shu (New Standard History of the Tan Dynasty).*
Sima, Guang (1019-1086), *History as a Mirror.*
Sima, Qian (145-86 BC), *Records of the Historian.*
Sun, Tze (c. 540-485 BC), *Art of War.*
Tian, Jangchu (5th Century) and others, *The Methods of the Minister of War.*
Tung, Douglas S. and Kenneth Tung (2003), *More than 36 Stratagems: A Systematic classification based on Basic Behaviors, Trafford Publishing, Canada.*
Tung, Douglas S. and Joseph K. Tung (2008), *Sun Tze's Stratagems: A systematic appraoch based on basis behaviors, Trafford Publishing, Canada.*

Wang, Renyu (907-960), *Anecdotes of the Kaiyan and Tianbao Reigns.*

Wu, Jingxu, *Poems of Different Dynaties Reviewed.*

Wu, Tze (c. 435-381 BC), *Art of Warfare.*

Xiao, Zixian (489-537), *Nan Qi Shi (History of the Southern Qi Dynasty).*

Zuo, Qiuming (c. 490 BC), *Zuo Qiuming's Chronicles.*

Index A

Stratagems* and Basic Behaviors

*Stratagems in bold letters.	Detailed in Section
A straw will show which way the wind blows.	3.1.1 (II)
Aim at swift victory and avoid prolonged campaign.	13.1.1 (II)
Avoid the important and dwell on the trivial.	11.1.1 (I)
Beat somebody at his own game.	6.2.1 (I)
Beat the grass to startle the snake.	9.2.1
Befriend a distant state while attacking a neighbour.	9.4.1 (I)
Besiege Wei to rescue Zhao.	6.1.1
Borrow a safe passage to conquer Guo.	10.1.9
Break the cauldrons and sink the boats.	10.1.6
Cast a brick to attract a piece of jade.	9.1.1 (I)
Create something out from nothing.	7.1.1 (I)
Cross the sea by deceiving the heaven.	4.3.1 (I)
Decorate the tree with bogus blossoms.	7.1.1 (III)
Defeat the enemy by capturing their chief.	10.1.7
Empty castle ploy.	5.1.1
Entice snakes out of their lairs.	9.1.1 (II)
Find the way in the dark by throwing a stone.	3.2.1
Fish in murky waters.	7.1.1 (II)
Gain the initiative by striking first.	10.1.3
Hide a dagger in a smile.	5.3.1
Hide one's light under a bushel.	4.1.1 (II)
In order to capture, one must let loose.	13.1.2
Inflict injury on one's self to win the enemy's trust.	12.1.1 (III)
Kill with a borrowed knife.	6.3.1 (I)
Lengthwise and breadthwise, opening and closing.	9.4.1 (II)
Let the enemy's own spy sow discord in the enemy's camp.	12.1.1 (II)
Loot a burning house.	3.5.1 (I)
Lure the tiger out of the mountain.	8.1.1

*Stratagems in bold letters	Detailed in Section
Make a cat's paw of someone.	6.3.1 (III)
Make a feint to the east and attack the west.	4.2.1 (I)
Not to be bound by fixed rules, but vary the plan according to the situation of the enemy.	10.3.1
Offend in order to defend.	10.1.2
Outwit by novelty.	10.1.5
Play double-faced and attack somebody from behind.	9.4.1 (III)
Play dumb.	4.1.1 (I)
Point at the mulberry only to curse the locust.	4.2.1 (III)
Pretend to advance along one path while secretly going along another.	4.2.1 (II)
Prod somebody into action.	9.3.1
Push the boat along with the current.	6.2.1 (II)
Raise a corpse from the dead.	5.2.1 (I)
Remove the firewood under the cooking pot.	8.2.1
Remove the ladder after the accent.	10.1.8
Retreat in order to go forward.	4.3.1 (II)
Retreat is the best option.	13.2.1 (II)
Shift the misfortune to somebody else by Moving the corpse to his place.	6.4.1
Shut the door to catch the thief.	10.2.1
Steal the beams and pillars and replace them with rotten timber.	5.2.1 (II)
Take away a goat in passing.	3.5.1 (II)
Take counsel in one's temple.	3.3.1 (I)
The beauty trap.	12.1.1 (I)
The cicada sheds its shells.	13.2.1 (I)
The Stratagem with a set of interlocking stratagems.	12.1.1 (IV)
The plum tree dies for the peach tree.	13.1.1
Their name is Legion.	10.1.1
To abandon	13.1
To attract	9.1
To avoid	11.1
To await	3.4
To be circuitous	6.1
To block the opponent's retreat path	10.2

*Stratagems in bold letters	Detailed in Section
To bluff	5.1
To borrow	8.3
To chart the best course for action	9.4
To conceal	5.3
To deceive	4.3
To feint by misleading	4.2
To find out	3.2
To make use of	6.2
To monitor	10.3
To plan	3.3
To pretend to be ignorant	4.1
To procreate	7.1
To prod	9.3
To reverse	11.2
To run away	13.2
To shift off	6.4
To strike	10.1
To substitute	5.2
To take advantage of	3.5
To take away	8.2
To transfer	8.1
To use some special stratagems to help	12.1
To warn	9.2
To watch	3.1
To win hands down.	3.3.1 (II)
Turn around one thousand catties with the strength of four liangs.	6.3.1 (II)
Turn the guest into the host.	11.2.1
Wait at one's ease for an exhausted enemy.	3.4.1
Watch the fire across the river.	3.1.1 (I)
Work on the hearts and minds of others.	10.1.4

Index B

Names of People

A

Achilles, 80
Adams John Quincy, 256-257
Adzhubei Alexei, 168
Ah-Yang, 104
Agenor Antoine Alfred, 201
Akechi Mitsuhide, 61
Alexander I Tsar, 52-54,199
Alexander II Tsar, 200
Alexander the Great, 226
Almonde Philip van, 58
Amiot J.J.M.,5
An Lushan, 150,233
Anne, 105
Aquino Benigno, 106
Aquino Corazon, 106-107
Arafat, Yasser, 32
Arlosoroff Lisa, 301
Arlosoroff Victor Chaim, 301
Ashby Ross, 337
Athena, 80
Attlee Clement, 71
Aziz Tareq, 40

B

Batiatus Lentulus, 322
Bell, Roderick, 224
Benedetti Vincent Count, 202
Bentinck William, 200
Bentov Cheryl, 281
Bergman Ingrid, 228-229
Betty (fictitious), 124-125
Bin Laden Osama, 39,222
Bismarck Otto von, 200-202,
    205-206

Black (fictitious), 272
Blomberg von Werner, 240-241
Bond James, 282
Bonaparte Joseph-Napoleon,
    200
Bonaparte Napoleon, 47-49,
    52-53,76-77,84,176,199-200,
    211,257-258,274
Bor-Komorowski (see
    Komorowski)
Bradley Omar N., 94
Brezhnev Leonid, 168,243,256
Brandon (fictitious) 217-218
Bryan (fictitious) 74
Bush George H. W., 44,263-264
Bush George W., 33,39-40, 57,
    199-200,222,248,251,252,267
Butt Joiyeo, 313

C

Cadel Raymond, 309
Callahan Richard, 310-311
Carton Sidney, 305-306
Cao Cao, 30-31,37-38,260-261,
    293
Cao Gui, 50
Cao Shuang, 70
Casey William, 263
Chamberlain Neville, 141,196-,
    197,297
Charles VI Emperor, 204
Charles VII Albert Emperor, 204
Charles XII of Sweden, 151-152
Chen Shou, 31,70,167,238
Chen Yu, 46
Cheney, Richard, 39,57
Cheng An Lord (see Chen Yu)
Chiang Kaishek, 27,140,181
Chien Chiao, 15,337

Chong Er, 238,317-318,320
Christian IX Denmark, 200
Chunshen Lady, 289
Chunshen Lord, 268-269,289
Churchill Winston S., 31-32,
    57,71,114,250,253,285,
    318-319,320,321
Cindy (see Bentov Cheryl)
Clarke Stanley, 308
Clemens Samuel Langhorne,
    270-271
Confucius, 2,37

D

Da Vinci Leonardo, 133-134
Darnay Charles, 305-306
David (fictitious), 71-72
Defarge, Therese, 306
Demirel Suleyman, 300
de Gaulle Charles, 319-320
Deng Xiaoping, 75
Dickens Charles, 305
Dickson Colonel, 300
Dikiy Alexei, 109
Dixin, (see Zhow, King)
Drexler Anton, 220
Dubcek Alexander, 243-244,256
Dugommier Jacques, 176
Dunyzad, 119

E

Eden Anthony, 146-147
Einstein Albert, 84
Eisenhower, Dwight D.,27
    81,155
Elizabeth Empress, 173
Emmanuel Victor King, 234
Enrile Juan Ponce, 106
Ernst Karl Gustav, 309
Euryblades, 239

F

Fabius Maximus Verrucosus
    Quintus, 51-52,54
Fan Chen, 170,195
Fan Li, 279-280
Fan Ye, 76
Fan Zeng, 284-285
Fontaney Father, 153
Ford Henry II, 246-248
Francis II of Austria, 211
Franco Francisco, 285,297
Franks Tommy, 5,235,250-251
Frederick II Prussia, 204-206
Friedlander Max, 300
Fritsch Werner von, 241
Fuchai King, 55,279
Fuchs Klaus, 72
Fujisawa Takeo, 210
Fulton, 84

G

Gallery Daniel V. 192
Galtieri Leopoldo, 65
Gaozong 138-139
Garretson Alan, 310-311
Geolitti Giovanni, 89
Giannini Amadeo Pietro, 315-
    316
Giles Lionel, 5
Giskes H.J., 287-288
Glad Tor, 290-291
Goebbels Joseph Paul, 108,153
    301
Goering, Hermann, 38,240-241
    290
Gong Ziqi, 242
Gongsun Kang, 30-31
Göring Hermann (see Goering
    Hermann)
Goujian King, 54-55,279-280
Gramont, 201
Gruhn Erna, 240
Guang Wu Lord (see Li Tsochun)
Gui Gu Zi, 118
Guilliani Rudolph, 57

H

Hamilton Duke, 290
Han Fetze, 2
Hann Xin, 46-47,79-80,284
Hannibal Barca, 51-53
"Harrison Al", 310-311
Hart Basil Henry Liddell, 7
Hayashi Kenji, 309-311
Hector, 80
Hegel John (fictitious), 181-182
Helen, 80
Helu King of Wu, 4-5,83
Henry (fictitious), 94-95
Hertz (fictitious), 192
Hess Rudolph, 289-290,292
Higuchi Toshio, 247-248
Himmler Heinrich, 140-141,146
    240-241
Hirohito Emperor, 116
Hitler Adolf, 31-32, 38-39, 65-
    66,84,108-109,114,131,136,
    140-141,153,167,191,196-
    198,214-215,220-222.234,
    240-241,273-274,285-286,
    289-290,292,295-298,315
Ho Yewbei, 86
Honda Soichiro, 210
Hood Admiral Lord, 176
Hoth Hermann, 208
Hoover Herbert, 196
Hounam Peter, 280
Huaiwang of Chu, 203-204,
    230
Huang Gai, 293
Huang Xie, (see Chunshen)
Huangong of Zheng, 129
Huigong Duke of Jin, 238,317
Huiwang, King of Yan, 227
Huiwang (Liang), King of Wei,
    4,118
Hussein Saddam, 39-40,43-45,
    108-109,222,235,248,267

I

Iacocca Lee, 187-188

Imagawa Yoshimoto, 95
Innes William, 152
Ito Hirobumi, 43, 45
Iwasaki Yataro, 171-172

J

Jackson (fictitious), 136-137
James M. E. Clifton, 113-114
Jean (fictitious), 67-68
Jeff (see Glad Tor)
Jia Sheren, 189-191
Jiang Ziya (see Lu Shang)
Jie Tyrant, 107
Jinggong Duke of Qi, 3
Johnson (fictitious), 161-162
Jones (fictitious), 114-5
Jesus Christ, 133
Judas, 133-134

K

Keiko Emperor, 176
Kell Vernon, 308-309
Kambe, 155-156
Kantaro, 161
Kausov Sergei, 281-282
Kaoliewang King of Chu, 268-
    269
Karzai, Hamid, 39
Kei Je, 227
Kennedy Edward, 261-262,264
Kennedy John F., 48-49
Kennedy Robert, 261
"Kerigan, Richard", 310
Khrushchev Nikita Sergeyevich,
    48-49,96-97,167-169
Kimura, 311-312
Kisaburo Nakazawa, 311
Kissinger Henry, 87-88
Komatsubara Michitaro, 294
Komorowski Tadeusz, 131
Koniev Ivan, 159
Konoe Fumimaro, 45
Kopechne Mary Jo, 261-262
Kurchatov Igor, 71

Kutuzov Marshal, 52-53

L

Laocoon, 80
Lauwers H.M.G., 287
Lawrence (fictitious), 97-98
Le Duc Tho, 89
Lenin Vladimir, 89-90
Leonidas I, King of Sparta, 239
Lewenhaupt Adam Ludwig,
    151-152
Ley Robert, 167
Li Ching (Weikung), 4
Li Linfu, 110
Li Ji, 238,317
Li Shimin, 4,138,158
Li Si, 2
Li Tsochun, 46-47
Li Yin, 104-105
Li Yuan, 4,158
Li Yuen, 268-269
Lian Po, 170
Lindbergh Charles, 191
Linghu Chao, 150-151
Liu Bang, 46,79-80,284-285
Liu Bei, 37-38,260-261,293
Liu Biao, 37,237
Liu Qi, 237-238
Liu Xiang, 196,204
Liu Xun, 166
Liu Yu, King of Liu-Song, 8
Liu Zhang, 37
Liu Zong, 238
Louis XVIII of France, 47-48
Lu Shang, 3-4,154,279
Ludwik Jan (see Maxwell, Ian
    Robert)
Luo Guanzhong, 38,261,293,
    308

M

MacArthur Douglas, 93,116
Magda (see Ritschel, Johanna
    Marie Magdalena)

Manette Alexandre, 305-306
Manette Lucie, 305-306
Mao Zedong, 115
Marcos Ferdinand, 106
Martin Edwin, 300
Masuda Takashi, 171,173
Matsushita Konosuke, 27,98
    102-103,323
Matt (see Moe Helge)
Maxwell Ian Robert, 101-103,
    280
McFarlane Robert C., 263-264
Meese Edwin, 264
Mencius, 2,288
Meng Huo, 307-308
Menelaus of Sparta, 80
Metternich, Klemens von, 211
Mingdi King of Southern Qi, 7-8
Moe Helge, 290-291
Mohiedin Zakaria, 73
Molotov Vyacheslav, 32,71
Montgomery Bernard L., 78,113-
    114,215,249-251
Monty (see Montgomery Bernard
    L.)
Morgan E., 300
Morgan John Pierpont, 315
Mountbatten Louis, Lord, 253
Mugong of Qin, 238,318
Mussolini Benito, 155,234-236,
    285
Mutsu Munemitsu, 42

N

Napoleon III, 201-202, 205-206
Naruse Jun, 311
Nasser Gamal Abdel, 73-74,126,
    221
Nehring Walther, 314
Nelson Mr., 258
Nelson Horatio, 77
Neurath Ernst von, 296
Ney Michel, 47-48
Nimitz Chester W., 143
Nixon Richard, 87,115
North Oliver, 263-264

Novotny Antonin, 243

O

Oda Nobunaga, 95
Odysseus, 80
Ohnishi Isao, 311
Oikawa Koshiro, 45
Okuma Shigenobu, 171-173
Onassis Aristotle, 281
Onassis Christina, 281-282
Ouyang Xiu, 151,234

P

Paley Maxwell, 309-310
Palmerston Lord, 206
Paris, 80
Pasa Halid Hamid, 231
Patton George S, 81
Perutz Max Ferdinand, 253
Pétain Philippe, 319
Peter III of Russia, 206
Peter the Great, 151,153
Petrovna Nina, 168
Poindexter John M., 263-264
Pong Quen, 118-119
Pong Tong, 293
Powell Colin, 40
Priam, 80
Psalmanazar George, 152-153
Puyi Henry (see Xuantong)
Pyke Geoffrey, 253

Q

Qian Chu, 223-224
Qin Shihuangdi, 4,196
Qingxiangwang King, 289
Quandt Gunther, 301
Qui Gu Zi, 189

R

Raeder Erich, 38
Rakousky Christian, 89-91
Ramsay Bertram, 318
Rashid, 109
Reagan Ronald, 263-264
"Reimers Tony Mrs.", 308-309
Reynaud Paul, 319
Ritschel Johanna Marie
    Magdalena, 300-301
Rochefort Joseph P., 142-143
Rommel Erwin, 77-78,215,
    249-250
Rooke George, 58,60
Roosevelt Franklin D., 32,84
    123-125,191,193,196
Roosevelt Theodore, 111-112
    115-116
Royall Anne Newport, 256-257
Rozhestvensky Z.P., 120
Rumantsiev Peter, 231,233,
    254
Rumsfeld Donald H., 235

S

Sachs Alexander, 84
Sadat Anwar El, 73-74
Saffaie Barry, 309
Sam (fictitious) 92
Sanchez Ricardo, 267
Schuschnigg Kurt von, 65-66
Schwarzkopf Norman, 5,44
    54
Semichastny Vladimir, 168
Sen Seng, 238,317
Seyss-Inquart Artur, 65-66
Sforza Carlo, 89-90
Sforza Ludovico, 133
Shahrazad. 119,121
Shahriyar King, 119
Shelepin Aleksandr, 168
Shibusawa Eiichi, 171,173

Shimoichi Lord, 133-134
Shultz George, 263
Sima Guang, 110
Sima Qian, 4,47,55,80,84,101,
    119,123,171,191,219,228,
    231,280,285,304,318
Sima Yi, 70
Sinon, 80
Sik Wei, 100
Skorzeny Otto, 154-156,234
Smanthers George, 261
Smith (fictitious) 62-63,114
Song Yi, 230
Sorge Richard, 294
Spartacus, 322-323
Stalin Josef, 31-32,54,70-72,96-
    97,108-109,146-147,159,167,
    181,182,197,294-295
Stanlea (fictitious), 71-72
Stedfast Johnny, 105
Steinhauer Gustav, 309
Strauss Johann II, 127-128
Stumme George, 250
Su Qin, 118,189-191,199
Suk Jim, 100
Sun Bin, 3,9,118,304
Sun Ce, 37,166
Sun Quan, 260-261,293
Sun Tze,
    2,3-6,7,9,15-16,24,27,30,33,
    34,36,41,42,44,45,46,50,51,
    56,64,65,66,70,73,75,78-79,
    81,83,86,89,118,125-126,
    132,135,156,165,169,170,
    176,180,182,183,189,193,
    194,198,203,213-216,219,
    223,227,230,232,237,245,
    248-250,260,265,267,277,
    283,288,291,304,307,321,
    325-338
Sun Wu (see Sun Tze)
Suvorov Vaslyevich Alexander,
    232,267

T

Tai Kung (see Lu Shang)
Taizong of Tang (see Li Shimin)

Tan Daoji, 8-9,317
Taylor, 192-193
Thatcher Margaret, 225
Themistocles, 239,241
Theresa Maria, (Maria Theresa
    Walburga Amalia Christina)
    204-205
Tian Dan, 227-228
Tien Jangchu, 3
Tien Ji, 118,304
Tokugawa Ieyasu, 301-302
Toyo Heihachiro, 120-121
Toyoda Kiichiro, 269
Toyotomi Hideyoshi, 61
Truman Harry S., 70-72,94,109
Tsetsui Junkeian, 61
Tukhachevsky Marshal, 108-109
Twain Mark (see Clemens
    Samuel Langhorne)

U

Urban II Pope, 129-130

V

Vanderbilt Cornelius, 174-175
Vanunu Mordechai, 280-281
Vatutin Nikolai Fyodorovish,
    208,314,316
Verdi Giuseppe, 228
Vinogradov Vladimir
    Mikhailovich, 90-91

W

Walker William, 174-175
Walsh Lawrence, 264
Wan Ziki, 233-234
Wang Empress, 138-139
Wang Jingze, 8
Wang Lu, 186
Wang Renyu, 186
Wang Yu, (see Gui Gu Zi)

Walters Peter, 258
Wee Duke, 129
Wei Liao, 4
Weinberger Caspar, 263-264
Weiwang King of Qi, 3,118,304
Wellesley Arthur, 200
Wellington Duke, (see Wellesley
    Arthur)
Wendi King of Liu-Song, 8
Wengong of Jin (see Chong Er)
Wengong of Zheng, 100
Wenhou Duke, 122
Wenwang, Duke of Chu, 100
Wenwang, King of Zhou, 3,279
Wheatly Dennis Yates, 66
Wheeler Burton K., 135-137
Wiener Norbert, 249
William I (Wihelm I) of Prussia,
    200-201
William II (Wihelm II), 45
Williams Spencer, 311
Wilson Harold, 90-91
Wilson Woodrow, 111
Woodward, J.F., 225
Wu Ch'i (see Wu Tze)
Wu Jingxu, 180
Wu Tze, 3,226,246
Wu Zetian, 138-139
Wuwang King of Zhou, 3

X

Xerxes I, King of Persia, 239,241
Xiang Liang, 219
Xiang Yu, 46,79,230-231,284-
    285
Xiangong Duke of Jin, 238,242-
    243,317
Xiao Baojuan, 8-9
Xiaochengwang of Zhao, 170
Ximen Pau, 122-123
Xishi, 9,279-280
Xong Qi, 151,234
Xuandi (see Sima Yi)
Xuantong Emperor, 140,196
Xuanzong of Tang, 110,150,186
    233

Xun Xi, 242
Xunzi, 2

Y

Yahya Agha Mohammed Klan,
    88
Yamagata Aritomo, 43
Yamaha Torakusu, 145
Yamamoto Isoroku, 123,125,
    142,143
Yamato Takeru 176-177
Yangdi Emperor of Sui, 158
Yin Tong, 219
Ying Zheng (see Qin Shihuangdi)
Yoshino Lord, 133-134
Yu Duke, 242-243
Yuan Shao, 30,37,260-261
Yuan Shikai, 55-56
Yuan Shu, 37
Yuan Xhang, 30-31
Yuan Xi. 30-31
Yue, 289
Yue Tzeki, 284-285
Yue Yi, 227
Yuen Marquis, 100
Yuri (fictitious), 85

Z

Zhan Ping, 284-285
Zhang Han, 230
Zhang Jian, 180
Zhang Xiu, 37
Zhang Yau, 99
Zhang Yi, 118,189-190,199
Zhang Zin, 150, 233
Zhao Gu 180
Zhao Guangyi, 224
Zhao Kuo, 170-171
Zhao Kuangyin, 223-224
Zhao She, 170
Zhaowang, King of Yan, 227

Zheng Dan, 279
Zheng Xiu, 203-204
Zhou Yu, 293
Zhow King of Shang, 107
Zhu Jiun, 76
Zhuanggong of Lu, 50

Zhuge Liang, 237-238,260-261,
    293,307-308
Zhukov Georgi K., 71,159-160,
    294-295,297,314
Zhung Limei, 284
Zuo Qiuming, 51,243